Edexcel GCSE (9-1)

Combined Science Support Edition

including entry level certificate

Pearson

Contents

Teaching and learning   iv

B1 Cells, genetics, inheritance and modification 1

B1a Cell structure   2
B1a Core practical – Using a light microscope   4
B1b Stem cells and specialised cells   6
B1c Growth   8
B1d The nervous system   10
B1e DNA   12
B1f Inheritance   14
B1g Variation   16
B1h Evolution and natural selection   18
B1i Selective breeding and genetic engineering   20
B1   Preparing for your exams   22

B2 Health, disease and the development of medicines 23

B2a Health and disease   24
B2b Lifestyle diseases   26
B2c Pathogens and disease   28
B2d Spread and control of pathogens   30
B2e Sexually transmitted infections   32
B2f Protection against infection   34
B2g Medicines   36
B2   Preparing for your exams   38

B3 Plants and ecosystems 39

B3a Photosynthesis   40
B3a Core practical – Light intensity and photosynthesis   42
B3b Movement of substances   44
B3b Core practical – Osmosis in potatoes   46
B3c Transpiration and translocation   48
B3d Ecosystems   50
B3d Core practical – Quadrats and transects   52
B3e Biotic factors in ecosystems   54
B3f Biodiversity   56
B3g Natural cycles   58
B3   Preparing for your exams   60

B4 Human biology 61

B4a Hormones   62
B4b Keeping things constant   64
B4c Menstrual cycle and contraception   66
B4d Enzymes   68
B4d Core practical – pH and enzyme activity   70
B4e Exchange and transport   72

B4f The circulatory system   74
B4g Cellular respiration   76
B4g Core practical – Respiration rates   78
B4   Preparing for your exams   80

C1 Atoms, compounds and states of matter 81

C1a States of matter   82
C1b Atomic structure   84
C1c The periodic table   86
C1d Metals and the periodic table   88
C1e Ionic bonding   90
C1f Covalent bonding   92
C1g Giant covalent substances   94
C1h Metallic bonding and bonding summary   96
C1   Preparing for your exams   98

C2 Separating mixtures 99

C2a Separating mixtures   100
C2b Chromatography   102
C2c Purifying mixtures   104
C2c Core practical – Investigating inks   106
C2d Electrolysis   108
C2d Core practical – Electrolysis of copper sulfate solution 110
C2   Preparing for your exams   112

C3 Acids and metals 113

C3a Acids and alkalis   114
C3b Neutralisation   116
C3b Core practical – Investigating neutralisation   118
C3c Making salts   120
C3c Core practical – Preparing copper sulfate   122
C3d Metals   124
C3e Recycling metals   126
C3f Calculations involving masses   128
C3   Preparing for your exams   130

C4 Elements and chemical reactions 131

C4a Group 1   132
C4b Group 7   134
C4c Group 0   136
C4d Energy changes   138
C4e Rates of reaction   140
C4e Core practical – Investigating reaction rates   142
C4f Reversible reactions   144
C4   Preparing for your exams   146

Contents

C5 Fuels and the Earth's atmosphere — 147

C5a	Hydrocarbons	148
C5b	Combustion	150
C5c	Fuel pollution	152
C5d	Cracking	154
C5e	Early Earth	156
C5f	Today's atmosphere	158
C5	Preparing for your exams	160

P1 Forces, movement and energy — 161

P1a	Stopping distances	162
P1b	Balanced and unbalanced forces	164
P1c	Measuring quantities	166
P1d	Journeys	168
P1e	Calculating speed and acceleration	170
P1f	Mass, weight and acceleration	172
P1f	Core practical – Investigating acceleration	174
P1g	Energy transfers	176
P1h	Wasted energy	178
P1i	Energy resources	180
P1j	Using energy resources	182
P1	Preparing for your exams	184

P2 Waves and radiation — 185

P2a	Describing waves	186
P2b	Wave speeds	188
P2b	Core practical – Investigating waves	190
P2c	Electromagnetic waves	192
P2c	Core practical – Investigating refraction	194
P2d	Using the long wavelengths	196
P2e	Using the short wavelengths	198
P2f	Dangers of electromagnetic radiation	200
P2g	Inside atoms	202
P2h	Radioactive decay	204
P2i	Half-life	206
P2j	Dangers of radioactivity	208
P2	Preparing for your exams	210

P3 Electricity and magnets — 211

P3a	Electrical circuits	212
P3b	Resistance	214
P3c	More about resistance	216
P3c	Core practical – Investigating resistance	218
P3d	Electrical power	220
P3e	Magnets and electromagnets	222
P3f	Electricity in the home	224
P3	Preparing for your exams	226

P4 Energy and particles — 227

P4a	Work and power	228
P4b	Particles and density	230
P4b	Core practical – Investigating densities	232
P4c	Energy and changes of state	234
P4c	Core practical – Investigating water	236
P4d	Stretching	238
P4d	Core practical – Investigating springs	240
P4	Preparing for your exams	242

Glossary	243
The periodic table of the elements	250
Index	251

Teaching and learning

The **topic reference** tells you which part of the course you are in. 'B1a' means 'Biology, unit 1, topic a'.

The **specification reference** allows you to cross-reference against the Entry Level Certificate (ELC) and GCSE specification criteria so you know which parts you are covering.

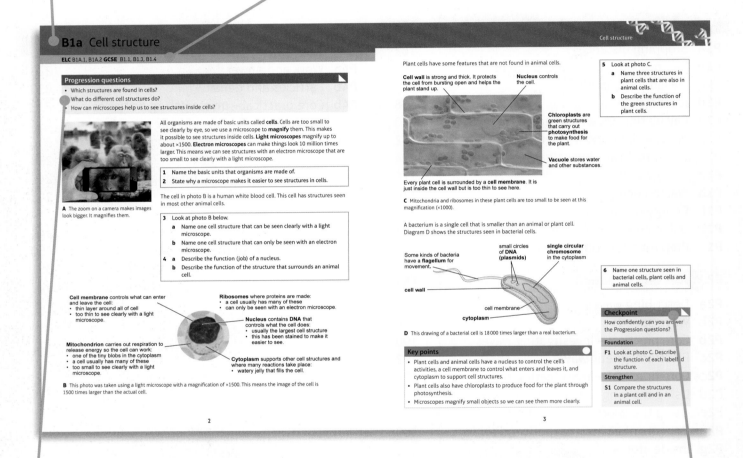

B1a Cell structure

ELC B1A.1, B1A.2 **GCSE** B1.1, B1.3, B1.4

Progression questions

- Which structures are found in cells?
- What do different cell structures do?
- How can microscopes help us to see structures inside cells?

All organisms are made of basic units called **cells**. Cells are too small to see clearly by eye, so we use a microscope to **magnify** them. This makes it possible to see structures inside cells. **Light microscopes** magnify up to about ×1500. **Electron microscopes** can make things look 10 million times larger. This means we can see structures with an electron microscope that are too small to see clearly with a light microscope.

1 Name the basic units that organisms are made of.

2 State why a microscope makes it easier to see structures in cells.

The cell in photo B is a human white blood cell. This cell has structures seen in most other animal cells.

A The zoom on a camera makes images look bigger. It magnifies them.

3 Look at photo B below.
   a Name one cell structure that can be seen clearly with a light microscope.
   b Name one cell structure that can only be seen with an electron microscope.
4 a Describe the function (job) of a nucleus.
   b Describe the function of the structure that surrounds an animal cell.

Cell membrane controls what can enter and leave the cell:
- thin layer around all of cell
- too thin to see clearly with a light microscope.

Mitochondrion carries out respiration to release energy so the cell can work:
- one of the tiny blobs in the cytoplasm
- a cell usually has many of these
- too small to see clearly with a light microscope.

Ribosomes where proteins are made:
- a cell usually has many of these
- can only be seen with an electron microscope.

Nucleus contains **DNA** that controls what the cell does:
- usually the largest cell structure
- this has been stained to make it easier to see.

Cytoplasm supports other cell structures and where many reactions take place:
- watery jelly that fills the cell.

B This photo was taken using a light microscope with a magnification of ×1500. This means the image of the cell is 1500 times larger than the actual cell.

2

Plant cells have some features that are not found in animal cells.

Cell wall is strong and thick. It protects the cell from bursting open and helps the plant stand up.

Nucleus controls the cell.

Chloroplasts are green structures that carry out **photosynthesis** to make food for the plant.

Vacuole stores water and other substances.

Every plant cell is surrounded by a **cell membrane**. It is just inside the cell wall but is too thin to see here.

C Mitochondria and ribosomes in these plant cells are too small to be seen at this magnification (×1000).

A bacterium is a single cell that is smaller than an animal or plant cell. Diagram D shows the structures seen in bacterial cells.

Some kinds of bacteria have a **flagellum** for movement.

small circles of DNA (**plasmids**)

single circular chromosome in the cytoplasm

cell wall

cell membrane

cytoplasm

D This drawing of a bacterial cell is 18 000 times larger than a real bacterium.

Key points

- Plant cells and animal cells have a nucleus to control the cell's activities, a cell membrane to control what enters and leaves it, and cytoplasm to support cell structures.
- Plant cells also have chloroplasts to produce food for the plant through photosynthesis.
- Microscopes magnify small objects so we can see them more clearly.

Cell structure

5 Look at photo C.
   a Name three structures in plant cells that are also in animal cells.
   b Describe the function of the green structures in plant cells.

6 Name one structure seen in bacterial cells, plant cells and animal cells.

Checkpoint

How confidently can you answer the Progression questions?

Foundation

F1 Look at photo C. Describe the function of each labelled structure.

Strengthen

S1 Compare the structures in a plant cell and in an animal cell.

3

By the end of the topic you should be able to confidently answer the **Progression questions**. Try to answer them before you start and make a note of your answers. Think about what you know already and what more you need to learn to be able to answer them.

When you've worked through the main student book questions, answer the **Progression questions** again and review your own progress. If you need to check your learning, answer the **Foundation question**. If you need to reinforce your learning then tackle the **Strengthen question**.

B1 Cells, genetics, inheritance and modification

All living organisms, such as trees, humans and dogs, are made of cells. The differences between cells help our bodies to do different things, such as move or sense things around us. The differences in DNA in our cells make us look different.

In this unit you will learn about how cells differ, and how the differences between cells help bodies work well.

The learning journey

Previously you will have learnt at KS3:

- that cells are the basic units of living organisms
- how to use a light microscope to view cells
- what the different parts of cells do
- about differences between individuals within a species.

In this unit you will learn:

- about the structure of animal and plant cells
- how organisms grow
- how the nervous system works
- about DNA and genes
- about variation and natural selection
- about selective breeding and genetic engineering.

B1a Cell structure

ELC B1A.1, B1A.2, B1B.4 **GCSE** B1.1, B1.3, B1.4

Progression questions

- Which structures are found in cells?
- What do different cell structures do?
- How can microscopes help us to see structures inside cells?

A The zoom on a camera makes images look bigger. It magnifies them.

All organisms are made of basic units called **cells**. Cells are too small to see clearly by eye, so we use a microscope to **magnify** them. This makes it possible to see structures inside cells. **Light microscopes** magnify up to about ×1500. **Electron microscopes** can make things look 10 million times larger. This means we can see structures with an electron microscope that are too small to see clearly with a light microscope.

> **1** Name the basic units that organisms are made of.
>
> **2** State why a microscope makes it easier to see structures in cells.

The cell in photo B is a human white blood cell. This cell has structures seen in most other animal cells.

> **3** Look at photo B below.
>
>   **a** Name one cell structure that can be seen clearly with a light microscope.
>
>   **b** Name one cell structure that can only be seen with an electron microscope.
>
> **4** **a** Describe the function (job) of a nucleus.
>
>   **b** Describe the function of the structure that surrounds an animal cell.

Cell membrane controls what can enter and leave the cell:
- thin layer around all of cell
- too thin to see clearly with a light microscope.

Ribosomes where proteins are made:
- a cell usually has many of these
- can only be seen with an electron microscope.

Nucleus contains **DNA** that controls what the cell does:
- usually the largest cell structure
- this has been stained to make it easier to see.

Mitochondrion carries out respiration to release energy so the cell can work:
- one of the tiny blobs in the cytoplasm
- a cell usually has many of these
- too small to see clearly with a light microscope.

Cytoplasm supports other cell structures and where many reactions take place:
- watery jelly that fills the cell.

B This photo was taken using a light microscope with a magnification of ×1500. This means the image of the cell is 1500 times larger than the actual cell.

Plant cells have some features that are not found in animal cells.

Cell wall is strong and thick. It protects the cell from bursting open and helps the plant stand up.

Nucleus controls the cell.

Chloroplasts are green structures that carry out **photosynthesis** to make food for the plant.

Vacuole stores water and other substances.

Every plant cell is surrounded by a **cell membrane**. It is just inside the cell wall but is too thin to see here.

C Mitochondria and ribosomes in these plant cells are too small to be seen at this magnification (×1000).

A bacterium is a single cell that is smaller than an animal or plant cell. Diagram D shows the structures seen in bacterial cells.

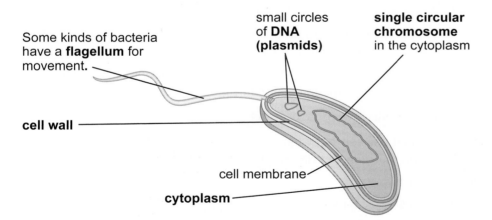

Some kinds of bacteria have a **flagellum** for movement.

small circles of **DNA (plasmids)**

single circular chromosome in the cytoplasm

cell wall

cell membrane

cytoplasm

D This drawing of a bacterial cell is 18 000 times larger than a real bacterium.

5 Look at photo C.

a Name three structures in plant cells that are also in animal cells.

b Describe the function of the green structures in plant cells.

6 Name one structure seen in bacterial cells, plant cells and animal cells.

Checkpoint

How confidently can you answer the Progression questions?

Foundation

F1 Look at photo C. Describe the function of each labelled structure.

Strengthen

S1 Compare the structures in a plant cell and in an animal cell.

Key points

- Plant cells and animal cells have a nucleus to control the cell's activities, a cell membrane to control what enters and leaves it, and cytoplasm to support cell structures.
- Plant cells also have chloroplasts to produce food for the plant through photosynthesis.
- Microscopes magnify small objects so we can see them more clearly.

A light microscope makes cells appear large enough to see clearly. A microscope also makes it easier to see what is inside a cell. You will use a light microscope to look at slides of cells.

Carefully draw a cell from each slide. Label the parts of the cell clearly. Add a title to your drawing to say what you were looking at.

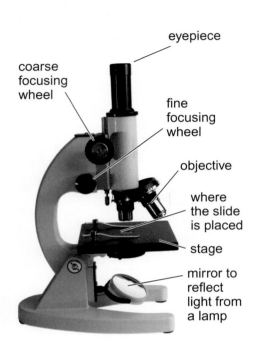

A parts of a light microscope

Method

Using a light microscope

A Look at the **magnification** numbers on the **objective** lenses (objectives).

B Make sure the objective with the lowest magnification number is below the eyepiece.

C Turn the coarse focusing wheel until the objective is as low as it can go.

D Place the slide on the stage under the clips, so that it cannot move easily.

E Move the mirror so that light from the lamp passes through the hole in the stage.

F Look through the eyepiece. Try to keep both eyes open as this will be less tiring.

G Turn the coarse focusing wheel slowly to move the objective up from the slide. Keep turning until what you see is clear (in **focus**).

H To see a bigger image, move a higher magnification objective so that it is above the slide. Only use the fine focusing wheel to focus.

I Record the magnification of the eyepiece and the objective you use. Then calculate the magnification of the cell that you draw.

Drawing a labelled scientific drawing

J Draw what you see, not what is shown in books. You may see lots of detail on the slide, but draw only what you have been asked to draw.

K When drawing:
- use a sharp HB pencil
- draw a clean line for each shape – if a line goes wrong, rub it out and draw it again
- don't add any shading.

L When labelling your drawing:
- label all the features you have been asked to label
- use a ruler to draw straight label lines
- make sure label lines don't cross each other
- write a clear label to say what the line is pointing to.

Safety

Do *not* use the coarse focusing wheel with higher magnification objectives. If you can't see something clearly, go back to a lower magnification objective. Refocus the specimen, then return to the higher magnification.

Exam-style questions

1 Name the type of microscope shown in photo A. *(1 mark)*

2 Name the part of a light microscope where you place the slide. *(1 mark)*

3 State what 'focusing' means. *(1 mark)*

4 A light microscope has objectives with these magnifications:
×10   ×40   ×100

   a State which objective you should use when you start looking at a slide. *(1 mark)*

   b Give a reason for your answer to part **a**. *(1 mark)*

5 Describe what you should do if the image is not in focus when you are using a higher magnification objective. *(2 marks)*

6 Look at the drawings in diagram B.

   a Give one reason why the top drawing of the cell is not drawn correctly. *(1 mark)*

   b Describe one mistake the student made when labelling this drawing. *(1 mark)*

7 Look at photo C.

   a Draw a clear scientific drawing of the cell in photo C. *(1 mark)*

   b Label your drawing to show the nucleus, cell membrane and cytoplasm. *(1 mark)*

8 Look at the caption of photo C. State what the magnification information means. *(1 mark)*

9 Explain why microscopes are used to look at cells. *(2 marks)*

10 Sam looks at a cheek cell. He uses an eyepiece magnification of ×10 and an objective magnification of ×20. Use the equation below to calculate the total magnification. This will tell you how much larger what he sees is than the actual cell. *(1 mark)*

$$\frac{\text{total}}{\text{magnification}} = \frac{\text{eyepiece}}{\text{magnification}} \times \frac{\text{objective}}{\text{magnification}}$$

11 When looking at plant root tissue under a microscope, Jenna notices that about 10 cells fit across the field of view. She calculates the field of view as 0.2 mm. Estimate the diameter of one cell. Show your working. *(2 marks)*

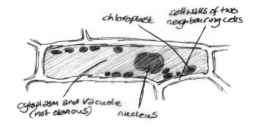

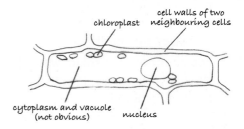

B A poor drawing of a cell at the top, and a well-drawn scientific diagram of the same cell at the bottom.

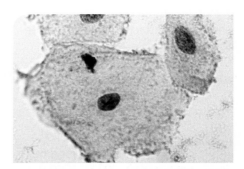

C a photograph of a human cheek cell seen under a light microscope (enlarged to magnification ×3500)

Progression questions

- What is a stem cell?
- How are some specialised cells adapted to their function?
- Why is cell differentiation important?

---

1 How do we begin life?

2 A human baby contains many more cells than an **embryo**. Name the process that increases the number of cells.

3 Look at photo A. Explain why the baby is so much larger than the embryo.

We begin life as a single cell that is formed when a sperm cell **fertilises** an egg cell. The fertilised egg cell divides in two. The two cells it forms also divide in two. This **cell division** continues again and again. By the time a baby is born, it contains trillions of cells.

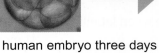
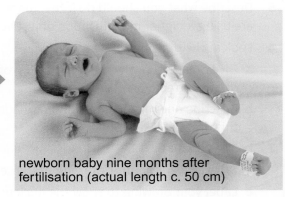

human embryo three days after fertilisation (actual diameter c. 0.1 mm)

newborn baby nine months after fertilisation (actual length c. 50 cm)

A It takes about nine months for the cells in a human embryo to divide and differentiate to form a baby.

All the cells in the embryo in photo A are identical and **unspecialised**. These cells are called **embryonic stem cells**. After more divisions, some stem cells start to **differentiate** into different types of **specialised cell**. Embryonic stem cells can differentiate into any type of specialised cell.

---

4 **a** State what is meant by 'stem cell'.

   b Describe the function of stem cells in embryos.

Specialised cells have features that help them carry out a particular **function**. We say they are **adapted** to their function. For example:

- **muscle cells** can **contract** (get shorter) to move other parts of the body
- **nerve cells** are very long to carry electrical impulses around the body.

Cell differentiation produces all the different types of cells that the body needs to carry out many different functions well.

---

5 **a** Describe how a muscle cell is adapted to its function.

   b Describe how a nerve cell is adapted to its function.

6 Explain why cell differentiation is important in the human body.

B Muscle cells move this athlete's legs when they contract and pull on his leg bones.

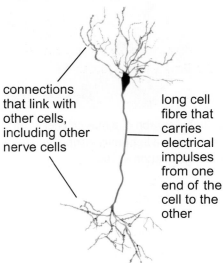

connections that link with other cells, including other nerve cells

long cell fibre that carries electrical impulses from one end of the cell to the other

C Nerve cells are adapted to detect and respond to changes.

Photo D shows that egg cells and sperm cells are specialised cells. They have special features that make it possible for fertilisation to take place.

special features of an egg cell:
- **haploid** nucleus containing DNA from mother
- many food molecules to provide energy for cell division and differentiation
- cell membrane that will thicken and harden after one sperm cell has broken through so other sperm cells cannot enter

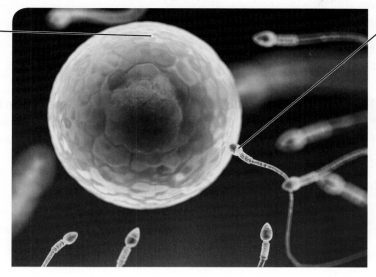

special features of a sperm cell:
- haploid nucleus containing DNA from father
- **acrosome** (bag of enzymes) at front of cell to digest a hole through the egg cell membrane
- long swimming tail
- many mitochondria to provide energy for swimming

D This artist's impression shows sperm cells swimming to reach an egg cell and fertilise it.

---

7 **a** Describe how the egg cell membrane changes at fertilisation to prevent other sperm cells entering it.

b Describe how the tail and mitochondria of a sperm cell help it to fertilise an egg cell.

There are a few stem cells left in our tissues even after most cells have differentiated. These are called **adult stem cells**. Adult stem cells can only produce a few types of new specialised cells. Adult stem cells are important for growth and for the replacement of damaged cells.

---

8 Describe the function of adult stem cells.

Plants also have stem cells. Plant stem cells are found in small areas called **meristems**. Meristems are found in shoot tips and root tips.

Key points

- Stem cells are unspecialised cells that divide to produce specialised cells. Specialised cells are adapted to carry out a particular function.
- Cell differentiation allows the body to produce different kinds of cells to carry out different functions.
- Embryonic stem cells can produce any type of specialised cell in the body.
- Adult stem cells produce new specialised cells for growth and repair of tissues.

Checkpoint

How confidently can you answer the Progression questions?

Foundation

F1 For each of these cells, describe one way in which they are adapted to their function:
a egg cell
b sperm cell
c nerve cell
d muscle cell.

Strengthen

S1 Describe the importance of stem cells in adult tissues.

B1c Growth

ELC B1A.3 **GCSE** B2.1, B2.2, B2.3, B2.5

Progression questions

- How does growth happen in animals and plants?
- How does mitosis produce new cells?
- Why is mitosis important?

A This baby's length is being measured. Length is a way of measuring its growth.

Young plants and animals grow as they get older. **Growth** means that they get bigger. Growth can be measured in different ways, such as:

- an increase in height
- an increase in mass.

In animals, growth happens by cell division. Cell division is when a cell divides and makes new cells. Cell division is part of the **cell cycle** in which cells grow and divide. The type of cell division that makes new body cells is called **mitosis**. Diagram B shows mitosis.

1. State what growth means.
2. Look at photo A.
   a. Suggest how the baby's length has changed since the measurement was taken a month earlier.
   b. Give a reason for your answer to part **a**.
3. Describe one way that growth of a plant could be measured.
4. Name the type of cell division that happens during growth.

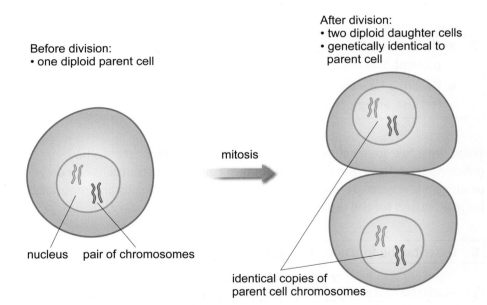

Before division:
- one diploid parent cell

mitosis

After division:
- two diploid daughter cells
- genetically identical to parent cell

nucleus   pair of chromosomes

identical copies of parent cell chromosomes

B In mitosis, one parent cell divides to produce two daughter cells.

5. a. Give the meaning of the term 'diploid'.
   b. Daughter cells formed in mitosis are genetically identical to the parent cell. Give a reason why.

The **parent cell** is **diploid**. This means it has pairs (two sets) of **chromosomes** in its nucleus. The chromosomes are copied exactly in mitosis. Each **daughter cell** has exact copies of the chromosomes in the parent cell. This means the daughter cells are genetically identical to the parent cell. After mitosis, cells differentiate into specialised cells, as you saw in topic B1b.

Plants also grow by mitosis. First, the cells divide in the shoot and root tips. Then the new cells get longer. We say that the cells undergo **elongation**. Finally, the plant cells differentiate into specialised types of plant cell.

Mitosis also produces new cells to replace any that get damaged. This repairs tissues and organs. For example, new skin forms if you cut yourself.

In some organisms, mitosis produces entire new individuals through **asexual reproduction**. Asexual reproduction is when offspring are produced without fertilisation. This means the offspring have only one parent. This makes them genetically identical to their parent and to each other.

- cell differentiation in older cells higher up the root
- produces specialised cells

- cell elongation in this area
- cells get longer

- cell division (mitosis) in this area
- new cells are small

root tip

C Cells in the tip of an onion root. The nucleus in each cell has been stained blue (magnification ×15).

plantlet with leaves and root

leaf of adult plant

D These plantlets were produced by asexual reproduction. When they separate from the parent, the plantlets will grow in the ground into new plants.

6 Compare the number of parents of offspring produced by asexual reproduction and by sexual reproduction.

7 The cells in the plantlets in photo D contain chromosomes that are identical to those in the cells of the parent plant. Give a reason why.

Key points

- Growth is an increase in size.
- Growth in animals happens by cell division. Growth in plants happens by cell division and cell elongation.
- Mitosis is cell division that produces two daughter cells from one parent diploid cell. The daughter cells are genetically identical to the parent cell.
- Mitosis produces new cells for growth, repair and asexual reproduction.

Checkpoint

How confidently can you answer the Progression questions?

Foundation

F1 Describe how growth takes place in animals and plants.

Strengthen

S1 Describe how the plantlets in photo D were formed.

B1d The nervous system

ELC B1A.7, B1A.8, B1A.9, B1A.10 **GCSE** B2.13, B2.14

Progression questions

- What do different types of neurones do?
- How do synapses work?
- Why are reflex arcs important?

A Our nervous system helps us to sense what is happening around us. It also helps us to respond to changes around us.

1 State the function of neurones.

2 Give an example of:
  a a sense organ
  b an effector.

3 a Name three different types of neurones.
  b Which type of neurone carries impulses between sensory neurones and motor neurones?

4 Describe the function of these parts of a neurone:
  a axon
  b dendron
  c myelin sheath.

The **nervous system** is made of nerve cells called **neurones**. Neurones carry electrical **impulses**. Neurones connect **receptor cells** in **sense organs**, such as the eyes and ears, with **effectors**, such as muscles. Receptor cells detect changes in the body or the surroundings. These changes are **stimuli** that cause the nervous system to respond.

There are three main types of neurones, with different functions (jobs).

- **Sensory neurones** carry impulses from receptor cells to relay neurones.
- **Relay neurones** in the **spinal cord** and brain (the central nervous system, or CNS) carry impulses from sensory neurones to motor neurones.
- **Motor neurones** carry impulses from relay neurones to effectors.

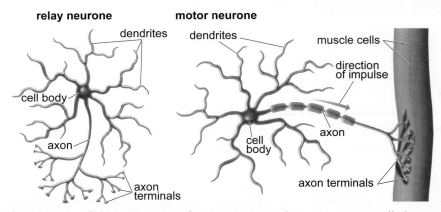

B The structure of the main types of neurones. Note that axons are usually longer than those in the diagram.

The parts of a neurone are adapted to their functions.

- The **axon** may be the longest part of a sensory or motor neurone. It carries the nerve impulse to other neurones, or to effector cells.
- The **dendron** is long in a sensory neurone. It carries the impulse from receptor cells.
- The **myelin sheath** is a fatty layer around the axon and dendron in many nerve cells. It **insulates** the neurone. This stops the nerve impulse

jumping to other nerve cells from the axon or dendron. The myelin sheath also makes the nerve impulse move faster along the neurone.

The point where two neurones meet is called a **synapse**. There is a small gap between the neurones. The electrical impulse cannot cross this gap. **Axon terminals** contain chemical **neurotransmitter**. When an impulse reaches the axon terminals of the first neurone, it triggers the release of neurotransmitter into the gap between the neurones. The neurotransmitter diffuses across the gap to a **dendrite** of the next neurone. This triggers an electrical impulse in that neurone.

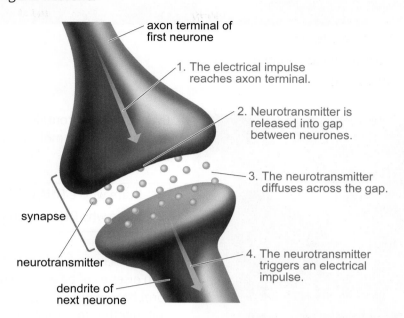

- 1. The electrical impulse reaches axon terminal.
- 2. Neurotransmitter is released into gap between neurones.
- 3. The neurotransmitter diffuses across the gap.
- 4. The neurotransmitter triggers an electrical impulse.

axon terminal of first neurone

synapse

neurotransmitter

dendrite of next neurone

C Chemical neurotransmitter allows an electrical impulse in one neurone to trigger an electrical impulse in the next neurone.

> **5 a** Define the term synapse.
>
> **b** Give a reason why neurotransmitter is needed to trigger an impulse in another neurone.
>
> **c** Give a reason why synapses make sure an electrical impulse can only pass in one direction between neurones.

A **reflex arc** is a simple pathway of neurones. It links receptor cells in a sensory organ to effector cells. These simple pathways allow very fast responses because the brain is not involved. Reflex arcs control automatic **reflex** responses that help to protect us. One example is the withdrawal reflex if you touch something hot. This reflex will cause you to automatically move away from the hot object.

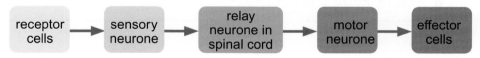

receptor cells → sensory neurone → relay neurone in spinal cord → motor neurone → effector cells

D the pathway of a reflex arc

> **6 a** State what is meant by a reflex arc.
>
> **b** Explain why reflex arcs are important for keeping us safe.

Key points

- Sensory neurones carry electrical impulses from receptor cells to relay neurones. Relay neurones pass the impulses to other relay neurones or to motor neurones. Motor neurones pass the impulses to effectors.
- A myelin sheath insulates some axons and dendrons.
- A synapse is where two neurones meet. Chemical neurotransmitter crosses the synapse gap and triggers an impulse in the next neurone.
- A reflex arc is a simple pathway of sensory neurone, relay neurone and motor neurone. It allows a quick, automatic response.

Checkpoint

How confidently can you answer the Progression questions?

Foundation

F1 State the function of the following: **a** sensory neurone, **b** relay neurone, **c** motor neurone, **d** neurotransmitter, **e** myelin sheath, **f** reflex arc.

Strengthen

S1 Your hand touches something hot. Draw a flow chart to show the stages of the withdrawal reflex. Include detail to show what happens at each stage of the reflex.

B1e DNA

ELC B1A.11, B1A.12 **GCSE** B3.4, B3.5, B3.6

Progression questions

- Where is DNA found?
- What is the structure of DNA?
- What is a gene?

A This staircase is like a DNA molecule. Each step has two colours, like the two bases of the base pairs that hold the two strands of the molecule together.

Every organism contains DNA. DNA is found in the nucleus of plant and animal cells. DNA molecules contain the **genetic code** that controls how our bodies work.

1 State where DNA is found in a cell.
2 State why DNA can control what happens in our bodies.

Each DNA molecule is made of two strands. Each strand has a 'backbone' with a series of bases attached to it. The bases on the two strands link to form **base pairs**. The base pairs hold the strands together. The two strands coil together to form a shape called a **double helix**.

3 Write a sentence to describe what diagram B shows. Use these words in your answer: DNA, chromosome, cell, nucleus.
4 Look again at diagram B.
   a How many DNA strands are in a DNA molecule?
   b What holds the strands of a DNA molecule together?
   c Which term describes the shape of a DNA molecule?
   d What forms the genetic code?

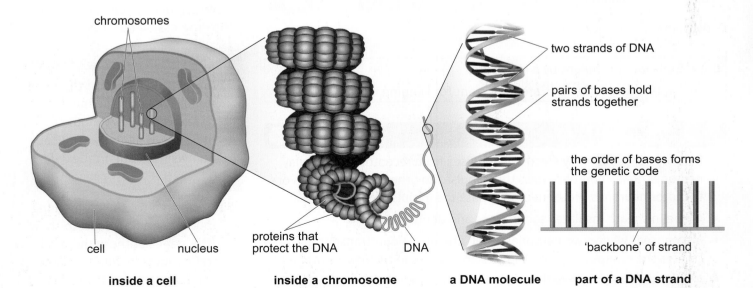

B DNA is tightly packaged inside chromosomes.

A **gene** is a section of a DNA molecule. Each gene contains the genetic code for making a specific **protein**. The order of the bases in each gene is different. This means different genes code for different proteins.

Each chromosome contains many genes. Each gene is found at a particular point on a chromosome. All the DNA of an organism is known as the organism's **genome**.

---

5 a What is a gene made of?

  b Describe the function of a gene.

6 a State what is meant by an organism's genome.

  b Suggest why different types of organisms have different proteins.

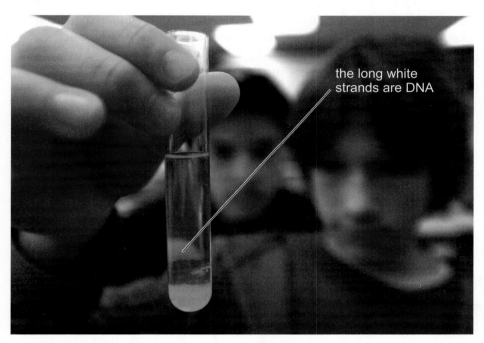

the long white strands are DNA

C DNA can be extracted from the cells of fruits, such as kiwi fruit.

---

7 The fruit in photo C was mashed with a mixture that breaks up the cells. Suggest which parts of the fruit cells were broken open by the mixture to release the DNA. Give a reason for your answer.

Key points

- A molecule of DNA has two strands. The strands are joined by base pairs. They coil to form a double helix.
- DNA is packaged into chromosomes in the cell nucleus.
- A gene is a section of a DNA molecule that codes for a specific protein.
- Chromosomes contain many genes. All the DNA of an organism is its genome.

Checkpoint

How confidently can you answer the Progression questions?

Foundation

F1 Describe the relationship between DNA, genes, chromosomes and a nucleus.

Strengthen

S1 Identify similarities between the structure of the staircase in photo A and DNA.

B1f Inheritance

ELC B1A.13, B1A.14, B1A.15 GCSE B3.12, B3.13, B3.14, B3.15

Progression questions

- How is a person's sex determined?
- What are dominant and recessive alleles?
- What are heterozygous and homozygous genotypes and phenotypes?

A In this family it looks like red hair is dominant over fair hair, because all the children have inherited red hair. Knowing about genes can show that this isn't true.

We inherit characteristics from our parents through chromosomes and genes. These chromosomes and genes are in the **gametes** (sex cells) that join at **fertilisation**.

Sex inheritance

The two **sex chromosomes** in each body cell determine if you are male or female. Human females have two X chromosomes (XX). Human males have one X chromosome and one Y chromosome (XY).

> **1** Give a reason why we inherit characteristics from our parents.
>
> **2** Which chromosomes determine if you are male or female?

Human gametes are sperm cells and egg cells. Each gamete contains only one set of chromosomes, so they have only one sex chromosome.

> **3** Look at diagram B. Which sex chromosome is found only in sperm cells?

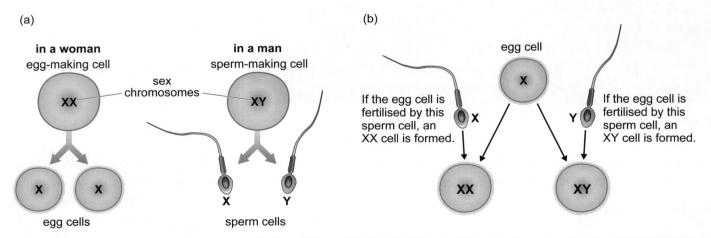

B (a) Gametes get only one set of chromosomes from the cell they are made from. This set includes one sex chromosome. (b) Sex is determined when a sperm cell and an egg cell join at fertilisation.

> **4** State whether the father's gamete or the mother's gamete determines the sex of their babies. Use part b of diagram B to help you.

The cell formed at fertilisation is a **zygote**. It always inherits an X chromosome from the egg cell. It also inherits a sex chromosome from the sperm cell. If the sperm cell contains an X chromosome, the zygote will be XX. If the sperm cell contains a Y chromosome, the zygote will be XY.

Monohybrid inheritance

A gene codes for a particular characteristic, such as hair colour. **Alleles** are different versions of a gene. For example, one allele of a hair colour gene causes red hair. A different allele of the same gene causes fair hair.

Body cells have two copies of each gene. The two copies may be the same allele or different alleles. The alleles an individual has for a particular gene are their **genotype**. The effect of these alleles is their **phenotype** (what the individual looks like).

A **dominant** allele always affects the phenotype if it is present in the genotype. **Recessive** alleles only affect the phenotype when there is no dominant allele present.

- If an individual has two identical alleles of a gene, they are **homozygous**.
- If their two alleles are different, the individual is **heterozygous**.

Monohybrid inheritance is the inheritance of alleles for one gene. We can show this using a **Punnett square**, like the one in diagram C.

> **5** Give a reason why one hair colour gene can cause red hair or fair hair.

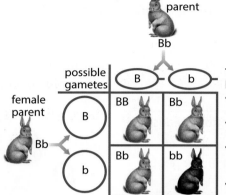

This gene for coat colour has two alleles.
- B is the allele for brown coat.
- b is the allele for black coat.
- genotypes BB and Bb both produce brown coat phenotype.
- genotype bb produces black coat phenotype.

The boxes show the possible combinations in the offspring.

C This Punnett square shows the possible coat colours of offspring from two parent rabbits that are heterozygous for the coat colour gene.

> **6** Look at diagram C.
>   **a** State the phenotypes (coat colour) and genotypes of the parent rabbits.
>   **b** Give a reason why there are two different possible gametes shown for both parents.
> **7** Use examples from diagram C to help you describe what these words mean: dominant, recessive, heterozygous, homozygous.
> **8** One possible outcome from a cross between two brown rabbits is a black rabbit. Use diagram C to help you explain why.

Another way to show inheritance is using a **family pedigree**. This shows the relationships between members of a family. It also shows which phenotype each person has for a particular characteristic.

Key points

- In humans, females have the sex chromosomes XX, males are XY. Sex is determined when an X or a Y sperm cell fertilises the X egg cell.
- Alleles are different versions of the same gene. A dominant allele in the genotype controls the phenotype. Recessive alleles only affect the phenotype when there is no dominant allele present.
- An individual with two identical alleles for a gene is homozygous. An individual with different alleles for a gene is heterozygous.
- Punnett squares can be used to show monohybrid inheritance.

Checkpoint

How confidently can you answer the Progression questions?

Foundation

F1 In pea plants, the dominant allele (R) produces purple flowers. The recessive allele (r) produces white flowers. State what the flower colour of pea plants with the alleles Rr will be.

Strengthen

S1 Write your own definitions for the following genetic terms: gene, allele, dominant, recessive, heterozygous, homozygous, genotype, phenotype.

B1g Variation

ELC B1A.16, B1A.17, B1A.18, B1A.19 GCSE B3.19, B3.20, B3.22, B3.23

Progression questions

- How is genetic variation caused?
- How can the environment affect characteristics?
- How do mutations result in variation in a population?

Animals or plants of the same species show **variation** in their characteristics. This means there are differences in characteristics such as height, mass, colour or the sound of their voice.

> 1 State what variation means.
> 2 Describe two examples of variation shown in the people in photo A.

A There are many examples of variation in this group of people.

Some of the variation between individuals is caused by the different combinations of alleles they inherit from their parents. Different allele combinations are produced when a male gamete fertilises a female gamete during sexual reproduction. Variation caused by different alleles is called **genetic variation**. For example, some people have alleles for blue eye colour. Others have alleles for brown eye colour. Like many of our characteristics, eye colour is controlled by more than one gene. This means that there are more eye colours than just brown and blue.

B Some of the children in this family have a mutation that stops them making the pigment that causes dark skin in their parents and other brothers and sisters.

> 3 A child has a long thin nose like his father. Suggest a reason for this.
> 4 Different fur colours in rabbits are an example of genetic variation. Explain what this means.

Different alleles of genes are produced by small changes to the structure of DNA. These changes in DNA are called **mutations**. Most mutations have no obvious effect. Some have a small effect. Rarely, a single mutation will significantly change a characteristic, as shown in photo B. Mutations cause variation between individuals in a population.

> 5 Give a reason for the genetic variation in skin colour shown in photo B.

Many characteristics change during life. For example, we may cut or colour our hair. These changes are caused by something in the environment. Characteristics that change because of the environment show **environmental variation**. Characteristics like this are also called **acquired characteristics**. They are acquired (they develop) during life.

C Exercise can change several characteristics, including muscle size, mass and body shape.

Most of our characteristics are affected by our genes and by the environment. For example, height is affected by genes that control how bones grow, and by other genes that control how well nutrients from food are used to make more bone. This explains why there is so much variation in height between people.

> **8** Explain how a person's height may be affected by several genes and by the environment.

Key points

- Variation is the differences in characteristics of individuals of the same species.
- Genetic variation is due to differences in alleles inherited from parents. Different alleles are produced by mutations (small changes to DNA). Most characteristics are affected by more than one gene.
- Environmental variation is differences in characteristics due to the environment.
- Most mutations have no effect on the phenotype. Only a very few have a significant effect on a characteristic.

> **6** Suggest an environmental cause of variation in hair length.
>
> **7** **a** Look at photo C. Does body mass show environmental variation?
>
> **b** Give a reason for your answer to part **a**.

Checkpoint

How confidently can you answer the Progression questions?

Foundation

F1 Zack is taller than his brother Jack. Suggest one genetic cause for this difference, and one environmental cause.

Strengthen

S1 A child has long, wavy blonde hair but his mother has straight, short brown hair. Give as many reasons as you can for these differences, explaining your answers.

Progression questions

- What evidence is there for human evolution?
- How did Darwin explain evolution by natural selection?
- What evidence supports Darwin's theory?

A Evidence from fossil skulls was used to make this model of a *Homo erectus* head.

Evolution is how things change over time. We can look at **fossils** to see how organisms changed over millions of years.

Diagram B shows skulls from some human-like species and from our own species, *Homo sapiens*. It also shows what scientists think these species looked like. This is based on evidence from their fossil bones. The evidence shows how human-like species evolved.

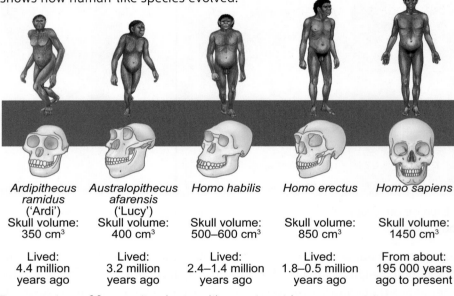

Ardipithecus ramidus ('Ardi')	*Australopithecus afarensis* ('Lucy')	*Homo habilis*	*Homo erectus*	*Homo sapiens*
Skull volume: 350 cm³	Skull volume: 400 cm³	Skull volume: 500–600 cm³	Skull volume: 850 cm³	Skull volume: 1450 cm³
Lived: 4.4 million years ago	Lived: 3.2 million years ago	Lived: 2.4–1.4 million years ago	Lived: 1.8–0.5 million years ago	From about: 195 000 years ago to present

B comparison of four ancient human-like species with our own species

> 1 State what evolution means.
>
> 2 Look at diagram B.
>
>   **a** Which human-like species lived 4.4 million years ago?
>
>   **b** Describe how skull volume evolved in human-like species over the last 4.4 million years.

C The stone chopper on the top was made about 2 million years ago. The stone knife on the bottom was made about 13 000 years ago.

> 3 **a** Use the photos in C to describe how stone tools changed over time.
>
>   **b** Suggest a reason why the stone tools changed.

Other evidence for human evolution comes from the stone tools that different human-like species made. The age of stone tools is worked out from the sediment they are found in.

Charles Darwin (1809–1882) developed the theory of **natural selection** to explain how evolution happens. Natural selection is how differences in an organism's characteristics affect its survival in certain environmental conditions. For example, dark skin in humans protects against cancer where light intensity from the Sun is high. Pale skin makes more vitamin D where light intensity is low. Vitamin D keeps us healthy.

Table D shows how Darwin's theory explains the evolution of pale skin colour from dark in some groups of humans.

Darwin's theory	Example of human skin colour
• There is variation in characteristics between individuals of a species because they have different alleles (genetic variation).	• Many thousands of years ago some humans left Africa. Over many generations, the people spread into northern Asia and Europe. The people who left Africa had dark skin, though some had slightly lighter skin than others.
• Some variations make individuals more likely to survive. We say they are better adapted to the environment.	• People living in northern areas who had lighter skin made more vitamin D than people with darker skin.
• Individuals that survive can reproduce. Their offspring can inherit the alleles for the better-adapted variations.	• Those people in northern areas who made more vitamin D grew better and had more children. These children inherited paler skin from their parents.
• In the next generation there will therefore be more offspring with the better-adapted variations.	• Over many generations human skin colour in northern Asia and Europe became paler and paler.

D how Darwin's theory explains the evolution of pale skin colour from dark in some human populations

> **4 a** Define the term natural selection.
>
> **b** State what 'being better adapted' means.
>
> **c** Explain why human skin colour evolved as people moved from Africa to northern Asia and Europe.

The evolution of antibiotic resistance in bacteria is another example of evolution through natural selection. **Antibiotics** kill bacteria. However, some bacteria have variations in their genes that stop them being killed by an antibiotic. We say they are **resistant** to it. The antibiotic-resistant bacteria survive and reproduce when other bacteria are killed. They pass on antibiotic resistance to their offspring.

> **5 a** State what is meant by antibiotic resistance in bacteria.
>
> **b** Explain why using antibiotics leads to an increase in the number of antibiotic-resistant bacteria.

Key points

- Charles Darwin developed a theory of evolution by natural selection. This states that individuals that are better adapted to their environment are more likely to survive and produce more young. More individuals in the next generation will have the better adaptations.
- Evolution is change over time.
- Human evolution is the change in human-like species over time. Evidence for this comes from fossil bones and from stone tools.

Checkpoint

How confidently can you answer the Progression questions?

Foundation

F1 Sketch a flow chart to show how Darwin explained evolution through natural selection.

Strengthen

S1 Some scientists think that environmental changes a few million years ago caused an increase in brain development of human-like species. Suggest evidence to support this idea.

B1i Selective breeding and genetic engineering

ELC B1A.21, B1A.22, B1A.23 GCSE B4.8, B4.10

Progression questions

- How can selective breeding change plants and animals?
- What is genetic engineering?
- What are the risks and benefits of genetic engineering?

A The Jack Russell terrier is a small dog breed developed to help people catch foxes and other animals that live in burrows, such as rabbits.

> **1** Define the term selective breeding.
>
> **2** State a characteristic of Jack Russells that makes them useful for catching foxes.

Selective breeding

Selective breeding is when people change the characteristics of animals or plants by selecting individuals with particular characteristics to breed together. This is done to make the plants and animals more useful to us.

For example, selective breeding of dogs has produced different **breeds**. Each breed has been developed for a different job. The Jack Russell breed was developed to catch foxes by:

- selecting small male and female dogs to breed together
- the offspring inherited the small size from their parents
- when the offspring grew up, the smallest were then bred together
- repeating this over many generations produced dogs small enough to get into fox holes.

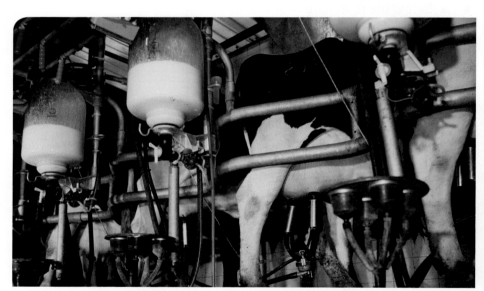

B One Holstein–Friesian cow can produce over 30 dm³ of milk each day. Other breeds of cow produce much less milk than this.

> **3 a** State which characteristic Holstein–Friesian cows have been selectively bred for.
>
> **b** Explain why this characteristic of Holstein–Friesian cows is useful to us.

Most of the **domesticated animals** that provide our food have been developed through selective breeding. Some breeds of cow have been selectively bred to produce lots of milk. This was done by breeding bulls whose female offspring produce lots of milk with cows that produce lots of milk.

Crop plants, such as wheat, are important sources of food. Wheat plants have been selectively bred to make them more resistant to disease. This has been done because diseases reduce the amount of food we get from each plant.

4 a State what is meant by a disease-resistant plant.

b Explain why selective breeding to make wheat plants resistant to disease is useful.

c Describe how selective breeding could be used to produce disease-resistant wheat plants.

Genetic engineering

Genetic engineering is used to give species new and desirable characteristics. This is done by:

- taking the gene for a desirable characteristic from the DNA of one species
- inserting this gene into the DNA of another species so that it produces the desirable characteristic.

AquAdvantage® GM Atlantic salmon

non-GM Atlantic salmon of the same age

C The AquAdvantage® salmon is a genetically modified (GM) breed. It contains a gene that non-GM breeds don't have. This gene helps the salmon grow faster than normal.

Genetic engineering can make organisms more useful, but it can also cause problems. For example, if the new gene is passed to wild organisms through breeding, it can change them too. This can change feeding relationships in the community and so harm other species.

5 AquAdvantage® salmon are produced in fish farms as food for us.

a Explain why AquAdvantage® salmon grow faster than non-GM salmon.

b Describe an advantage of growing AquAdvantage® salmon compared with non-GM salmon.

c AquAdvantage® salmon have also been genetically modified so they cannot breed with wild salmon. Suggest a reason for this.

Key points

- In selective breeding, individuals with the best characteristics are bred together. Over many generations, new and more useful breeds are developed.
- In genetic engineering, a gene for a desirable characteristic is taken from one species. The gene is inserted into the DNA of an individual of another species. This individual then has the useful characteristic.
- There are both benefits and risks of selective breeding and genetic engineering.

Checkpoint

How confidently can you answer the Progression questions?

Foundation

F1 Describe how one characteristic of a species has been changed by selective breeding.

F2 Describe one example of how a species has been changed by genetic engineering.

Strengthen

S1 A farmer plans to plant a field with genetically modified wheat. This wheat is resistant to attack by an insect that eats its leaves. Give one benefit of this for the farmer and one problem that this could cause.

Cell adaptations

1   Explain how an egg cell is adapted so that it can only be fertilised by one sperm cell.   (2 marks)

Student answer

Fertilisation is when a sperm cell joins with an egg cell [A]. *The egg cell membrane blocks other sperm from entering after one sperm has fertilised the cell* [B].

[A] This statement does not answer the question, so does not qualify for a mark.

[B] This is correct. However, the student should also have explained that this happens because the cell membrane changes or hardens after the sperm cell has entered.

Verdict

This is a poor answer. When the question says 'explain', you need to say *what* happens and also *why* it happens. The student has only said what happens.

Interpreting a Punnett square

2   Hair colour is controlled by genes. In one hair colour gene the dominant allele F produces fair hair, and the recessive allele f produces red hair.

Complete the Punnett square to determine the phenotype of the children of a man with fair hair and a woman with red hair.   (2 marks)

		Man	
		F	F
Woman	f		
	f		

Student answer

		Man		
		F	F	[A]
Woman	f	Ff	Ff	
	f	Ff	Ff	

All the children have fair hair [B].

[A] The student has correctly paired the alleles to complete the genotypes of the children in the Punnett square.

[B] They have correctly identified the phenotype from the genotypes.

Verdict

This is a good answer. Take care when completing a Punnett square or genetic diagram to pair the alleles correctly. Make sure you know the difference between the terms genotype and phenotype, so that you can give the correct answer.

B2 Health, disease and the development of medicines

Some microorganisms can cause disease if they get past our natural defences. If this happens, our immune system attacks and tries to destroy the microorganisms. If this does not work, we have medicines to help control the disease and make us better.

Not all diseases are caused by microorganisms. Some are caused by unhealthy changes inside the body. A healthy lifestyle can help prevent some of these diseases.

In this unit you will learn about diseases caused by microorganisms. You will also learn about diseases that are caused by changes in the body.

The learning journey

Previously you will have learnt at KS3:

- how to calculate energy requirements in a healthy daily diet
- how imbalances in the diet can lead to obesity, starvation or deficiency diseases
- how smoking can affect the human gas exchange system.

In this unit you will learn:

- about different pathogens that cause some common infections
- how infections are spread
- how the spread of infections can be reduced or prevented
- about the natural defences of the body, including the immune system
- how medicines are developed, including antibiotics
- how some diseases are caused by other factors, such as diet, lifestyle and genes.

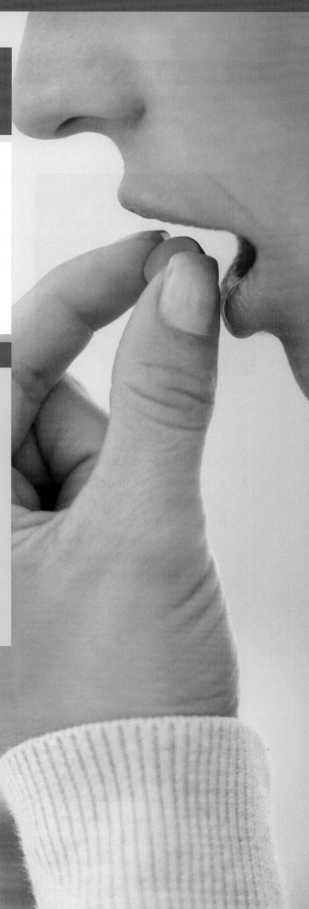

B2a Health and disease

ELC B1B.1, B1B.17, B1B.19, B1B.20 **GCSE** B5.1, B5.2, B5.23, B5.24

Progression questions

- What are communicable and non-communicable diseases?
- How is obesity affected by exercise and diet?
- How can BMI be used to measure obesity?

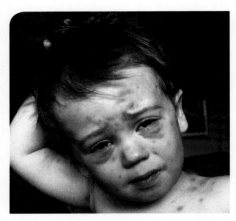

A This child caught chickenpox from a child who already had the disease.

> 1 Define the term health.
> 2 **a** What is a communicable disease?
> **b** Look at photo A. Is chickenpox a communicable disease? Give a reason for your answer.

Health is more than just not having a disease. It includes being physically fit and feeling good about yourself and about the way you live.

If a person has a disease, their body is not working properly. Some diseases are caused by infections passed from person to person. These are called **communicable diseases**. Examples include colds and flu.

Other diseases are caused by factors like our diet, our genes and the way we live. These diseases cannot be passed from person to person. They are called **non-communicable diseases**. Examples include cancer and **cardiovascular diseases** (diseases of the heart and blood vessels). The more factors we have that increase our **risk** of a disease, the more likely we are to develop the disease.

B Someone who is very overweight is said to be obese. Obesity is a factor that increases the risk of developing some non-communicable diseases.

> 3 Name three factors that can affect our risk of developing a non-communicable disease.
> 4 **a** State what obesity means.
> **b** Suggest why doctors advise people who are obese to lose weight.

Obesity can be measured using **BMI (body mass index)**. BMI is calculated using the equation:

$$BMI = \frac{mass\ (kg)}{(height\ (m))^2}$$

People who are taller are also usually heavier. BMI takes height into account, and so can give an estimate of how much body fat a person has. The higher the BMI, the more likely the person is to be overweight or even obese.

Worked example W1

A woman is 1.6 m tall and has a mass of 64 kg. Calculate her BMI.

$$BMI = \frac{mass\ (kg)}{(height\ (m))^2}$$

$$BMI = \frac{64}{1.6 \times 1.6}$$

$$= \frac{64}{2.56} = 25.0$$

Another way to estimate body fat is to use **waist : hip ratio**. This is calculated using the equation:

$$waist : hip\ ratio = \frac{waist\ measurement}{hip\ measurement}$$

Worked example W2

A man has a waist measurement of 94 cm and a hip measurement of 104 cm. Calculate his waist : hip ratio.

$$waist : hip\ ratio = \frac{waist\ measurement}{hip\ measurement}$$

$$waist : hip\ ratio = \frac{94}{104}$$

$$= 0.90$$

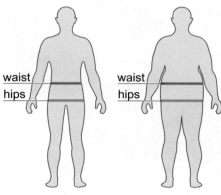

C taking waist and hip measurements to calculate waist : hip ratio

BMI and waist : hip ratio increase as body fat increases. Body fat increases if the diet contains more energy than the body needs to stay alive and be active. Body fat can decrease if the diet contains less energy. It can also decrease if a person does more exercise, because energy is used to make muscles work.

5 **a** State the two measurements needed to calculate each of the following.
  i BMI   **ii** waist : hip ratio
  b A man has a height of 1.85 m and a mass of 88 kg. Calculate his BMI.
6 Describe two ways in which people who are obese might reduce their body fat.

Key points

- Communicable diseases can be passed from an infected person to other people.
- Non-communicable diseases cannot be passed from person to person. They are caused by many factors, including diet, the way we live and our genes.
- BMI (body mass index) and waist : hip ratio can be used to measure obesity.
- Both exercise and a healthy diet can help reduce obesity.

Checkpoint

How confidently can you answer the Progression questions?

Foundation

F1 State whether cardiovascular disease is a communicable or non-communicable disease. Give a reason for your answer.

Strengthen

S1 Health advice for people with a high BMI is to eat a healthier diet and exercise more. Explain this advice.

B2b Lifestyle diseases

ELC B1B.17, B1B.18, B1B.21, B1B.22 GCSE B2.4, B5.23, B5.24

Progression questions

- What causes cancer?
- How can smoking harm the body?
- How is alcohol related to liver disease?

A Our lifestyle can increase the risk of developing cardiovascular diseases or cancer.

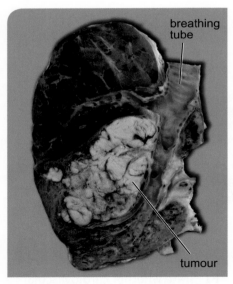

B This lung came from a person who died of lung cancer. The person smoked many cigarettes when they were alive.

The way we choose to live is our **lifestyle**. This includes things like what we eat, how much we exercise, whether we smoke, and how much alcohol we drink. Tobacco smoke and alcohol can both harm the body and lead to disease. Diseases caused by lifestyle are examples of non-communicable diseases.

> **1** **a** State what lifestyle means.
>
> **b** Give two examples of lifestyle factors that can harm the body.

Cancer is caused when changes in cells lead to uncontrolled cell division. Cancer can produce a lump called a **tumour**. This damages healthy cells around it as it grows. Your risk of developing cancer depends partly on your genes. However, some substances increase the risk that cells will change and become cancerous. Such substances are found in tobacco smoke.

> **2** Give a reason why smoking can cause cancer.

Cardiovascular disease

Substances in tobacco smoke can also increase the risk of cardiovascular disease. These substances enter the blood from the lungs. Diagram C shows how these substances can cause cardiovascular disease.

Substances from tobacco smoke damage the artery lining.

Fat builds up in the artery wall at the site of damage, making the artery narrower.

A blood clot may block the artery here, or break off and block an artery in another part of the body – causing a heart attack or **stroke**.

C how damage to an artery by substances in tobacco smoke can cause cardiovascular disease

> **3** Look at diagram C.
>
> **a** Describe what some substances in tobacco smoke do to arteries.
>
> **b** Describe the effect of fat build-up on arteries.
>
> **c** State why a blood clot in an artery is dangerous.

Cardiovascular disease can be treated in different ways:

- Medicines can reduce health problems that may cause cardiovascular disease. These problems include high blood pressure and high blood cholesterol. Such medicines must be taken for life.
- **Surgical procedures** (operations) can repair the heart or widen blood vessels that have been narrowed by fat build-up.
- A healthier diet and more exercise can reduce the health problems that may cause cardiovascular disease. Giving up smoking and making other lifestyle changes may also help.

> **4** Describe three ways in which cardiovascular disease may be treated.

Liver disease and alcohol

Liver cells are more likely than other cells to be damaged by alcohol. This is because the liver is where alcohol is broken down by the body. Drinking too much alcohol can lead to liver disease, which can kill.

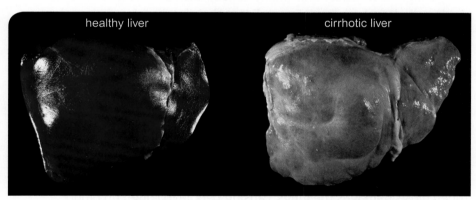

healthy liver   cirrhotic liver

D A healthy liver is dark red, smooth and soft. A liver damaged by alcohol may be larger and paler. It may also be much harder because of cell damage.

> **5 a** Use photo D to describe two effects on the liver of drinking too much alcohol.
>
> **b** Give a reason why most deaths linked to alcohol are deaths from liver disease.

Key points

- Cancer is caused by changes in cells leading to uncontrolled cell division.
- Tobacco smoke increases the risk of developing lung cancer and cardiovascular disease.
- Cardiovascular disease may be treated by taking medicines for life, surgery or lifestyle changes.
- Drinking too much alcohol can lead to liver disease.

Checkpoint

How confidently can you answer the Progression questions?

Foundation

F1 Give one reason why the woman in photo A is more likely than a non-smoker to suffer lung cancer.

Strengthen

S1 Give one reason why too much alcohol over a long time is a problem for each of the following:

 a the person who drinks it

 b the person's family.

B2c Pathogens and disease

ELC B1B.2, B1B.3, B1B.5, B1B.6, B1B.7 **GCSE** B5.4, B5.5

Progression questions

- What is a pathogen?
- What causes some common infections?
- What are the effects of some common infections?

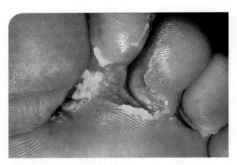

A Tinea (athlete's foot) is caused by a fungus that digests skin cells. This causes a rash and pain where skin splits.

> **2 a** Describe how fungi get their food.
>
> **b** Name one pathogenic fungus that attacks animals and one that attacks plants.
>
> **c** For each fungus named in **b**, describe the harm it can cause.

A **pathogen** is an organism that can cause disease. Pathogens include fungi, bacteria, protists and viruses. Pathogens can spread from an infected organism to others, causing disease in them. We say that pathogens cause communicable diseases or **infections**.

> **1 a** What is a pathogen?
>
> **b** Name four groups of organisms that are pathogens.

Many **fungi** are **multicellular** (many-celled), such as mushrooms. Others are single-celled, such as yeast. Fungi **digest** their food while it is outside the fungus. They then absorb the digested substances. Pathogenic fungi, such as the one that causes **tinea** (**athlete's foot**), cause harm when they digest living cells.

Some pathogenic fungi attack plants. For example, one fungus causes **chalara dieback** in ash trees. The fungus kills cells and causes leaf loss and **lesions** (splits) in the tree bark.

Bacterial infections include **cholera** and **tuberculosis**. Cholera causes **diarrhoea**. This can make people lose too much water and mineral salts. Tuberculosis damages the lungs, causing people to cough up blood.

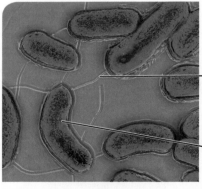

each bacterium has a **flagellum** (tail) for movement

the single circular chromosome (DNA) is in the cytoplasm, not in a nucleus

B Cholera is caused by a bacterium. A bacterium is a single cell with typical bacterial structures (magnification ×1350).

> **3 a** Give two examples of diseases caused by bacteria.
>
> **b** For each disease named in **a**, describe one way in which the pathogen causes harm.

Viruses are tiny particles that contain genetic material. They are said to be non-living because they cannot reproduce on their own. They only reproduce inside living cells. The cells are often damaged when the new viruses leave, causing disease. **Influenza** viruses cause sudden cold-like 'flu' **symptoms**. **HIV** (human immunodeficiency virus) is an example of another virus. HIV viruses destroy white blood cells. This means the body cannot defend itself from other pathogens, which can lead to infections that result in **AIDS**.

> **4 a** Describe two symptoms of infection with the influenza virus.
>
>   **b** Give a reason why HIV viruses harm the body.

Most **protists** are single-celled organisms. A few are pathogens. For example, **malaria** is a disease caused by a protist. The protist multiplies inside blood cells and liver cells and damages them.

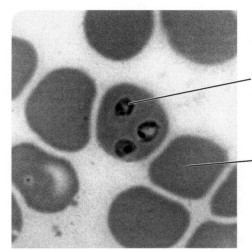

malaria protist inside red blood cell

uninfected red blood cell

D Malaria protists inside red blood cells. They will destroy the blood cells when they break out (magnification ×1500).

> **5 a** What type of organism is the pathogen that causes malaria?
>
>   **b** Describe the harm caused by malaria pathogens.

Key points

- Pathogens are disease-causing organisms. They include some bacteria, fungi, viruses and protists.
- Cholera and tuberculosis are bacterial infections. Cholera causes diarrhoea. Tuberculosis damages the lungs.
- Tinea (athlete's foot) and chalara dieback in ash trees are caused by fungal infections.
- Viruses are non-living particles that can only reproduce inside living cells. Examples include influenza and HIV.
- Malaria is caused by a protist that damages liver and blood cells.

C Flu symptoms appear suddenly and usually include **fever**, aches and pains. Other possible symptoms are a runny nose, sore throat or diarrhoea.

Checkpoint

How confidently can you answer the Progression questions?

Foundation

F1 Describe the symptoms of one disease caused by:

 a bacteria

 b viruses

 c fungi

 d protists.

Strengthen

S1 Draw up a table with the following headings: Name of disease, Type of pathogen, Symptoms of disease. Complete your table with all the examples of diseases in this topic.

B2d Spread and control of pathogens

ELC B1B.8, B1B.9 **GCSE** B5.6

Progression questions

* How are pathogens spread?
* What is a vector?
* How can we stop pathogens spreading?

A A sneeze or cough releases tiny droplets from the body. These can spread pathogens up to 5 m away.

Pathogens spread from one organism to another. Different pathogens spread in different ways, as shown in diagram B.

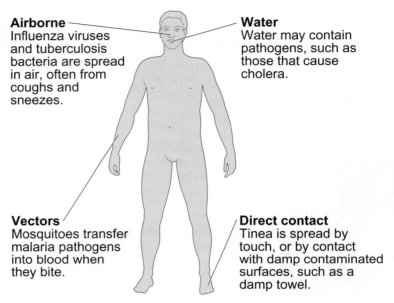

Airborne
Influenza viruses and tuberculosis bacteria are spread in air, often from coughs and sneezes.

Water
Water may contain pathogens, such as those that cause cholera.

Vectors
Mosquitoes transfer malaria pathogens into blood when they bite.

Direct contact
Tinea is spread by touch, or by contact with damp contaminated surfaces, such as a damp towel.

B different ways in which pathogens spread

---

1 Look at photo A. How far can pathogens in a cough or sneeze spread?

2 Look at diagram B. Describe how the pathogens that cause each of these diseases are spread:

   a cholera   **b** tinea   **c** influenza

   d malaria   **e** tuberculosis

Controlling the spread of infection

Knowing how pathogens spread can help us prevent diseases spreading. For example, you should catch a cough or a sneeze in a tissue, then bin the tissue. Washing your hands then removes pathogens left on your hands. This prevents airborne diseases, such as tuberculosis, spreading to other people.

---

3 Look at photo A and diagram B.

   a Name two diseases that could be spread by sneezes.

   b Describe one way in which the spread of these diseases could be prevented.

Washing your hands after a sneeze is an example of good **hygiene**. Hygiene means keeping things clean, and can help to stop the spread of disease. For example, cleaning floors in places where people walk barefoot can help to stop the spread of tinea.

Drinking water is usually treated with chlorine to kill pathogens. The water is then carried to houses and workplaces in pipes. This helps to stop the clean water coming into contact with pathogens before we use it. In areas where there is no piped drinking water, water can be heated to make it safe to drink.

> **5** Describe two ways in which dirty water can be treated to make it safe for drinking.

Some diseases are spread by **vectors**. Vectors are other organisms that spread pathogens. The malaria pathogen is carried in human blood that a mosquito has sucked from an infected person. So mosquitoes are a vector for malaria. Killing the mosquito before it can bite another person will stop the spread of malaria. For example, mosquitoes can be killed by spraying them or the surfaces they land on with **insecticide**.

D Spraying doorways with insecticide can help control the spread of malaria.

> **6 a** State what is meant by a vector of disease.
>
> **b** Explain why spraying with insecticide that kills mosquitoes can help to control the spread of malaria.

Key points

- Pathogens may be spread: in water (cholera), by air (influenza and tuberculosis), by direct contact (tinea), by an animal vector (malaria).
- An animal vector is an animal that spreads pathogens.
- The spread of pathogens can be reduced or prevented by hygiene (keeping clean), such as washing hands and surfaces, by treating water and by killing animal vectors.

> **4 a** State what hygiene means.
>
> **b** Describe one way to stop the spread of tinea at a swimming pool.

C Heating water to over 65 °C for a few minutes kills most of the pathogens in it.

Checkpoint

How confidently can you answer the Progression questions?

Foundation

F1 Give a reason why you should cover your nose and mouth when you sneeze or cough.

Strengthen

S1 Explain why it is important to wash your hands thoroughly after going to the toilet.

B2e Sexually transmitted infections

ELC B1B.10, B1B.11 **GCSE** B5.8

Progression questions

- What are STIs?
- How are *Chlamydia* and HIV spread?
- How can the spread of *Chlamydia* and HIV be reduced?

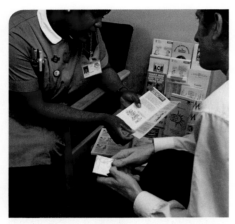

A Sexual health clinics provide advice on how to protect against being infected with STIs. They also do screening tests.

Sexually transmitted infections (**STIs**) are caused by pathogens that can spread through sexual activity. One example is the virus HIV (human immunodeficiency virus). Another is the bacterium **Chlamydia.**

> **1** **a** What is an STI?
>
> **b** Give two examples of pathogens that cause STIs.

In an infected person, HIV is found in **sexual fluids** such as semen and vaginal fluid. These fluids can be exchanged during sexual activity. HIV is also found in blood, and so can be spread by touching fresh blood. HIV cannot survive outside the body for long.

A person may not have any signs of HIV infection for a long while. HIV damages the immune system. This makes the body less able to fight off pathogens that cause other infections. A person who has other infections with HIV is said to have AIDS. Eventually this may cause death.

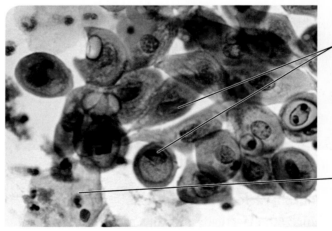

Chlamydia multiply inside cells, such as vaginal cells in a woman's reproductive system

vaginal cell that has broken open to release more bacteria

B *Chlamydia* bacteria multiply inside cells in organs of the reproductive system. When they break out of the cells, they can be spread to another person in sexual fluids (magnification ×400).

Chlamydia is found in sexual fluids. Contact with sexual fluid containing *Chlamydia* during sexual activity, or through touch, can lead to infection. Many people who are infected with *Chlamydia* have no symptoms and don't know they are infected. After a while, the infection can cause pain and fever. It may make the person **sterile**.

---

2 a State how HIV can be spread from an infected person to others.

    b State how *Chlamydia* can be spread from an infected person to others.

    c Explain why an infected person may spread *Chlamydia* or HIV without realising it.

Reducing the spread of STIs

The spread of HIV and *Chlamydia* can be reduced by avoiding contact with sexual fluids. This includes using a condom during sexual activity.

Simple tests can be used to test for STIs. Carrying out a test to see if somebody has a disease is known as **screening**.

---

3 a State what is meant by screening for a disease.

    b State what type of sample is needed for a *Chlamydia* screening test.

    c What type of sample could be used for an HIV screening test? Give a reason for your answer.

C A small sample of urine or swab of sexual fluids can be used to screen for *Chlamydia*.

Screening for STIs is recommended for anyone who has unprotected sex. Screening can help to prevent harm caused by long-term infection. *Chlamydia* can easily be treated with antibiotics to kill the pathogens. HIV can be destroyed if treated with medicines within a few days of infection. After that, its effects on the immune system can be controlled by other medicines.

---

4 Explain why it is important to be tested for STIs soon after having unprotected sex.

Checkpoint

How confidently can you answer the Progression questions?

Foundation

F1 Give a reason why using a condom during sexual activity can reduce the risk of catching an STI.

Strengthen

S1 In the UK, *Chlamydia* screening is recommended every year for people under 25. Suggest a reason for this recommendation.

Key points

- STIs are sexually transmitted infections. Pathogens that cause STIs include the bacterium *Chlamydia* and the HIV virus.
- STIs can be spread during sexual activity and contact with sexual fluids.
- The spread of STIs can be reduced or prevented by using a condom during sexual activity.
- STIs can be screened for by simple tests to show if a person is infected.

ELC B1B.12, B1B.13, B1B.14 GCSE B5.12, B5.13

Progression questions

- Which physical barriers protect against infection?
- Which chemical defences protect against infection?
- How does the immune system defend against infection?

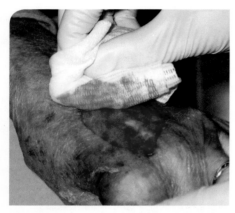

A Large wounds should be covered with a clean dressing to stop pathogens getting into blood. The dressing can be removed when a scab has sealed the wound.

Our bodies have **physical barriers** to help stop pathogens entering. Skin is a physical barrier because it is a thick layer that microorganisms cannot easily get through.

> 1 State why skin is a physical barrier.
> 2 **a** Explain why a wound should be covered with a clean dressing.
>   **b** Describe how the body naturally seals a wound.

Another physical barrier is **mucus**. Mucus is a sticky liquid that traps dust and pathogens. Mucus is produced in many parts of the body, including the nose, throat and lungs.

Cilia are tiny hair-like structures that line tubes, such as those in the lungs. Cilia wave from side to side, moving things across their surface. Cilia in the lungs help to move mucus out of the lungs to the throat, where it can be swallowed.

> 3 **a** Describe how mucus is a physical barrier to infection.
>   **b** Describe how cilia support mucus as a barrier to infection.

B These cilia wave from side to side. This movement moves mucus containing dust and pathogens out of the lungs.

Chemical defences are substances made by the body that protect against infection. For example, hydrochloric acid is made in the stomach. The acid destroys most pathogens in food and water, or in mucus from the throat.

Lysozymes are substances that are made in tears. Lysozymes destroy pathogens and so help to prevent infection of the eyes.

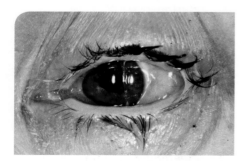

C This person's eye is infected with a pathogen. The eye is producing extra tears. The tears contain lysozymes to destroy the pathogen.

> 4 **a** Describe how the stomach protects against infection.
>   **b** Explain why lysozymes are an example of a chemical defence of the body.

The immune system

If pathogens enter blood or tissues, they are attacked by the **immune system**. The function of the immune system is to defend against disease.

White blood cells are part of the immune system. Some white blood cells, called **phagocytes**, **ingest** and destroy pathogens. Other white blood cells, called **lymphocytes**, produce **antibodies** that destroy pathogens (diagram D).

5 State the function of the immune system.

6 Describe two ways in which white blood cells attack pathogens.

3 This makes the lymphocyte divide over and over again. Many identical lymphocytes are produced.

1 Pathogens have antigens on their surface. Different pathogens have different antigens.

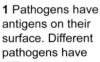
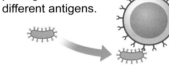
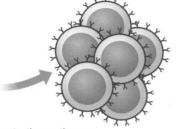
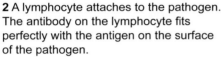

2 A lymphocyte attaches to the pathogen. The antibody on the lymphocyte fits perfectly with the antigen on the surface of the pathogen.

4 Some of the lymphocytes release a lot of antibodies. The antibodies stick to the antigens and destroy the pathogens.

D how the immune system attacks a pathogen by responding to **antigens**

After the pathogens have been destroyed, some lymphocytes stay in the blood. These are called **memory lymphocytes**, because they are how the body 'remembers' an infection. If you are infected by that pathogen again, the memory lymphocytes trigger a much faster and larger immune response. This **secondary response** destroys the pathogens *before* you become ill. This makes you **immune** to that pathogen.

7 Give the function of a memory lymphocyte.

8 a Describe two ways in which a secondary response of the immune system differs from the response after a first infection.

   b Explain why you usually don't feel ill when you are infected by a pathogen for a second time.

Key points

- Physical barriers stop pathogens getting into the body. These barriers include the skin, mucus and cilia.
- Chemical defences are substances produced by the body to destroy pathogens. They include hydrochloric acid and lysozymes.
- The immune system destroys pathogens inside the body. Some white blood cells ingest pathogens. Others, called lymphocytes, produce antibodies to destroy pathogens.
- Memory lymphocytes cause a fast secondary response if you are infected by the same pathogen again. This makes you immune to the pathogen.

Checkpoint

How confidently can you answer the Progression questions?

Foundation

F1 Cells in the lining of the nose produce mucus. Explain how this helps to protect against infection.

Strengthen

S1 Explain how the body responds if a pathogen gets past the body's physical and chemical defences.

B2g Medicines

ELC B1B.15, B1B.16 **GCSE** B5.20

Progression questions

- What are antibiotics?
- How are new medicines discovered?
- How are new medicines tested?

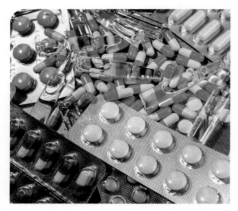

A Different antibiotics are used to treat different bacterial diseases.

Some medicines help us get better if pathogens have made us ill. Different medicines have different effects. For example, **antibiotics** can help to kill bacteria that are causing disease. However, antibiotics do not harm other groups of pathogens.

> **1** What are antibiotic medicines used for?
>
> **2** A person has a bad cold. Colds are caused by viruses. Would antibiotics help the person get better? Give a reason for your answer.

We need new medicines to replace those that don't work as well as they did, and to treat new diseases. Scientists study many sources to discover possible new medicines. One source is the substances that plants make to protect themselves from pathogens.

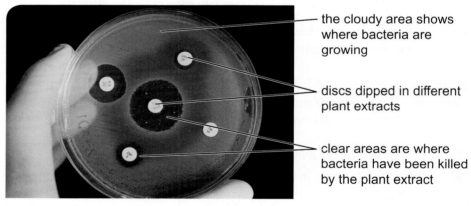

the cloudy area shows where bacteria are growing

discs dipped in different plant extracts

clear areas are where bacteria have been killed by the plant extract

B A bigger clear area around a disc shows that the plant extract in the disc is better at killing the bacteria.

> **3** State one way in which scientists are trying to discover possible new medicines.
>
> **4** Look at photo B.
>
> **a** Identify which disc contains the plant extract that is best at killing the bacteria in the dish.
>
> **b** Give a reason for your answer to **a**.

Possible new medicines are developed to make them more effective without harming human cells.

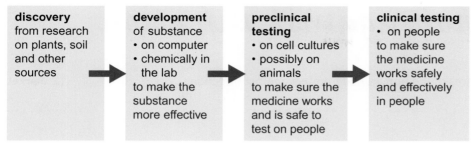

C Possible new medicines go through different stages of development before they can be given to people by doctors.

Preclinical testing

Stages of testing before medicines are tested on people are called **preclinical testing**. First, the medicines are tested on diseased human cells or tissues. This checks that the medicine can get into the human cells without harming them. It also checks that the medicine works, such as by killing the pathogen. Possible new medicines may then be tested on animals. This is the best way to test how a whole body is affected without risking harm to people.

Clinical testing

New medicines that are effective in preclinical tests are then tested on people. Tests on people are called **clinical testing**. The first stage of clinical testing is usually on a few healthy people. This makes sure the medicine is safe for people to take.

The last stage of clinical testing is on many people. These people have the disease that the medicine is meant to treat. The results from different groups of people (e.g. different age, sex or ethnic group) are compared. This test checks that the medicine is safe and effective in many different people. The new medicine must pass all the testing stages before it is allowed to be given by doctors to their patients.

> **6 a** Describe two stages of clinical testing.
>   **b** Explain why each stage you have described in **a** is done.

> **5 a** Describe two possible stages of preclinical testing.
>   **b** Explain why each stage you have described in **a** is done.

D Clinical tests of possible new medicines are carefully carried out by doctors.

Checkpoint

How confidently can you answer the Progression questions?

Foundation

F1 Give a reason why you are not given antibiotics to treat flu.

Strengthen

S1 A new antibiotic has been made. Describe how the antibiotic will be tested before doctors are allowed to use it on their patients.

Key points

- Antibiotics are used to treat bacterial diseases but not other diseases.
- Possible new medicines are discovered by studying plants and other sources, and developing the substances to make them more effective.
- New medicines must pass a series of tests before they can be used. Preclinical tests are on cell or tissue cultures, and sometimes on animals. Clinical tests are on people. The tests check that the medicine is safe and effective.

Protection against infection

1 Describe how two physical defences of the human body protect against infection. **(2 marks)**

. . . .

Student answer

Skin is very thick. This stops germs [A] *from getting in easily except when you have a cut* [B].

[A] 'Germs' is not a scientific term, so will not gain marks. Use 'pathogens' or 'infection' instead.

[B] The student has described only one defence. The question asks for two. Other suitable examples include sticky mucus that traps pathogens in the nose and lungs, or cilia that help move mucus out of the lungs.

. . . .

Verdict

This is a poor answer because it gives only one example. If a question asks for two things, make sure you include two examples. Remember that 'describe' questions only need facts, not reasons.

Calculating BMI

2 BMI (body mass index) is used to identify people who may be overweight and at risk of certain diseases.

BMI is calculated using the equation:

$$BMI = \frac{mass\ (kg)}{(height\ (m))^2}$$

A woman has a height of 168 cm and a mass of 82 kg. Calculate her BMI. **(2 marks)**

. . . .

Student answer

$$BMI = \frac{82}{1.68 \times 1.68} = \frac{82}{2.82} = 29.05$$
$$\quad\;\; [A] \qquad\qquad [B]$$

[A] The student has correctly converted the height units from centimetres in the question to metres for the answer.

[B] They have also clearly shown all their working.

. . . .

Verdict

This is a good answer because it gives the correct value and shows all the working. Remember that correct working will get a mark even if the final answer is wrong.

B3 Plants and ecosystems

Plants are green because they contain chlorophyll. Having chlorophyll means plants can photosynthesise. Photosynthesis needs light and makes food that plants use for growth. Herbivores are animals that eat plants. Carnivores are animals that eat other animals. So all organisms in an area depend on each other for food.

In this unit you will learn about how plants exchange substances with the environment and get what they need for growth. You will also learn about how organisms depend on each other, and how communities can change.

The learning journey

Previously you will have learnt at KS3:

- how plants are adapted for photosynthesis, and that almost all life depends on photosynthesis
- that plants take in mineral nutrients and water through their roots, and that leaf stomata are important in gas exchange
- how organisms in an ecosystem depend on each other and are affected by their environment
- the importance of pollination for plants and the importance of maintaining biodiversity
- about respiration and the carbon cycle.

In this unit you will learn:

- the effect of the environment on photosynthesis
- how substances are exchanged with the environment and transported into and out of cells
- how organisms in a community are affected by their environment and each other
- how human activity is affecting ecosystems
- how materials cycle through ecosystems.

B3a Photosynthesis

ELC B2A.1, B2A.2, B2A.3, B2A.4, B2A.5 **GCSE** B6.1, B6.2, B6.3

Progression questions

- What is photosynthesis?
- How do plants make biomass?
- What changes the rate of photosynthesis?

A During daylight, plants release a gas. In water, the gas can be seen as bubbles.

Plants and green algae are green because they have green **chlorophyll** in their cells. Chlorophyll is needed for **photosynthesis**. Photosynthesis is the process that makes **glucose** using energy transferred from light. Glucose is the plant's food. It can be changed into other substances to build more cells. This increases the **biomass** of the plant or alga and allows it to grow.

> 1 State why plants and green algae are green.
>
> 2 Name the substance produced in photosynthesis that plants and green algae use as food.
>
> 3 Explain why photosynthesis can increase a plant's biomass.

Photosynthesis uses energy transferred by light to react carbon dioxide with water. This produces glucose and oxygen. The word equation for the reaction is shown in diagram B. The carbon dioxide for photosynthesis comes from the air. The water usually comes from the soil.

> 4 **a** Name the products of photosynthesis.
>
> **b** Name the gas in the bubbles in photo A. Give a reason for your answer.

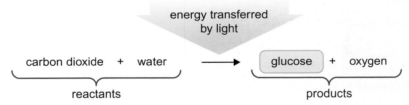

B the equation for photosynthesis

Photosynthesis only happens when there is enough light. This is because the reaction needs a supply of energy and is **endothermic**.

> 5 Name the source of energy for photosynthesis.

Rate of photosynthesis

A faster rate of photosynthesis means the plant will grow faster.

Some factors in the environment can affect the rate of photosynthesis. For example:

- carbon dioxide concentration – Carbon dioxide concentration in the air is quite low. Increasing the carbon dioxide concentration can increase the rate of photosynthesis.
- temperature – At low temperatures, photosynthesis may not happen at all. As temperature increases, the rate of photosynthesis can increase – up to a point.

- light intensity – Graph C shows how increasing **light intensity** increases the rate of photosynthesis, up to a point. At that point, some other factor starts to limit how fast the reaction can go. The other factor may be temperature or carbon dioxide concentration.

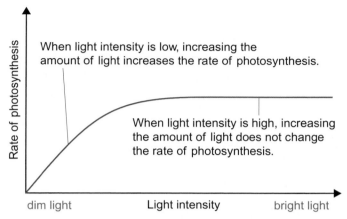

C the effect of changing light intensity on the rate of photosynthesis

We call factors such as carbon dioxide concentration, temperature and light intensity **limiting factors** in photosynthesis. This is because they can limit the rate of photosynthesis.

carbon dioxide generator

D Carbon dioxide generators add carbon dioxide to the air inside this glasshouse.

6 **a** Name three environmental factors that may limit the rate of photosynthesis.

  b Describe how changing each factor named in **a** can affect the rate of photosynthesis.

7 Tomato plants are often grown in glasshouses. Explain why carbon dioxide might be added to the air in a glasshouse where tomato plants are growing.

Key points

- Plants and green algae use photosynthesis to make food (glucose). They use this food to make more biomass.
- In photosynthesis, carbon dioxide and water react to form glucose and oxygen. The process needs energy transferred by light. So the reaction is endothermic.
- The rate of photosynthesis may be affected by light intensity, temperature or carbon dioxide concentration in the air.

Checkpoint

How confidently can you answer the Progression questions?

Foundation

F1 Describe how plants and green algae make food.

Strengthen

S1 Explain why a plant grower keeps young plants in a bright, warm place to grow.

A Plants photosynthesise faster on a sunny day than on a cloudy day.

Energy for photosynthesis is transferred by light. Brighter light transfers more energy than dimmer light. The rate of photosynthesis is therefore affected by light intensity.

You will investigate how light intensity affects the rate of photosynthesis in algal cells. The algal cells are trapped in balls of jelly. Bottles containing algal balls are placed at different distances from a lamp. Each bottle has the same number of balls, so all bottles contain the same quantity of algae. The further a bottle is from the light, the lower the light intensity.

The rate of photosynthesis is measured by the change in pH of the solutions in the bottles. Photosynthesis takes carbon dioxide from the solution. The solution becomes less acidic, which can be shown using a pH indicator. The faster the rate of photosynthesis, the greater the change in pH.

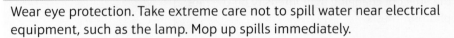

Method

Wear eye protection. Take extreme care not to spill water near electrical equipment, such as the lamp. Mop up spills immediately.

A You will be given four bottles. Place 20 algal balls into each bottle.

B Add enough indicator solution to the bottles to cover the algal balls. Use the same amount of indicator solution in each bottle. Put the cap on each bottle.

C Compare the colour of the indicator in your bottles with the colour range that your teacher has. Write down the pH of the colour that matches the indicator in your bottles.

D Place the ruler as shown in diagram B, so that zero is at the lamp. Place the bottles at different distances from the lamp, along the ruler to a maximum distance of 50 cm.

E Turn the lamp on. Leave the equipment until there are obvious colour changes in the bottles.

F Use the colour range to identify the pH of the solution in each bottle. Record the pH value for each bottle.

G Display your results in a line graph using axes like those in diagram C.

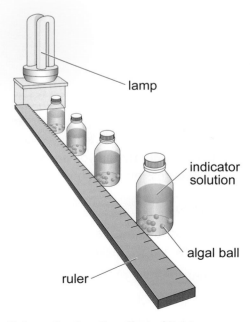

B investigating the effect of light intensity on the rate of photosynthesis

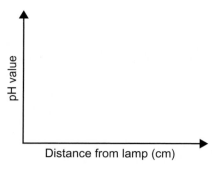

C axes for graph to show results of light intensity practical

Exam-style questions

1 State why algae are able to photosynthesise. *(1 mark)*

2 **a** Explain why the algae in this experiment need a good supply of carbon dioxide. *(2 marks)*

 b Explain why the colour of the indicator changes in the bottles when the lamp is on. *(2 marks)*

3 **a** State the independent variable in this experiment. *(1 mark)*

 b State the dependent variable. *(1 mark)*

4 Write an equipment list for the method shown on the previous page. *(2 marks)*

5 Graph D shows results from an experiment using the method shown on the previous page. Use graph D to draw a conclusion for this experiment. *(2 marks)*

D results for question 5

B3b Movement of substances

ELC B2A.6, B2A.7, B2A.8, B2A.9, B2A.10 **GCSE** B1.15, B6.7

Progression questions

- What is diffusion?
- How does water move by osmosis?
- Why do cells use active transport?

A The plant on the left has wilted because its cells do not contain enough water. On the right, water absorbed from the soil has filled the plant cells.

Substances are continually moving into and out of organisms by different processes. These processes are diffusion, osmosis and active transport.

> **1** Look at photo A. Name the substance that moved into the plant from the soil.

Diffusion

The images in photo B show what happens to a manganate crystal in water. As the crystal dissolves, the purple manganate particles can move between the water particles. The manganate and water particles move randomly. This random movement causes the manganate particles to spread out.

start

water

manganate crystal starting to dissolve

after 6 hours

The concentration of manganate particles is the same throughout the solution.

B experiment to show the diffusion of purple manganate particles in water

> **2** Name the process shown in photo B.
>
> **3** Describe how the concentration of manganate particles changed during the experiment in photo B.
>
> **4** Define the term diffusion.

This gradual spread of particles from where there are lots of them (higher concentration) to where there are fewer of them (lower concentration) is known as **diffusion**.

Small molecules can diffuse through cell membranes. They diffuse from the side of the membrane where they are in higher concentration to the side where they are in lower concentration. Examples of substances that diffuse into and out of cells include oxygen, carbon dioxide and glucose.

> **5** Oxygen concentration is usually low in a cell, due to respiration. Blood passing the cell has a higher concentration of oxygen.
>
> **a** In which direction will oxygen diffuse, from the blood to the cell or from the cell to the blood?
>
> **b** Give a reason for your answer to part **a**.

Osmosis

Water molecules are small enough to diffuse through a cell membrane. The diffusion of water is called **osmosis**. Osmosis is important for cells, because many cell reactions can only happen when the substances are in solution.

Cells lose water by osmosis when placed in a concentrated solution. Cells gain water when placed in a dilute solution.

> **6** Define the term osmosis.
>
> **7** Look at the images in photo C. Explain why the onion cells look different in the two images.

Active transport

Some cells need substances that are in lower concentration outside the cell than inside. For example, plants absorb mineral ions from the soil, but the concentration of mineral ions in their cells is higher than in the soil water around the root. So the mineral ions cannot diffuse into the cell.

Instead the cells pump mineral ions from the soil water into the cell. This pumping needs energy to move the mineral ions through the cell membrane. Movement of molecules through a cell membrane that needs energy is called **active transport**.

Adaptations for exchange

Cells that exchange substances with the environment have adaptations that help them do this well. Many of these cells have a large surface area. This makes it easier for more substances to enter or leave the cell at the same time.

> **8 a** Define the term active transport.
>
> **b** Explain why root hair cells absorb mineral ions from the soil by active transport, not diffusion.
>
> **9** Explain how the root hair cells in photo D are adapted for absorbing substances from the soil.

Key points

- Diffusion is the movement of particles from an area of their higher concentration to an area of lower concentration.
- Osmosis is a type of diffusion where water molecules move across a cell membrane. Cells that are in a concentrated solution will lose water. Cells in a dilute solution will gain water.
- Active transport is the movement of substances across a cell membrane from a lower concentration to a higher concentration. This requires energy.
- Root hair cells have a large surface area. This helps them absorb substances faster from soil water.

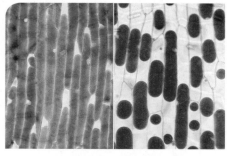

C The red onion cells on the left have been kept in a dilute solution. These cells contain as much water as can get in. The cytoplasm fills the cells. The cells on the right have been kept in a concentrated solution. Water has left the cells, so the cytoplasm no longer fills the cells (magnification ×55).

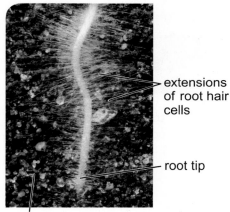

extensions of root hair cells

root tip

soil

D Root hair cells near a root tip have long hair-like extensions that spread out into the soil. This increases the surface area of each cell's cell membrane.

Checkpoint

How confidently can you answer the Progression questions?

Foundation

F1 Describe three different ways in which substances can enter or leave a cell.

Strengthen

S1 Describe how water and mineral ions enter a plant from the soil.

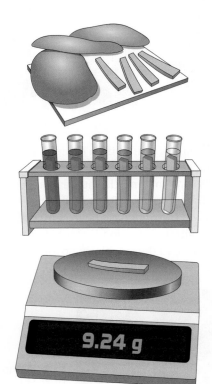

A some of the apparatus used in the osmosis in potatoes practical

Water enters and leaves cells by osmosis. The amount of water that moves into or out of cells depends on the concentration of the solution that the cells are in.

If water enters cells, the mass of the cells increases. If water leaves cells, the mass of the cells decreases. We can use the change in mass to measure how much osmosis has taken place.

You are going to measure the gain and loss of mass due to osmosis in strips of potato in solutions of different concentration. Different pieces of potato will have different starting masses. The fairest way to compare them is by calculating the percentage change in mass for each piece:

$$\text{percentage change in mass} = \frac{(\text{final mass} - \text{starting mass})}{\text{starting mass}} \times 100\%$$

If the answer is a positive number, then the potato piece gained mass. If it is a negative number, then the potato piece lost mass.

Method

A You will be given some boiling tubes. Label each tube with one of the sucrose concentrations you will test. Each tube should be labelled with a different concentration. Place all the labelled tubes in a rack.

B Cut similar-sized potato strips. Make sure the potato strips will fit in a boiling tube. You need one potato strip for each tube.

C Draw up a table to record your results.

D Blot one potato strip dry. Measure the starting mass of the strip to 2 decimal places. Record the starting mass of the strip in your table.

E Place the potato strip into an empty tube. Record in your table the concentration marked on the tube.

F Repeat steps D and E for each potato strip.

G Fill each tube with the solution that has the concentration marked on the tube. Make sure the potato strip in the tube is covered with solution. Leave the tubes for at least 15 minutes.

H Remove each potato strip from its solution. Blot each strip dry. Then measure the final mass of each strip and record the mass in your table. Make sure you match the correct final mass with the starting mass for each strip.

I Calculate the percentage change in mass for each strip and record it in your table.

Exam-style questions

1 Give a reason why the mass of the potato strips changed during the experiment. *(1 mark)*

2 Write an equipment list for the method shown on the previous page. *(2 marks)*

3 **a** Identify the independent variable in this experiment. *(1 mark)*

   b Identify the dependent variable in this experiment. *(1 mark)*

4 Explain why each strip of potato was blotted dry before its mass was measured. *(2 marks)*

5 Explain why you need to compare the percentage change in mass of the potato strips, not just the change in mass. *(2 marks)*

6 Table B shows the results from an experiment similar to the one described in the method on the previous page.

   a For each solution, calculate the gain or loss in mass of the potato strip to 2 decimal places. *(2 marks)*

   b For each solution, calculate the percentage change in mass of the potato strip to 1 decimal place. *(2 marks)*

   c Plot the results using a line graph. Put the concentration of solution on the *x*-axis and percentage change in mass on the *y*-axis. (Note that you will need to place the *x*-axis part way up the *y*-axis, as in diagram C. This is so you can display both negative and positive values for percentage change in mass.) *(2 marks)*

   d Explain the result in tube A. *(2 marks)*

   e Explain the results in tubes B, C and D. *(2 marks)*

   f When the concentration of the cell cytoplasm is the same as the concentration of sucrose in the surrounding solution, there will be no osmosis.

   Use your graph to identify the concentration of the potato cell cytoplasm. Give a reason for your answer. *(2 marks)*

Tube	A	B	C	D
Sucrose concentration (%)	0	10	30	50
Starting mass of potato strip (g)	4.81	5.22	4.94	4.86
Final mass of potato strip (g)	4.90	4.96	4.39	3.69

B the effect of sucrose concentration on the change in mass of potato strips (results for question 6)

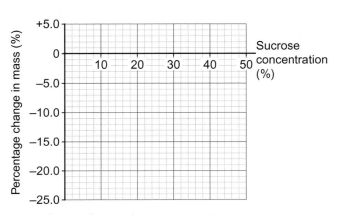

C axes for results graph in question 6c

B3c Transpiration and translocation

ELC B2A.11, B2A.12, B2A.13 **GCSE** B6.8, B6.9, B6.10, B6.12

Progression questions

- How do water and mineral ions move through a plant?
- What is transpiration?
- How is sucrose moved through a plant?

A Indoor plants need regular watering. They need more watering when it is hot and sunny.

1 a Name two types of tissue in a plant vein that transport substances.

b State what is transported in each tissue that you named in **a**.

Plant **veins** contain two types of tissue that transport substances around the plant.

- **Xylem** carries water and mineral ions.
- **Phloem** carries **sucrose** dissolved in water.

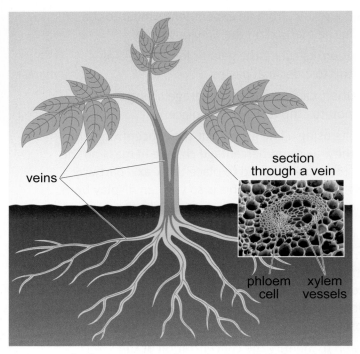

B A network of veins reaches from the tips of roots to the tips of leaves.

Transpiration

Water evaporates out of leaves through tiny pores called **stomata**. Each stoma is surrounded by two **guard cells**. These cells can change shape to open or close the stoma. Stomata are usually open when it is light. This allows carbon dioxide into the leaf for photosynthesis.

2 Name the tissue involved in transpiration.

3 Give a reason why stomata can open and close.

Water that evaporates out of stomata is replaced by water from xylem. This causes water to flow in xylem from plant roots up through the stem to the leaves. This flow of water is called **transpiration**. Anything that increases the rate of transpiration will increase the rate of water uptake by the plant.

For example:

- light intensity – Water uptake is faster during the day (when it is light) than at night.
- air movement – Water uptake is faster in windy conditions than in still conditions.
- temperature – Water uptake is faster when it is warmer.

> **4** **a** Sketch a flow chart to show the path of water flow from soil to air through a plant.
>
> **b** Give a reason why water uptake by a plant is greater on a warm, windy day than on a cool, still day.

Translocation

Glucose is formed during photosynthesis in leaf cells. Glucose is used to make sucrose. Sucrose then enters the phloem in the leaves and is transported around the plant to cells where it is used as a source of energy. This transport is called **translocation**.

> **5** What is translocation?

Xylem and phloem adaptations

Xylem and phloem have adaptations that help them carry out their functions.

A xylem vessel is a long tube made from dead cells. Water can flow easily through the empty vessel. The walls of the vessels are lignified. This means they contain **lignin**, which is a strong material. Lignin stops the vessel walls collapsing or bursting.

Phloem tissue is made of living cells. Some of the cells carry the sucrose solution. Other cells provide energy to help the sucrose move through the phloem.

> **6** Describe how xylem is adapted for its function.
> **7** Describe how phloem is adapted for its function.

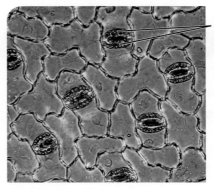

Two guard cells surround one stoma.

C Stomata are mostly found on the lower surface of a leaf (magnification ×170).

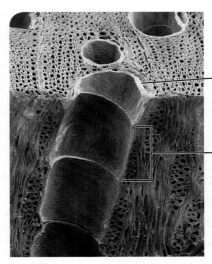

thick, lignified wall of vessel

remains of one xylem cell – the end walls of the dead, empty cells have gone, forming a long tube

D features of a xylem vessel (magnification ×100)

Key points

- Transpiration is the flow of water through a plant.
- Xylem transports water and mineral ions through a plant. Xylem has long empty vessels with strong lignified walls.
- Stomata are pores in the leaf surface that open or close due to changes in the shape of guard cells.
- Translocation is the movement of sucrose through plants in phloem. Phloem is made of living cells. Some of the cells supply energy that helps transport the sucrose around the plant.

Checkpoint

How confidently can you answer the Progression questions?

Foundation

F1 Sucrose is made in plant leaves. Describe how sucrose moves to other parts of the plant.

Strengthen

S1 Compare and contrast transpiration and translocation.

B3d Ecosystems

ELC B2A.14, B2A.15, B2A.18 **GCSE** B9.1, B9.2, B9.6

Progression questions

- What are the parts of an ecosystem?
- How are communities affected by abiotic factors?
- Which methods are used to investigate the number of organisms in an area?

A This African savannah ecosystem contains a community of populations of zebras, giraffes, grasses, different bushes and many other species.

An **ecosystem** is all the organisms in an area and the environment that affects them. Diagram A shows that an ecosystem has a **community** of organisms, made up of **populations** of different species. The non-living factors of the ecosystem that affect organisms are called **abiotic factors**.

1 State what these words mean.
  a ecosystem
  b community
  c population

2 Use photo A to identify an example of each of the following.
  a a population
  b a community
  c an ecosystem

---

ecosystem: all the organisms in an area and the abiotic factors that affect them (e.g. African savannah)

abiotic factors: non-living factors that affect organisms, such as:
- light
- nutrients
- water
- temperature
- space

community: all the populations of different species living in the ecosystem

population: all the individuals of a species living in an area, such as the:
- savannah grass population
- zebra population
- acacia tree population
- lion population

B the relationship between an ecosystem, its community and the populations in it

Abiotic factors that affect a community of organisms include:

- light – Plants need light for photosynthesis, although some plants grow better in shade. Animals are also affected by light. For example, day length may affect when animals breed.

- temperature – High temperatures damage cells, as do very low temperatures. Different species are adapted to living in different temperatures. So different species are found in different ecosystems.

C A northern forest ecosystem contains many species of conifer tree (trees with needle leaves). Conifer trees are not easily damaged by cold and snow.

- water – All organisms need water. Some ecosystems, such as deserts, lack water. Where it rains a lot, organisms may need adaptations to cope with too much water.
- pollution – **Pollutants** are substances that harm organisms and the environment. For example, some substances from industry are poisonous to living organisms. Increasing carbon dioxide in the atmosphere from burning fossil fuels is also a pollutant, because it is causing **climate change**. Climate change is changing the temperature and other abiotic factors in many places.

> **4** Describe one way in which each of these abiotic factors can affect a community.
>
> **a** light **b** temperature **c** water **d** pollution

Sampling ecosystems

It can be difficult to count the number of organisms in an area if the area is large or the organisms are difficult to see. Instead we use fieldwork techniques that **sample** the population. These include using a:

- **quadrat** – A quadrat is a square frame that is placed on the ground. The number of organisms of the species being studied inside the frame are counted. We can use the numbers from the quadrats to estimate the number in the whole area. Quadrats are useful for sampling organisms that either do not move at all or do not move during the sampling time, such as plants or snails.
- **pitfall trap** – This trap is set into the ground so that small animals fall into it. It is important to check the trap frequently and to release any animals so that they do not die.

> **5** Explain why sampling techniques are used to investigate how many organisms are living in an area.
>
> **6** Describe one fieldwork technique that could be used for counting the number of ground beetles in an area.

> **3** Give one reason why northern forest ecosystems have larger populations of conifer trees than of broad-leaved trees.

D This pitfall trap is covered to protect any animals that fall into it from rain.

Key points

- Ecosystems are made up of a community of organisms and the environment in which they live. The community is made up of populations of different species. Each population contains all the individuals of a species living in the area.
- Abiotic factors are non-living factors in the environment, such as temperature, light, water and pollutants.
- The number of organisms in a given area can be estimated using techniques such as quadrats and pitfall traps.

Checkpoint

How confidently can you answer the Progression questions?

Foundation

F1 Write your own definitions for the key words in this topic.

Strengthen

S1 Give a reason why plants in a community are affected by the amount of light they get.

B3d Core practical – Quadrats and transects

A This student is studying how changes in abiotic factors along a belt transect affect plant species on a school field.

The effect of abiotic (non-living) factors on organisms can be studied by sampling along a straight line called a **belt transect**. Quadrats are placed at regular intervals along the transect. The number of organisms inside each quadrat is counted. Abiotic factors are also measured in each quadrat. These measurements might include temperature, light intensity, soil nutrients or humidity (amount of water in the air or soil).

The number of organisms at each point along the transect is then compared with the values for the abiotic factors. This will show if changes in numbers of organisms have a similar pattern to changes in abiotic factors.

Good places to use a transect are where changes in the numbers of particular species can clearly be seen, such as from under a shady tree to out into the open.

Method

A Peg out a long tape measure (at least 20 m) on the ground. Start the tape measure where there is heavy shade and end it where there is no shade. This is the transect.

B Decide how many quadrat samples you will take along the transect. Work out how to space this number at regular intervals along the transect.

C Your teacher will suggest which plant species to record. These species should clearly change in number along the transect.

D Your teacher will suggest abiotic factors to measure. Choose which to use and make sure you know how to measure them.

E Use a suitable table to record all your measurements.

F Place the top left-hand corner of the quadrat at a measurement point on the transect. Count the number of individuals of each species you are studying. Only count those inside the quadrat. Record the numbers.

G Measure the abiotic factors in the middle of the quadrat and record them.

H Repeat steps F and G at each measurement point along the transect.

I Back in school, use your measurements to draw a chart to display your results clearly.

B Quadrats are placed at regular intervals along a transect.

Exam-style questions

1 State what a transect is. *(1 mark)*

2 a What are abiotic factors? *(1 mark)*

   b Look at diagram B. Suggest a reason why the student might choose to measure light intensity along the transect. *(2 marks)*

   c Name a piece of equipment that could be used to measure light intensity. *(1 mark)*

3 The number of quadrat samples taken along the transect may affect the results.

   a Describe a possible problem with sampling at every metre along a transect that is 30 metres long. *(1 mark)*

   b Describe a possible problem with sampling at only two or three points along this transect. *(1 mark)*

4 Describe how you would identify the plant species in the study. *(1 mark)*

5 Table C shows the results from an investigation like the one in diagram B. The investigation used a quadrat that was 1 m × 1 m square.

Quadrat distance from tree trunk (m)	0	5	10	15	20
Number of daisy plants	0	0	4	8	9
Light intensity (lux)	523	745	938	2833	5679

C results for question 5

   a Describe how the number of daisy plants changes with distance from the tree. *(1 mark)*

   b Describe how light intensity changes with distance from the tree. *(1 mark)*

   c Compare the pattern of change in number of daisy plants with the change in light intensity. Start your answer with: The change in daisy number… *(1 mark)*

   d Suggest a reason why light intensity might affect where daisy plants grow. *(1 mark)*

B3e Biotic factors in ecosystems

ELC B2A.16, B2A.17 **GCSE** B9.2, B9.3, B9.4

Progression questions

- How are communities affected by biotic factors?
- How does interdependence affect communities?
- How are organisms interdependent in parasitism and mutualism?

A This lioness has killed a zebra. She is hiding with her food in bushes so that leopards do not take her food.

1. Give two examples of resources in an ecosystem.
2. Give a reason why organisms in a community are interdependent.
3. Look at photo A. Identify the resource that the lioness gets from:
   - **a** the zebra
   - **b** the bush.

Organisms in a community are **interdependent**, because they depend on each other for **resources** such as food and shelter. Being interdependent means that if the number of one species changes in the community, this will affect other species. For example, if trees in a wood are chopped down, ground-level plants will get more light and may grow better, but birds may have nowhere to nest.

Biotic factors in an ecosystem are factors caused by other organisms that affect the community. Two examples of biotic factors are predation and competition.

- **Predation** is when one animal kills and eats other animals. The animal that kills and eats others is the **predator**. The animals the predators feed on are their **prey**.
- **Competition** is when organisms struggle with each other to get the resources they need.

4. **a** Define the term biotic factor.
   b Give one example of a biotic factor.
5. **a** What is meant by predation?
   b Identify the predator and prey in photo A. Give a reason for your answers.
6. Describe the competition that the lion in photo A is trying to avoid.

Parasitism and mutualism

Some organisms have special relationships that make them highly interdependent. **Parasitism** is where one organism (the **parasite**) lives on or in another organism (the **host**). The parasite benefits from the relationship by getting food or other resources from the host. The host is harmed by the parasite.

> **7** Explain why the relationship between head lice and humans in photo B is an example of parasitism.

Mutualism is a special partnership between species where both species benefit. If one of the species in the partnership changes in number, the other species may be affected too.

B Head lice are parasites of humans. They pierce the skin on the head and suck blood, which is their food.

C Bees visit flowers to collect nectar for food. The bees then carry pollen from flower to flower. The transfer of pollen allows the plants to reproduce.

> **8** Explain why the relationship between bees and flowers in photo C is an example of mutualism.

Key points

- Organisms in a community are interdependent, because they depend on each other for resources.
- Biotic factors are caused by organisms. Predation is when an animal kills and eats other animals. Competition is when different species struggle with each other for resources such as food or light.
- Parasitism is a close relationship between species where the parasite benefits but the host is harmed. Mutualism is a close relationship where both species benefit.

Checkpoint

How confidently can you answer the Progression questions?

Foundation

F1 Describe an example of interdependence between organisms described in this topic.

Strengthen

S1 Compare parasitism and mutualism.

B3f Biodiversity

ELC B2A.19, B2A.20 **GCSE** B9.9, B9.10

Progression questions

- What are the benefits of animal conservation?
- What are the benefits of reforestation?
- What are the benefits and risks of human activities for ecosystems?

A People now grow crops in places where elephants used to feed on wild plants. Now elephants sometimes eat the crops. They can do a lot of damage.

The human population is increasing. More land is needed for people to live, work and grow food. This has left many other species at risk of going **extinct** (dying out), because they cannot get the resources they need.

> 1 Give one reason why species may go extinct.
> 2 Look at photo A.
>   a Describe one problem for people living in areas where wild animals live.
>   b Describe one problem for wild animals living in areas where people live.

Conservation

Conservation is the protection of a species or an area to prevent damage. Human activities such as building and clearing land may be stopped in a conservation area.

Conservation of an area preserves the **habitats** where organisms live. It can help to protect **biodiversity** (the number of species in an area). Conservation can also encourage people to visit to see the wildlife, which is called **wildlife tourism**. This may have an economic benefit, as it can help local people earn money.

> 3 a State what conservation means.
>   b Explain why conservation of an area can help protect biodiversity.
>   c Explain how conservation of an area can increase wildlife tourism.

Reforestation

Planting new trees in an area where trees have been cut down is called **reforestation**. Reforestation can create new habitats. This can increase biodiversity, as more species come to live in the area.

B Millions of trees have been planted in the National Forest in England over the last 20 years. Each young tree is protected by a plastic sleeve when it is planted. Many rare species, such as otters and barn owls, are increasing in number. New species have also moved into the area.

Trees are also important because they take carbon from the air during photosynthesis and store it in their wood. This can reduce the amount of carbon dioxide in the air, which may help to reduce the effects of climate change.

> 4 a Explain why reforestation can increase biodiversity.
>   b Explain how reforestation could help to reduce climate change.

Fish farming

Fish farming is growing fish in pens or ponds to feed people. Eating farmed fish means that we take fewer wild fish. This can protect wild fish and their habitats. However, farming fish can risk polluting nearby habitats.

C Salmon are farmed in pens. They grow faster than wild salmon, because they are fed well. They are also protected from predators and disease.

Non-indigenous species

Non-indigenous species are species that have been introduced to an area where they do not normally live. This can happen by accident, such as rats spreading to many parts of the world on ships. Species can also be introduced on purpose, perhaps because a plant is pretty or an animal is useful. Non-indigenous species can change indigenous communities by competition or predation.

> **6 a** Define the term non-indigenous species.
>
> **b** Explain why non-indigenous species can be a problem.

> **5 a** Explain how farming fish is useful to people.
>
> **b** Explain how farming fish can protect wild fish.

Key points ⬤

- Conservation is the protection of a species or an area. Benefits include preserving habitats and biodiversity and promoting wildlife tourism.
- Reforestation is planting new trees where others have been cut down. Benefits include providing habitats, increasing biodiversity and reducing climate change.
- Fish farming is growing fish in pens or ponds to provide food. It may harm nearby habitats by adding pollutants. It can help to protect wild fish.
- Non-indigenous species are species introduced to an area where they do not normally live. They can harm communities through competition or predation.

Checkpoint ◤

How confidently can you answer the Progression questions?

Foundation

F1 Describe one reason for protecting wild animals in conservation areas.

Strengthen

S1 How can planting an area of grassland with different kinds of trees increase biodiversity?

B3g Natural cycles

ELC B2A.21 GCSE B9.12, B9.13, B9.14

Progression questions

- What is the carbon cycle?
- Why are decomposers important?
- What happens in the water cycle?

A Food and drink are sources of carbon and water.

Substances such as carbon and water constantly cycle through the living (biotic) and non-living (abiotic) parts of an ecosystem.

> **1** **a** Name one source of the carbon in our bodies.
>
> **b** Name one source of the water in our bodies.

Carbon cycle

Diagram B shows how carbon cycles through an ecosystem. The processes that exchange carbon between organisms and the air are:

- **photosynthesis** – carbon dioxide is taken in by plants to make carbon compounds
- **respiration** – carbon dioxide is released from carbon compounds by all organisms, including plants and animals
- **combustion** – burning releases carbon dioxide to the atmosphere.

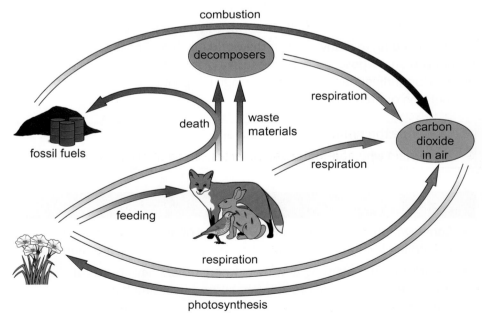

B the carbon cycle

2 Look at diagram B.

    a Identify two processes that add carbon dioxide to the atmosphere.

    b Identify one process that removes carbon dioxide from the atmosphere.

3 **a** Give one example of a decomposer.

    b Give a reason why decomposers are important in the carbon cycle.

Decomposers are microorganisms, including fungi and bacteria. Decomposers break down large compounds in dead bodies and in animal waste. Decomposition releases smaller compounds into the environment, including carbon dioxide into the air.

If dead organisms are not decomposed, over thousands or millions of years they may form **fossil fuels** such as coal, oil and peat. Combustion of fossil fuels releases a lot of carbon dioxide.

Water cycle

Diagram C shows the water cycle. The processes in this cycle include:

- **evaporation** – where liquid water changes to water vapour
- **condensation** – where water vapour changes to liquid water.

Organisms need water in their cells, because many cell reactions take place in solution. Plants absorb water from the soil and lose it to the air through transpiration. Animals take in water through food and drink. Animals lose water by evaporation from their surface and in urine and waste.

In **drought** areas, there may not be enough **potable** (drinking) water. We can produce drinking water from salty water by **desalination**. This means separating the dissolved salts from the water.

As air rises it cools, so water vapour in it condenses to form clouds.

As water droplets get too large and heavy they fall as rain or snow.

Water evaporates from oceans, lakes and rivers to form water vapour.

river

lake

river

ocean

Transpiration in plants takes in water from the soil and gives out water vapour from leaves.

Rivers flow into lakes and eventually the water returns to the ocean.

C the water cycle

---

5 a Describe how water is exchanged between plants and the environment.

   b Describe how water is exchanged between animals and the environment.

6 Explain how potable water can be produced from salty water.

---

4 Look at diagram C.

   a Identify where evaporation occurs in an abiotic part of the water cycle.

   b Identify where condensation occurs.

Key points

- The carbon cycle shows how carbon cycles through the biotic and abiotic parts of an ecosystem. Processes in the cycle include respiration, photosynthesis and combustion.
- Decomposers break down dead organisms and animal waste. Decomposers include microorganisms. Decomposition releases carbon dioxide.
- The water cycle shows how water cycles through an ecosystem. It involves abiotic processes such as evaporation and condensation. It also involves biotic processes such as drinking and transpiration.
- Potable (drinking) water can be made from salty water using desalination.

Checkpoint

How confidently can you answer the Progression questions?

Foundation

F1 Describe two processes in living organisms that affect the amount of carbon dioxide in the atmosphere.

Strengthen

S1 A gardener puts dead plant material in a compost heap. After a few weeks the heap is smaller. It is also covered in fungi. Explain these observations.

Transport in plants

1 Compare and contrast how water and dissolved mineral ions enter and are transported around a plant.

(2 marks)

Student answer

Water and mineral ions dissolved in the water enter through the plant's roots [A] and are transported in xylem vessels [B] [C].

[A] Plants only absorb substances through root hair cells, not the whole root. It is important to be specific in the answer.

[B] The student has correctly identified the similarity that xylem vessels transport both water and dissolved mineral ions.

[C] The answer doesn't state how water and dissolved mineral ions enter the plant. Remember that different processes are involved: water enters by osmosis, dissolved mineral ions enter by active transport.

Verdict

This is a poor answer. The words 'compare and contrast' indicate that the answer should include similarities *and* differences between the examples. This answer has not given any differences.

The effect of fertiliser

2 All the fish died in a small lake. Scientists carried out tests and concluded that overuse of fertiliser by farmers on nearby fields caused the fish to die. Explain this conclusion.

(3 marks)

Student answer

- [A] Too much fertiliser on the field means that some can get into the lake. This causes eutrophication [B] of the lake.

- Eutrophication causes algae to grow quickly, blocking light to plants below.

- The plants die and are decomposed by bacteria [C].

- Bacteria take oxygen from the water for respiration, so that there is not enough oxygen for the fish.

[A] Setting out a long answer in bullet points can help to arrange your thoughts in a good order.

[B] Remember to use correct scientific words where you can.

[C] Make sure you understand and explain the role of decomposers in this process, and that they cause the decrease in oxygen in the water.

Verdict

This is a good answer. 'Explain' questions need to give a reason for a statement. This answer gives reasons that link the cause (fertiliser) with the effect (dying fish).

B4 Human biology

Conditions inside your body are continually changing as reactions take place. Some substances are broken down, while new substances are made. These new substances include enzymes that control reactions. They also include hormones that affect how cells work.

We have so many blood vessels in our bodies that if you take everything else away you can still see the shape of the body. We need all these blood vessels because substances must be continually exchanged between cells and the blood. Blood travels along the vessels, bringing substances that cells need more of and carrying away substances that the cells do not need.

The learning journey

Previously you will have learnt at KS3:

- about the menstrual cycle
- that enzymes digest food in the gut
- about how gas exchange happens in lungs
- about aerobic and anaerobic respiration.

In this unit you will learn:

- about hormones, including hormones that control the menstrual cycle
- how insulin controls blood glucose concentration
- about the causes and treatment of type 1 and type 2 diabetes
- how enzymes work
- about the structure and function of blood, blood vessels and the heart
- how aerobic and anaerobic respiration release energy.

B4a Hormones

ELC B2B.1, B2B.2, B2B.8 **GCSE** B7.1, B7.13

Progression questions

- What are hormones?
- Where are some hormones made?
- What is the function of insulin?

A Some characteristics of a boy change during **puberty**. These changes are caused by the hormone **testosterone**.

Hormones are chemical messengers that are made in the body. Hormones help to control what happens in the body.

> **1** **a** State the meaning of the term hormone.
>
>   **b** Describe the function of hormones.
>
> **2** Look at photo A. Describe one effect of the hormone testosterone.

Hormones are made by special cells in **endocrine glands**. Different hormones are produced in different endocrine glands, as shown in diagram B.

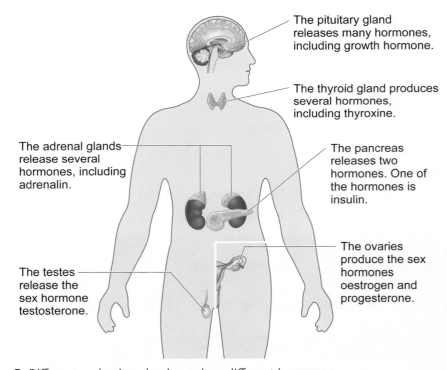

The pituitary gland releases many hormones, including growth hormone.

The thyroid gland produces several hormones, including thyroxine.

The adrenal glands release several hormones, including adrenalin.

The pancreas releases two hormones. One of the hormones is insulin.

The testes release the sex hormone testosterone.

The ovaries produce the sex hormones oestrogen and progesterone.

B Different endocrine glands produce different hormones.

> **3** Look at diagram B.
>
>   **a** Name the endocrine gland in which oestrogen is made.
>
>   **b** Name a hormone that is produced in the pancreas.

Hormones are released into the blood from their endocrine gland. They travel around the body in the blood. Some organs are affected by the hormone in the blood and change how they work. These organs are called **target organs**.

Insulin

Insulin is a hormone that is produced in the pancreas. The function of insulin is to stop the concentration of glucose in the blood getting too high.

When we eat a meal, we absorb glucose into the blood from digested food. Our blood glucose concentration then increases. The higher concentration of glucose makes the pancreas release more insulin into the blood. The blood carries insulin around the body.

C Sugary and starchy foods are broken down to glucose when food is digested in the gut. They cause an increase in blood glucose concentration when the glucose is absorbed.

Insulin particularly affects cells in organs such as muscles and the liver. Insulin causes these cells to take in glucose from the blood. As glucose is absorbed into cells, blood glucose concentration falls.

6 **a** Give a reason why blood glucose concentration increases.

 b Describe the effect of increased blood glucose concentration on the pancreas.

 c Give a reason why insulin causes blood glucose concentration to fall.

Key points

- Hormones are chemical messengers that are produced in endocrine glands.
- Hormones are carried in the blood and affect target organs by changing what they are doing.
- Insulin is a hormone released by the pancreas to help control blood glucose concentration.
- Insulin causes target cells in muscles and the liver to absorb glucose from the blood.

4 State what is meant by a target organ.

5 Sketch a flow chart to show how a hormone is transported from where it is made to where it has an effect. Use the terms target organ and endocrine gland in your diagram.

Checkpoint

How confidently can you answer the Progression questions?

Foundation

F1 Give an example of a hormone and the endocrine gland where it is made. State where your chosen hormone has an effect.

Strengthen

S1 Write bullet notes for an item on hormones in a web dictionary. Use insulin as the example.

B4b Keeping things constant

Progression questions

- Why are some conditions inside the body kept constant?
- How is type 1 diabetes controlled?
- How is type 2 diabetes controlled?

A This person has diabetes. The diabetes was not controlled properly. This caused so much damage to the nerves and blood vessels in his foot that his foot had to be cut off.

Many conditions inside the body must be kept constant, for example:

- blood glucose concentration
- body temperature
- amount of water in the body.

These conditions are controlled to keep the body working well.

> **1** State three conditions in the body that need to be kept constant.

Some people are not able to control their blood glucose concentration properly. This condition is known as **diabetes**. Diabetes needs treatment to stop blood glucose concentration going too high. High blood glucose concentration can cause unconsciousness. Over a long time, high blood glucose concentration also damages many organs. For example, it may cause blindness.

There are two different types of diabetes. Each type has a different cause and so needs different treatment.

> **2** Name the condition in which people cannot control their blood glucose concentration properly.
>
> **3** Give a reason why blood glucose concentration needs to be controlled properly.
>
> **4** How many types of diabetes are there?

B A person with type 1 diabetes injects insulin to control blood glucose concentration. The insulin is injected into the fat below the skin, where it can enter the blood.

C This machine measures blood glucose concentration. This helps people with diabetes to work out how much insulin to inject.

Type 1 diabetes

People with **type 1 diabetes** do not produce insulin. This is because the cells in the **pancreas** that make insulin do not function.

People with type 1 diabetes have to control their blood glucose concentration by injecting insulin. The right amount of insulin must be injected to make sure blood glucose concentration does not go too high or too low. This helps to protect the body from harm.

> **5 a** Describe the cause of type 1 diabetes.
>
>   **b** Describe the treatment for type 1 diabetes.
>
> **6** Describe how insulin injected into the fat below the skin causes blood glucose concentration to fall. Look at topic B4a if you need help to answer this.
>
> **7** Explain why blood glucose concentration should be measured before injecting insulin.

Type 2 diabetes

Type 2 diabetes can be caused by the pancreas not producing enough insulin to control blood glucose concentration well. It can also be caused by target cells not responding properly to insulin. The result in both cases is that not enough glucose is absorbed from the blood.

A low-sugar diet can help people with type 2 diabetes. This diet helps stop blood glucose concentration increasing too much. Exercise can also help, because it takes glucose from the blood without the need for insulin.

> **8 a** Describe two causes of type 2 diabetes.
>
>   **b** Explain how the following can help someone with type 2 diabetes.
>
>   **i** changing the diet   **ii** taking more exercise

D During exercise, muscle cells absorb glucose from the blood. The glucose is used in respiration to release energy for movement.

The proportion of people in the UK with type 2 diabetes is increasing. This may be because more people are obese. Obese people are more likely to have type 2 diabetes than people who are not overweight. **Obesity** may be increasing because of unhealthy diets and lack of exercise.

> **9** Give one possible cause of the increase in people with type 2 diabetes.

Checkpoint

How confidently can you answer the Progression questions?

Foundation

F1 Give a reason why someone who has type 1 diabetes must inject insulin every day.

Strengthen

S1 Describe the similarities and differences between type 1 diabetes and type 2 diabetes, and how they are treated.

Key points

- Blood glucose concentration, body temperature and water content need to be kept constant.
- Type 1 diabetes is caused by cells in the pancreas not producing insulin.
- Type 1 diabetes is controlled by injecting insulin to keep blood glucose concentration at safe levels.
- Type 2 diabetes is caused by insulin-producing cells not producing enough insulin, or by target cells not responding to insulin.
- Type 2 diabetes may be controlled by a low-sugar diet and exercise.

B4c Menstrual cycle and contraception

ELC B2B.3, B2B.4, B2B.5, B2B.6 **GCSE** B7.4, B7.6

Progression questions

- What happens in the menstrual cycle?
- How does hormonal contraception work?
- How do barrier methods of contraception work?

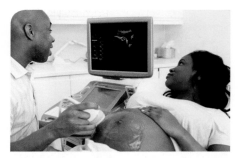

A This woman became pregnant when one of her egg cells was fertilised by a sperm cell. The scan shows her baby developing inside her uterus.

Pregnancy is the result of the **fertilisation** of an egg cell by a sperm cell. Pregnancy is possible due to the menstrual cycle.

The **menstrual cycle** is a cycle of changes that happen in a woman's reproductive system. The changes help prepare her body for pregnancy. The first cycle begins at puberty (around 12 years old), and cycles stop at **menopause** (around 50 years old). Each cycle takes about 28 days, although some women have longer or shorter cycles. The cycle is controlled by hormones, including **oestrogen** and **progesterone**.

> 1   What is the menstrual cycle?
> 2   How long does one menstrual cycle usually take?

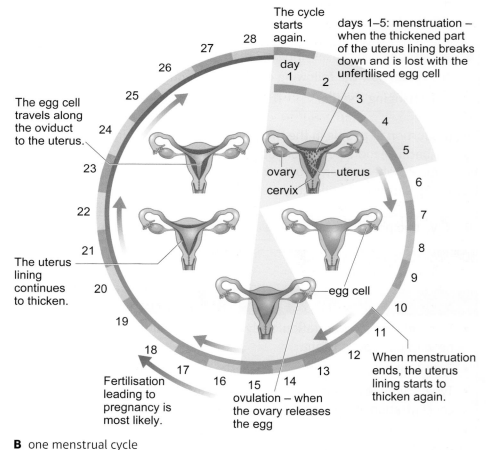

The cycle starts again.

days 1–5: menstruation – when the thickened part of the uterus lining breaks down and is lost with the unfertilised egg cell

The egg cell travels along the oviduct to the uterus.

ovary   uterus

cervix

The uterus lining continues to thicken.

egg cell

When menstruation ends, the uterus lining starts to thicken again.

Fertilisation leading to pregnancy is most likely.

ovulation – when the ovary releases the egg

B one menstrual cycle

> 3   Look at diagram B.
>   **a** On which day of the cycle does menstruation begin?
>   **b** Within which three days of the cycle does ovulation take place?

- Day 1 of the menstrual cycle is the start of **menstruation**. Menstruation is also known as a period. The thickened part of the uterus lining and the unfertilised egg leave the body.
- After menstruation, the amount of oestrogen released by the ovaries increases. When the oestrogen concentration is high enough, it triggers the release of an egg from the ovary. The release of an egg is called **ovulation**.

At ovulation, the concentration of oestrogen in the blood falls and the concentration of progesterone increases. This causes the uterus lining to thicken more. A thick uterus lining is needed if the egg cell is fertilised.

If the egg is not fertilised, then the concentrations of oestrogen and progesterone fall. This allows menstruation to happen.

Contraception

Contraception prevents pregnancy if used properly. There are different types of contraceptive methods.

- Hormonal contraception contains progesterone, or progesterone with oestrogen. One example is the **contraceptive pill**. Hormonal contraception works by keeping hormone concentrations high, to prevent ovulation. Hormonal contraception can also change conditions inside the woman's body, making it difficult for sperm to reach an egg.
- Barrier contraception methods include the **male condom**. Barrier methods work by preventing sperm from reaching the egg. The male condom can also help prevent the spread of STIs (sexually transmitted infections).

> 5 State what is meant by contraception.
> 6 a Give one example of hormonal contraception.
>   b Describe how hormonal contraception works.
> 7 a Name one example of a barrier method of contraception.
>   b Describe how the barrier method you named in **a** works.
> 8 Give one advantage of using a male condom compared with hormonal methods of contraception.

> **4** a Describe the role of oestrogen before ovulation.
>   b Describe the role of progesterone after ovulation.

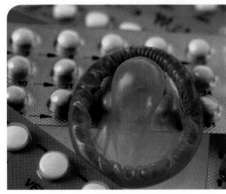

C Contraceptive methods include the contraceptive pill and the male condom.

Key points

- The menstrual cycle is a cycle of changes in a woman's reproductive system. The menstrual cycle is controlled by hormones.
- Increase in oestrogen concentration causes ovulation. Increase in progesterone after ovulation causes thickening of the uterus lining.
- Decreases in progesterone and oestrogen cause menstruation.
- Contraception is used to prevent pregnancy.
- Hormonal contraceptive methods, such as the contraceptive pill, contain hormones that prevent ovulation.
- Barrier methods, such as the male condom, prevent sperm cells reaching the egg cell and can protect against the spread of STIs.

Checkpoint

How confidently can you answer the Progression questions?

Foundation

F1 Describe what happens in the following stages of the menstrual cycle.
   a days 1–5
   b about day 14
   c days 16–28

Strengthen

S1 Explain how the contraceptive pill prevents pregnancy.

B4d Enzymes

ELC B2B.11, B2B.12, B2B.13, B2B.14 **GCSE** B1.7, B1.8, B1.9, B1.12

Progression questions

- What are enzymes?
- How do enzymes work?
- How are enzymes affected by temperature, pH and substrate concentration?

A Saliva contains enzymes that start the digestion of starch (a large carbohydrate).

Enzymes are substances made by the body that speed up reactions. This means they are biological **catalysts**. For example, many enzymes are made in the digestive system. These enzymes speed up the **digestion** (breakdown) of large food molecules into smaller molecules that the body can absorb.

> 1 What is an enzyme?
>
> 2 Describe the role of enzymes in the digestive system.

Some enzymes inside cells speed up reactions that build larger molecules from smaller ones. These are **synthesis** reactions. Diagram B shows some digestion reactions and some synthesis reactions.

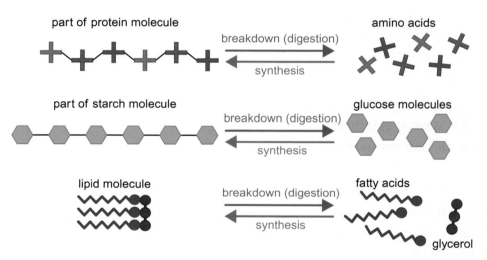

B Enzymes control the digestion and synthesis of many substances inside the body.

> 3 Look at diagram B.
>
> **a** Name the substance produced by the synthesis of amino acids.
>
> **b** Name the simple sugar produced from the digestion of starch.
>
> **c** Name the two substances needed for the synthesis of lipids.

substrate in active site   3D model of enzyme

C The blue shape is a 3D model of an enzyme. The yellow shape shows the enzyme's substrate.

Enzyme molecules have a 3D shape. Within the enzyme is a pocket shape called the **active site**. The substance that is changed in a reaction is called the **substrate**. The substrate has the right shape to fit neatly into the active site. Other molecules will not fit the active site. We say the substrate is **specific** to the enzyme and enzymes are specific to a particular reaction.

4 **a** State what is meant by the active site of an enzyme.

b Give a reason why an enzyme will only work with a specific substrate.

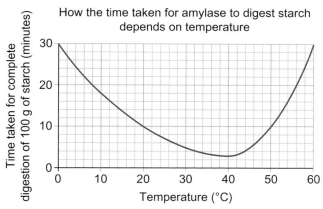

How the time taken for amylase to digest starch depends on temperature

D The time taken for human amylase to digest starch changes with temperature.

Changing enzyme activity

Changes in temperature, pH or substrate concentration can change how long it takes an enzyme-controlled reaction to happen. Graph D shows how temperature affects human amylase enzyme. Many enzymes are affected by temperature like this.

Graph D shows that:

- as the temperature increases from 0 °C to about 40 °C, the time taken for all the starch to be digested gets shorter
- there is a temperature at which the reaction is fastest – we call this temperature the **optimum temperature** for the enzyme
- as temperature increases above the optimum, the reaction slows down.

If the temperature gets high enough, the reaction stops. This is because the active site changes shape and cannot hold the substrate. At this point the enzyme is said to be **denatured**.

Key points

- Enzymes are catalysts that speed up reactions inside the body.
- Some enzymes help the body break down large molecules into smaller molecules. Other enzymes synthesise larger molecules from smaller ones.
- The substrate of an enzyme has the right shape to fit into the enzyme's active site. Each substrate is specific to its enzyme.
- Changes in temperature, pH and substrate concentration can affect the time that a reaction takes. High temperatures can stop a reaction, because the enzyme is denatured.

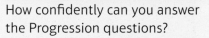

5 Sketch a copy of graph D.

a Add labels to your sketch to describe how the time taken for all the starch to be digested changes between:

i 0 °C and 40 °C

ii 42 °C and 60 °C.

b State the optimum temperature for human amylase. Give a reason for your answer.

6 Give a reason why human amylase enzyme that has been heated to 65 °C cannot digest starch.

Checkpoint

How confidently can you answer the Progression questions?

Foundation

F1 Give a reason why an enzyme that digests protein cannot digest starch.

Strengthen

S1 Biological clothes detergents contain enzymes. The instructions for some detergents state that they should be used at 30 °C. Give a reason why you should not use a higher or lower temperature than this.

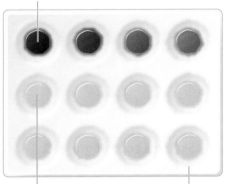

A blue/black colour indicates the presence of starch.

A yellow/orange colour that no longer changes indicates that the reaction is complete.

well tray

A A sample of starch/amylase solution was taken every 20 seconds and mixed with the next drop of iodine solution in a well tray.

Changes in pH can change how long an enzyme-controlled reaction takes. This is because a change in pH can change the shape of the active site of the enzyme.

The effect of pH on amylase can be investigated using starch and iodine solution. Iodine solution turns from yellow/orange to blue/black when it is mixed with starch. Amylase digests starch to simple sugars. Iodine solution does not change colour when mixed with simple sugars.

At the start of each experiment, amylase is mixed with starch in a solution at a particular pH. The time taken for all the starch to be broken down is recorded. The experiment is repeated at different pHs. The results from all the experiments are then used to draw a graph.

Method

Wear eye protection.

A Set up a water bath as shown in diagram B. Light the Bunsen burner to heat the water.

B When the water reaches 40 °C, adjust the collar on the Bunsen to produce a flame that keeps the water at this temperature. Check after a couple of minutes that the water stays at 40 °C and adjust the Bunsen collar again if needed.

C Place one drop of iodine solution into each depression of a well tray (dimple tile).

D Measure 2 cm³ of amylase solution into a tube.

E Add 1 cm³ of a particular pH solution to the tube. Your teacher will tell you which solution to use. Record the pH of the solution you have used.

F Add 2 cm³ of starch solution to the tube. Place the tube carefully into the water bath. Start the stop clock. Gently stir the mixture.

G After 20 seconds, take a small amount of mixture and place one drop into a fresh drop of iodine in the well tray.

H Repeat step G every 20 seconds. Stop testing when the iodine solution stops changing colour.

I Record the time at which the iodine solution no longer reacted with a drop of the mixture.

J Collect results for other pHs from other groups. Plot all the results on a graph. Put pH on the x-axis and time taken to stop reacting on the y-axis.

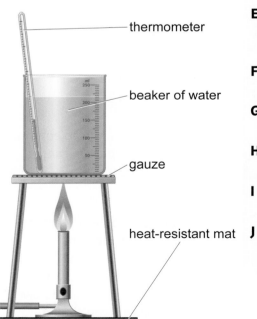

thermometer

beaker of water

gauze

heat-resistant mat

B water bath apparatus for keeping the experiment at 40 °C

Exam-style questions

1 Name the enzyme in this experiment. *(1 mark)*

2 a Name the substrate in this experiment. *(1 mark)*

b Give a reason why a different substrate could not be used in this experiment with this enzyme. *(1 mark)*

3 Name the independent variable in this experiment. *(1 mark)*

4 Name the dependent variable in this experiment. *(1 mark)*

5 Give a reason why iodine solution is used to identify when the reaction has stopped. *(1 mark)*

6 Explain the importance of carrying out the experiment in a water bath kept at the same temperature. *(2 marks)*

7 Write an equipment list for the method given on the previous page. *(2 marks)*

8 Table C shows results from experiments carried out by a class using amylase, starch and a range of different pH solutions.

pH	Time taken to stop reacting (s)
4	160
5	120
6	80
7	60
8	100
9	140

C results for question 8

a Use table C to identify the optimum pH for the amylase. *(1 mark)*

b Give a reason for your answer to **a**. *(1 mark)*

c Use the results to draw a graph of time taken to stop reacting (*x*-axis) against pH (*y*-axis). Join the points with a smooth curve. *(2 marks)*

9 Describe one change to the method that could give a more accurate value for the optimum pH.
Give a reason for your answer. *(2 marks)*

10 At pHs higher or lower than those used in the experiments, the amylase stops being able to digest starch.

a Describe the evidence from iodine solution that would show that the amylase had stopped working. *(1 mark)*

b Explain why amylase stops working at very low or very high pHs. *(2 marks)*

B4e Exchange and transport

ELC B2B.15, B2B.16 **GCSE** B8.1, B8.2, B8.3

Progression questions

- Which substances do organisms need to take in and get rid of?
- What are alveoli?
- How are alveoli adapted for gas exchange?

A Urine contains water and dissolved substances that the body does not need, including urea.

All organisms need to exchange substances with their environment. Organisms need to take in substances to make new cells. They also need to get rid of substances that their cells do not need.

Plants absorb water and dissolved mineral ions from the environment through their root hair cells. Most animals absorb water and dissolved food molecules into their body through their digestive system.

In plants, substances travel around the plant in xylem and phloem. In most animals, substances travel around their body in blood.

Gas exchange

Plants exchange gases with the environment through their leaves. We exchange gases with the environment through our **lungs**. Lungs have millions of **alveoli**. Alveoli are tiny pockets where gases are exchanged between the blood and the air in the lungs. The millions of alveoli create a large surface area. This is an adaptation for exchanging gases quickly.

1 Give a reason why organisms need substances from their environment.

2 a Name the part of an animal that absorbs water from the environment.

  b Name the part of a plant that absorbs water from the environment.

3 State how substances are transported inside:

  a plants

  b most animals.

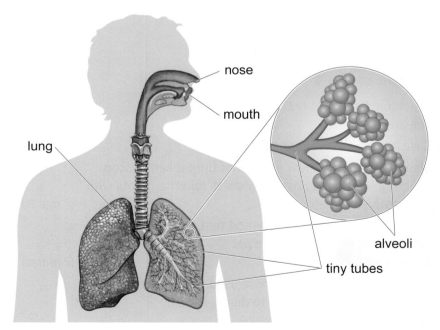

B The lungs are filled with millions of tiny tubes that connect to the breathing tube that comes from the mouth and nose. At the end of each tiny tube are alveoli.

4 Describe the function of alveoli.

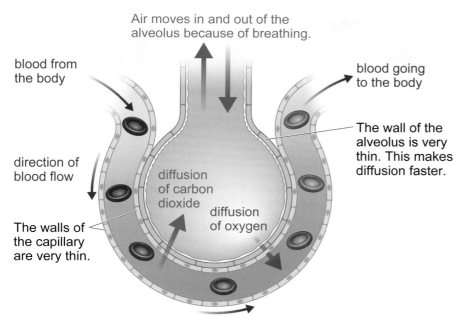

Air moves in and out of the alveolus because of breathing.

blood from the body

blood going to the body

The wall of the alveolus is very thin. This makes diffusion faster.

direction of blood flow

diffusion of carbon dioxide

diffusion of oxygen

The walls of the capillary are very thin.

C Oxygen and carbon dioxide are exchanged between air in the alveolus and blood in a capillary by diffusion.

Each alveolus is surrounded by tiny blood vessels called **capillaries**. Oxygen diffuses from air in the alveolus into blood in the capillary. Carbon dioxide diffuses from blood into the air in the alveolus.

The alveoli and capillaries are adapted for fast **diffusion** of gases by being very close together. They also have very thin walls, which means that gases have a short distance to diffuse between them.

---

5 a Describe two adaptations shown in diagram C for rapid diffusion of gases in the lungs.

b State which of the following contains more oxygen.

i blood arriving at the lungs, or blood leaving the lungs

ii air that is breathed out, or air that is breathed in

Key points

- Organisms exchange substances with their environment.
- Animals absorb water and dissolved food molecules in their digestive systems. Dissolved substances such as urea leave the body in urine. We exchange gases in our lungs.
- Transport systems carry substances around the body.
- Alveoli are adapted for exchanging gases between the body and air. They have thin walls and are close to capillaries.

Checkpoint

How confidently can you answer the Progression questions?

Foundation

F1 Describe how oxygen gets from air into blood in humans.

Strengthen

S1 Give a reason why lungs contain millions of alveoli and capillaries.

B4f The circulatory system

ELC B2B.17, B2B.18, B2B.19 **GCSE** B8.6, B8.7, B8.8

Progression questions

- What does blood contain?
- How does the structure of blood vessels affect their function?
- How does the structure of the heart affect its function?

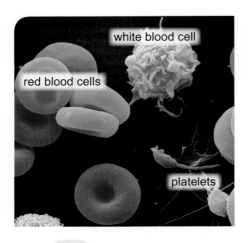

Blood

Blood is a mixture of cells carried in a liquid called **plasma**. Plasma transports dissolved substances such as glucose and carbon dioxide.

There are three main types of blood cell. Each has a different function.

- **Red blood cells** (**erythrocytes**) contain the red pigment **haemoglobin**. Haemoglobin carries oxygen.
- **White blood cells** include **phagocytes** and **lymphocytes**. They help the body to attack infections.
- **Platelets** are tiny pieces of larger cells. They help blood to clot if a blood vessel is damaged.

> **1** Name the liquid part of blood.
>
> **2** Describe the function of each type of blood cell.

Blood vessels

Blood vessels carry blood around the body. **Arteries** carry blood away from the heart. **Veins** carry blood towards the heart. Arteries are connected to veins by large networks of capillaries. Capillaries pass close to all the cells in the body. Capillaries are where substances are exchanged between the blood and the cells.

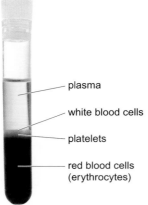

A The photo at the top shows different types of blood cells (magnification ×3350). The tube contains blood that has had the cells and plasma separated out.

> **3 a** State the function of each of the three main types of blood vessel.
>
> **b** Give a reason why veins contain valves.
>
> **c** Give a reason why capillaries have very thin walls.

network of fine capillaries in the lungs

Veins have valves that make sure blood can only flow towards the heart.

wide tube so blood flows easily

thin, flexible wall

heart

Arteries carry blood away from the heart under high pressure.

narrow tube

thick muscular wall that can withstand high pressures

capillaries in tissues
wall is only one cell thick, to allow faster diffusion of substances into and out of the capillary

very narrow tube

B a very simple diagram of the human circulatory system

Heart

The **circulatory system** is made up of blood vessels and the **heart**. When the muscular walls of the heart contract, blood is pushed through the heart and out into blood vessels that carry it around the body.

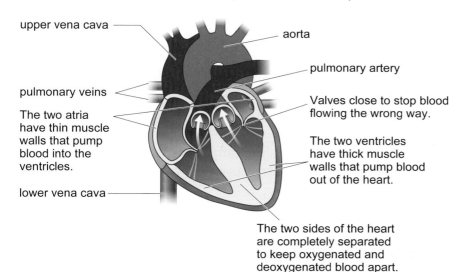

upper vena cava

aorta

pulmonary artery

pulmonary veins

Valves close to stop blood flowing the wrong way.

The two atria have thin muscle walls that pump blood into the ventricles.

The two ventricles have thick muscle walls that pump blood out of the heart.

lower vena cava

The two sides of the heart are completely separated to keep oxygenated and deoxygenated blood apart.

C The structure of the heart is related to its function. (Note that the heart is always drawn as if you are looking at the front of the person. So the left side of the heart is shown on the right.)

Blood from the body passes twice through the heart before it returns to the body. Blood from the body is **deoxygenated**, which means it contains little oxygen. Deoxygenated blood passes from the **vena cava** through the right side of the heart and is pumped to the lungs through the **pulmonary artery**. Gas exchange in the lungs adds oxygen to the blood, making it **oxygenated**. Oxygenated blood in the **pulmonary vein** then passes through the left side of the heart and is pumped to the rest of the body through the **aorta**.

---

5 Give a reason why blood from the body must go to the lungs before returning to the body.

Key points

- Blood is made of liquid plasma, red blood cells, white blood cells and platelets.
- Arteries carry blood away from the heart at high pressure. Veins contain valves that help blood move back to the heart. Capillaries have thin walls and exchange substances with cells.
- Deoxygenated blood from the body is pumped through the heart to the lungs. Oxygenated blood from the lungs is pumped through the heart to the rest of the body.

---

4 Look at diagram C.

a State whether the aorta is an artery or a vein. Give a reason for your answer.

b State whether the pulmonary artery carries oxygenated or deoxygenated blood. Give a reason for your answer.

Checkpoint

How confidently can you answer the Progression questions?

Foundation

F1 Describe one adaptation each of arteries, veins and capillaries that helps each carry out its function.

Strengthen

S1 Draw a table to compare arteries and veins. Include their structures and the substances in the blood inside them.

B4g Cellular respiration

ELC B2B.20, B2B.21 **GCSE** B8.9, B8.10

Progression questions

- Why do cells carry out respiration?
- What is aerobic respiration?
- What is anaerobic respiration?

All organisms need a source of energy. Energy is needed for many **metabolic processes** such as:

- growth and reproduction – Energy allows cells to build the new molecules needed to make more cells.

- maintenance – Energy allows cells to carry out other processes such as moving substances by active transport, or breaking down waste substances.

- movement – Energy allows muscle cells to contract and move the body.

A When exercising, we need extra energy for muscle contraction.

The energy that cells need is released mainly by breaking down glucose. The process that releases energy from glucose is called **respiration**. In plants, the glucose comes from photosynthesis. In animals, the glucose comes from digested food.

Respiration takes place inside cells all the time. It happens in structures called **mitochondria**. Because respiration releases energy, we say that it is an **exothermic** process.

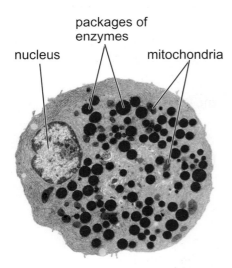

nucleus packages of enzymes mitochondria

B This pancreas cell contains many mitochondria. Respiration in the mitochondria releases energy that the cell needs for making the hormone insulin.

1	Name the process that releases energy in cells.
2	Name the substance that is the main source of energy in cells.
3	Give a reason why cells continually need energy.
4	State why respiration is described as an exothermic process.

There are two types of respiration, **aerobic respiration** and **anaerobic respiration**.

Aerobic respiration

Aerobic respiration happens in most plant and animal cells most of the time. The process is called aerobic respiration because it needs oxygen from the air.

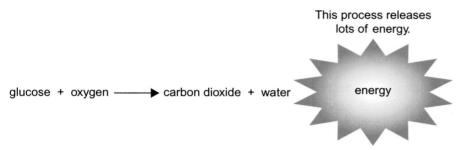

This process releases lots of energy.

glucose + oxygen ⟶ carbon dioxide + water   energy

C the process of aerobic respiration

The carbon dioxide produced by aerobic respiration diffuses out of the cells into the blood, for transport to the lungs.

Anaerobic respiration

The other type of respiration is anaerobic respiration. This does not need oxygen. Different cells carry out different forms of anaerobic respiration. Plant cells and yeast cells break down glucose to form ethanol and carbon dioxide. In humans, muscle cells break down glucose to **lactic acid** when there is not enough oxygen for aerobic respiration to release all the energy that the cell needs. This releases less energy than aerobic respiration.

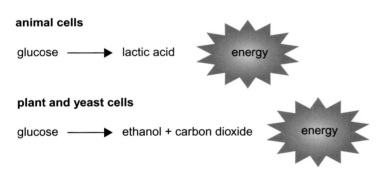

animal cells

glucose ⟶ lactic acid   energy

plant and yeast cells

glucose ⟶ ethanol + carbon dioxide   energy

D Different types of anaerobic respiration happen in different cells.

Key points

- Respiration is an exothermic reaction. It releases energy from glucose inside cells. The energy is needed for metabolic processes.
- Aerobic respiration needs oxygen. Glucose reacts with oxygen to produce carbon dioxide and water. This reaction releases lots of energy.
- Anaerobic respiration does not need oxygen. In animal cells, glucose is broken down to lactic acid. In plant and yeast cells, glucose is broken down to ethanol and carbon dioxide.

5 Describe how cells are supplied with the oxygen they need for aerobic respiration.

6 Use diagram C to identify the products of aerobic respiration.

7 Use diagram D to identify what anaerobic respiration produces in:
   a animal cells
   b plant and yeast cells.

8 Give a reason why muscle cells carry out anaerobic respiration during vigorous exercise.

Checkpoint

How confidently can you answer the Progression questions?

Foundation

F1 Describe the function of respiration.

Strengthen

S1 Describe one similarity and one difference between aerobic and anaerobic respiration.

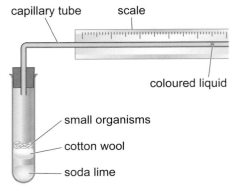

A a simple respirometer

The rate of respiration in living organisms can be measured using a **respirometer**.

The respirometer shown in diagram A measures the decrease in volume of gas inside the apparatus. As the volume of gas decreases, the blob of coloured liquid moves along the capillary tube towards the organisms. The scale shows how much the volume of gas has decreased.

The volume of gas decreases because organisms take oxygen from the air when they respire. Respiration produces another gas: carbon dioxide. Carbon dioxide is removed from the air in the respirometer by reacting it with soda lime. The decrease in volume of gas in the respirometer is therefore the decrease in the volume of oxygen due to the organisms respiring.

The faster the liquid blob moves among the tube, the more rapidly oxygen is being used by the organisms. This means the rate of respiration of the organisms is faster.

Method ◣

Wear eye protection.
The cotton wool is to protect you and the organisms.

A Collect a tube with some soda lime, held in place with cotton wool.

B Carefully collect some of the small organisms. Gently shake the organisms into the tube.

C Insert the bung and capillary tube into the top of the tube as shown in diagram A. Attach a scale to the tube so that the zero lines up with the open end of the capillary tube.

D Set up an identical respirometer, but without the organisms. This is the control tube.

E Place both tubes into a rack in a warm water bath. Tilt the rack slightly so that the capillary tubes hang over the side of the water bath at an angle.

F Wait for 5 minutes to allow the organisms to get used to the temperature of the water bath.

G Hold a beaker of coloured water to the ends of both capillary tubes. A little blob of coloured water should enter each capillary tube.

H Read off the starting position of the liquid blob on the scale for each capillary tube. Record these values and start the timer.

I After 5 minutes, read off the position of both blobs on the scales. Record these as the final positions.

J Calculate the distance each blob travelled using the formula:

distance travelled = final position − starting position

K Repeat the experiment at different temperatures no more than 40 °C.

Exam-style questions

1 a Write the equation for aerobic respiration. *(1 mark)*

 b Use the equation to explain why the volume of oxygen decreases in the respirometer. *(1 mark)*

 c Identify the part of the respirometer that removes carbon dioxide inside the apparatus. *(1 mark)*

 d Use the respiration equation to explain why carbon dioxide must be removed. *(2 marks)*

2 a Name the independent variable in this experiment. *(1 mark)*

 b Name the dependent variable in this experiment. *(1 mark)*

3 Explain why the experiment is carried out in a water bath. *(2 marks)*

4 The control respirometer contains no organisms.

 a Give a reason why the liquid blob in the control respirometer:

   i moves at the start   **ii** then stops moving. *(2 marks)*

 b Explain why the control tube is needed. *(2 marks)*

5 A student suggests using a small paintbrush for moving the organisms into the tube. State why this is a good idea. *(1 mark)*

6 Explain why the equipment is left in the water bath for 5 minutes before the experiment is started. *(2 marks)*

7 Scatter graph B shows results from five experiments using waxworms. Each experiment was carried out at a different temperature. A line of best fit has been plotted, with roughly the same number of points above the line as below it.

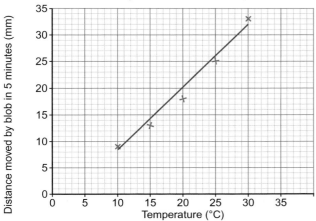

B results for question 7

 a Look at graph B. How far did the blob move in 5 minutes when the temperature was 20 °C? (Note: look at the point, not the line.) *(1 mark)*

 b The line of best fit drawn through the results for all five temperatures suggests the 20 °C value is a little low. Suggest a reason why it is lower than it should be. *(1 mark)*

 c Describe the correlation between the two variables in the graph. Start with the phrase: As temperature increases… *(1 mark)*

Treating diabetes

Explain the different treatments for type 1 diabetes and type 2 diabetes.

(6 marks)

Plan your answer

An 'explain' question means you need to give a reason for each statement that you make. So a student plan might look like this:

— type 1 — insulin injection <u>because</u> no insulin made

— type 2 — low-sugar diet <u>because</u> stops blood glucose going too high

— type 2 — more exercise <u>because</u> more glucose taken out of blood

. . . .

Student answer

Type 1 diabetes is when a person doesn't release any insulin from their pancreas [A]. Treatment [B] of type 1 diabetes is by injecting insulin. The insulin causes muscle and liver cells to take glucose out of the blood.

Type 2 diabetes is caused by the pancreas not making enough insulin, or by muscle and liver cells not responding to insulin properly [C]. Treatment for type 2 diabetes includes a healthy diet that is low in sugar. This stops the body absorbing lots of glucose after a meal. Treatment can include more exercise because [D] muscle cells take more glucose out of the blood during exercise [E].

[A] To help explain the treatments, you need to describe the causes of each type of diabetes first.

[B] Giving the treatment straight after the cause helps to set the answer out clearly.

[C] The effect of insulin on target cells (liver and muscle) and how this reduces blood glucose concentration is spread through the answer. This doesn't matter as long as it is all included and is given at relevant points, as in this answer.

[D] Conjunctions (linking words) like 'because' help to join cause and effect clearly in a sentence.

[E] As this is an 'explain' question and not 'compare', it is best to arrange the answer to cover type 1 diabetes first and then type 2.

. . . .

Verdict

This is a good answer. It is clearly organised so that it is easy to follow the points that the student is making. It also includes key scientific points about how diabetes and insulin are linked, and how this affects the body. Cause and effect are also linked in the explanations of why the different treatments work.

Before writing an answer to a 6-mark question, take a few minutes to plan out what you are going to write. You could do this by jotting down headings or key words to include. Check that you have these in a sensible order before you start writing your answer.

C1 Atoms, compounds and states of matter

Everything in the world is made from atoms, including you. Materials that contain only one type of atom are called elements. There are just over 100 elements. The periodic table below shows photos of most of these elements.

Compounds are formed when different atoms join together in different ways. Countless different compounds are possible, and you use many of these in your everyday life. You are even made from some of them.

The learning journey

Previously you will have learnt at KS3:

- about a simple model of the atom
- about the properties of metals and non-metals
- about periods and groups in the periodic table
- about metals and non-metals, their properties and their positions in the periodic table.

In this unit you will learn:

- about the structure of atoms
- what the periodic table is like and how it developed
- about the structure of metals, non-metals and different compounds
- how to explain the properties of different substances.

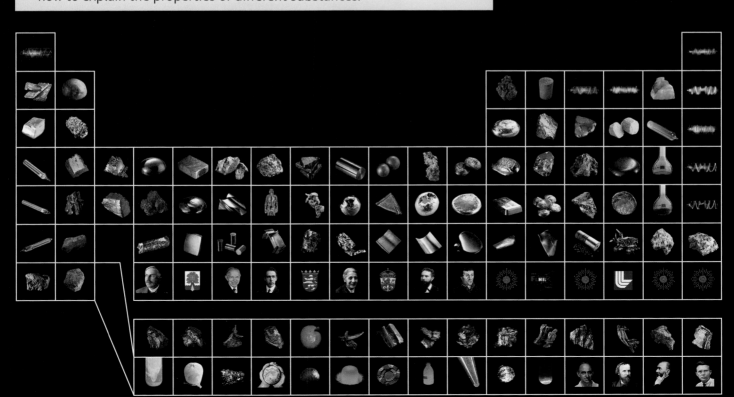

C1a States of matter

ELC C1A.29, C1A.30, C1A.31, C1A.32 **GCSE** C2.1, C2.2, C2.3

Progression questions

- What is the arrangement and movement of the particles in solids, liquids and gases?
- What are state changes, and why are they described as physical changes?
- What happens to the particles during the different changes of state?

A What happens to the particles in ice cream when it melts?

The three **states of matter** are solid, liquid and gas. Ice is solid water, water from a tap is a liquid, and steam is water in the gas state.

1	Name the three states of matter.

Particles

The particles in solids, liquids and gases are arranged differently, and move in different ways.

State	Particle diagram	Arrangement of particles	Movement of particles
gas		random far apart no attractive forces between particles	fast in all directions
liquid		random close together some attractive forces between particles	move around each other
solid		regular close together attractive forces hold particles in position	vibrate about fixed positions

B Particles in solids have the least stored energy. Particles in gases have the most stored energy.

2 Use table B to help you name the state(s) in which particles:
   a are close together
   b are randomly arranged
   c cannot move from place to place.

State changes

In a chemical change, particles join together in different ways to make new substances. In a **physical change** they do not. State changes are physical changes. Only the arrangement, movement and amount of stored energy of the particles change. No new substances are made.

3	Why are state changes physical changes?

Diagram C shows the different state changes that happen between the three states of matter.

> **4** **a** Name the state change that happens when a gas changes to a liquid.
>
> **b** During subliming, what state does a solid become?

Explaining state changes

Attractive forces hold particles together:

- during melting, some forces are overcome so particles can move around each other
- during evaporating and boiling, all remaining forces are overcome so particles can move far apart.

Energy must be transferred to overcome the attractive forces between particles. This is why ice cream melts on a sunny day, and why you boil water by heating it in a kettle.

> **5** What must happen to overcome the attractive forces between particles?

When a substance is cooled, its particles slow down enough for condensing or freezing to happen:

- during condensing, some attractive forces form and particles can stay close together
- during freezing, many attractive forces form and particles are held in fixed positions.

Energy is transferred from the particles to the surroundings as attractive forces form. This is why water droplets form on a cold window, and why you put tap water in a freezer to make ice.

> **6** What happens when attractive forces form between particles?

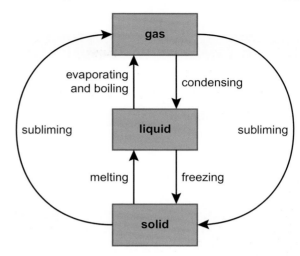

C the different state changes

D Water vapour in the air condenses as water droplets on a cold drinks can.

Checkpoint

How confidently can you answer the Progression questions?

Foundation

F1 Solid carbon dioxide, 'dry ice', turns into a gas above −78 °C. Describe what happens to its particles during this state change.

Strengthen

S1 Explain why energy is transferred to or from the surroundings during state changes.

Key points

- The three states of matter are solid, liquid and gas.
- Particles in a solid are close together and held in a regular arrangement. Particles in a liquid are close together but can move past each other. Particles in a gas are far apart and move quickly.
- State changes include melting, evaporating, condensing and freezing. They are physical changes.

C1b Atomic structure

ELC C1A.1, C1A.2, C1A.3, C1A.4, C1A.5, C1A.6 **GCSE** C1.2, C1.3, C1.4, C1.5, C1.6, C1.7, C1.8

Progression questions

- What does an atom contain?
- What are the parts of an atom like?
- What do atomic number and mass number mean?

A The London Eye has a diameter of 120 m. If an atom was as wide as the London Eye, its nucleus would only be 1.2 mm wide.

Everything is made from tiny particles called **atoms**. A single atom is too small to see. There are over a billion times more atoms in the ball of your ballpoint pen than there are people on Earth.

Nucleus and shells

Atoms are made from three types of **subatomic particle**. These are the **proton**, the **neutron** and the **electron**. There is a **nucleus** at the centre of an atom. The nucleus contains protons and neutrons. Electrons surround the nucleus and are arranged in **electron shells**. Atoms contain equal numbers of protons and electrons.

electron
shells

 protons  neutrons • electrons

B a diagram of a lithium atom

1 Name the subatomic particles that a nucleus contains.

2 Name the subatomic particles that surround the nucleus.

A nucleus is very small compared to an atom. The diameter of a nucleus is about 100 000 times smaller than the diameter of an atom. This means that 100 000 nuclei could fit across the width of an atom.

3 Describe the size of a nucleus compared to an atom.

Subatomic particles

The masses of subatomic particles are tiny, so it is easier to use their **relative masses**. A relative mass is the mass of a particle compared to the mass of a proton. We also use **relative charges** to describe the tiny electrical charges of subatomic particles.

Subatomic particle	Relative mass	Relative charge
proton	1	+1 (positive)
neutron	1	0 (no charge)
electron	$\frac{1}{1835}$ (very small)	−1 (negative)

C properties of subatomic particles

> **4** Use table C to help you to:
>
> **a** name the particle that has the same mass as a proton, but no charge.
>
> **b** give the relative mass of the particle that has a negative charge.

The mass of a proton or neutron is 1835 times greater than the mass of an electron. The nucleus is made up of protons and neutrons, so most of the mass of an atom is concentrated in the nucleus.

Atomic number and mass number

The **atomic number** of an atom is the number of protons in the nucleus. The atoms of any **element** all have the same atomic number.

The **mass number** of an atom is the total number of protons and neutrons in its nucleus. The mass numbers of different elements can be the same or different.

> **5** Diagram B shows a lithium atom.
>
> **a** State the number of protons in the nucleus of a lithium atom.
>
> **b** Give the atomic number of lithium. Use your answer to part **a** to help you.
>
> **c** State the number of neutrons in the nucleus of a lithium atom.
>
> **d** Calculate the mass number of lithium. Use your answers to parts **a** and **c** to help you.

D These objects are coated with zinc. Zinc atoms have 30 protons and 35 neutrons. The atomic number of zinc is 30. Its mass number is 30 + 35 = 65.

Checkpoint

How confidently can you answer the Progression questions?

Foundation

F1 Draw a labelled diagram to show the structure of an atom.

F2 Describe the differences between atomic number and mass number.

Strengthen

S1 Explain why atoms have no electrical charge overall.

Key points

- An atom has a nucleus containing protons and neutrons. The nucleus is surrounded by electrons in shells.
- Atomic number is the number of protons in a nucleus.
- Mass number is the total number of protons and neutrons in a nucleus.

C1c The periodic table

ELC C1A.8, C1A.9, C1A.10, C1A.13 GCSE C1.13, C1.14, C1.17, C1.20

Progression questions

- How did Mendeleev arrange the elements?
- What does the modern periodic table show?
- What are the links between the periodic table and electrons in atoms?

A How would you arrange all these vehicles into groups?

Dmitri Mendeleev was a Russian chemist. He arranged elements into tables that gradually developed into the modern **periodic table** we know today.

Relative atomic mass

Atoms have so little mass that calculations with their mass are difficult. To make things easier, we use **relative atomic mass** instead. An element's relative atomic mass is the mean mass of its atoms compared with the mass of a carbon atom. The relative atomic mass of carbon is 12. Magnesium atoms have twice the mass of carbon atoms, so the relative atomic mass of magnesium is 24.

> **1** What is the relative atomic mass of an atom?

Using properties

Mendeleev used the properties of the elements and their **compounds** to make his table. At the start, he put the elements in order of increasing relative atomic mass. He then arranged them into **groups**. These are vertical columns containing elements that have similar chemical and physical properties. For example, he put chlorine, bromine and iodine in group 7. These elements are non-metals with low melting points and other similar physical properties, and they all react in a similar way.

B These flasks contain chlorine, bromine and iodine (left to right). All three form coloured gases.

Making predictions

Sometimes, Mendeleev left gaps in his table. Diagram C shows these gaps in white. Mendeleev suggested that the gaps were there because some elements hadn't been discovered yet. He could predict the relative atomic masses of these unknown elements (the numbers with question marks in the diagram).

> **2** How did Mendeleev start his table?
>
> **3** What are groups in the periodic table?

Group 1	Group 2	Group 3	Group 4	Group 5	Group 6	Group 7
H 1						
Li 7	Be 9.4	B 11	C 12	N 14	O 16	F 19
Na 23	Mg 24	Al 27.3	Si 28	P 31	S 32	Cl 35.5
K 39	Ca 40	? 44	Ti 48	V 51	Cr 52	Mn 55
(Cu 63)	Zn 65	? 68	? 72	As 75	Se 78	Br 80
Rb 85	Sr 87	Y 88	Zr 90	Nb 94	Mo 96	? 100
(Ag 108)	Cd 112	In 113	Sn 118	Sb 122	Te 125	I 127

C Chlorine, bromine and iodine (in red) were in group 7 in Mendeleev's 1871 table.

Mendeleev also predicted some of their other properties by looking at the properties of known elements in the same group. The missing elements were discovered a few years later. Their properties were similar to those he had predicted.

> **4** What were the gaps for in Mendeleev's table?

The modern periodic table

In the modern periodic table:

- the elements are arranged in order of increasing atomic number (not relative atomic mass)
- elements are in horizontal rows called **periods**
- elements with similar properties are found in the same vertical columns, called groups.

> **5** In the modern periodic table:
>   **a** How are the elements arranged?
>   **b** What is a period?

Atomic structure and position in the periodic table

The structure of an element's atoms is related to its position in the periodic table. The electrons are not arranged randomly around the nucleus of an atom. They have a particular arrangement that is different for each element:

- the number of electron shells is the same as the period number
- the number of electrons in the outer shell is the same as the group number.

In group 0 elements, the outer shells of the atoms are full and cannot hold any more electrons.

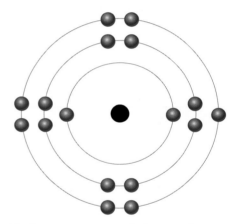

D the arrangement of electrons in a chlorine atom

> **6** Diagram D shows the electrons in a chlorine atom.
>   **a** How can you tell from this diagram that chlorine is in period 3?
>   **b** How can you tell from this diagram that chlorine is in group 7?

Key points

- Mendeleev arranged the elements in his table in order of increasing relative atomic mass. He put elements with similar properties together in vertical columns, even if this meant leaving gaps.
- In the modern periodic table, elements are arranged in order of increasing atomic number. They are in rows called periods, with vertical groups of similar elements.
- An element's position in the table is related to the arrangement of electrons in its atoms.

Checkpoint

How confidently can you answer the Progression questions?

Foundation

F1 Describe how Mendeleev arranged the elements in his periodic table.

Strengthen

S1 Describe how the position of an element in the modern periodic table is linked to its atomic structure.

C1d Metals and the periodic table

ELC C1A.11, C1A.12, C1A.14 **GCSE** C1.9, C1.10, C1.15, C1.16, C1.18, C1.42, C1.43

Progression questions

- What are the differences between metals and non-metals?
- What happens to atoms when elements react together?
- Why were elements in Mendeleev's table not always in order of relative atomic mass?

A How can you tell that copper, used in computer heat sinks and circuit boards, is a metal?

---

1 Sulfur is a non-metal. Where is it in the periodic table?

Metals and non-metals in the periodic table

The **metal** elements are placed on the left-hand side of the modern periodic table. The **non-metal** elements are placed on the right.

1	2											3	4	5	6	7	0
										metals			H				He
Li	Be									non-metals			B	C	N	O	F	Ne
Na	Mg											Al	Si	P	S	Cl	Ar
K	Ca	Sc	Ti	V	Cr	Mn	Fe	Co	Ni	Cu	Zn	Ga	Ge	As	Se	Br	Kr
Rb	Sr	Y	Zr	Nb	Mo	Tc	Ru	Rh	Pd	Ag	Cd	In	Sn	Sb	Te	I	Xe
Cs	Ba	La	Hf	Ta	W	Re	Os	Ir	Pt	Au	Hg	Tl	Pb	Bi	Po	At	Rn
Fr	Ra	Ac	Rf	Db	Sg	Bh	Hs	Mt	Ds	Rg							

B Most elements are metals rather than non-metals.

Properties of metals and non-metals

Table C shows some typical **physical properties** of metals and non-metals.

Property	Metals	Non-metals
appearance	shiny	dull
melting point	high	low
boiling point	high	low
density	high	low
electrical conduction	good conductors	poor conductors

C Metals and non-metals usually have opposite properties.

---

2 Look at photo A. Give one property you can see that suggests that copper is a metal.

Elements and compounds

When an element reacts, its atoms join with other atoms to form compounds. Metals do not react with each other. However, non-metals can react with other non-metals. For example, carbon reacts with oxygen to form carbon dioxide, which is a compound:

carbon + oxygen → carbon dioxide

Non-metals can also react with metals. For example, sodium reacts with chlorine to make sodium chloride, which is a compound:

sodium + chlorine → sodium chloride

---

3 Name the two types of element that non-metals can react with.

Atoms and the periodic table

Before the proton was discovered, the atomic number of an element was just its position in the periodic table. We now know that atomic number is the number of protons in the nucleus of an atom. The mass number is the number of protons and neutrons in the nucleus of an atom.

The atomic number and mass number are shown in full chemical symbols. Diagram D shows the chemical symbol for a beryllium atom. It explains how to work out the number of neutrons, protons and electrons in the atom.

Isotopes are atoms with the same number of protons but different numbers of neutrons. This means they are all the same element and their atomic number is the same, but their mass number is different.

> **4** Beryllium exists as two isotopes, $^9_4$Be and $^{10}_4$Be.
>
> **a** How many protons are in an atom of $^{10}_4$Be?
>
> **b** Calculate the number of neutrons in an atom of $^{10}_4$Be.

Explaining swaps

Mendeleev began his table by arranging the elements by relative atomic mass. However, he had to swap the positions of some elements so they were in the correct groups. Mendeleev did not know about isotopes, so he could not explain why ordering by relative atomic mass did not work. In fact, some elements have some isotopes with high mass numbers, giving them a higher relative atomic mass than expected.

This problem does not occur in the modern periodic table, because the elements are arranged in order of atomic number. Atoms of the same element always have the same atomic number, and every element has its own atomic number.

> **5** Tellurium is placed before iodine in the periodic table (diagram E).
>
> **a** Why was this an unexpected order in Mendeleev's table?
>
> **b** Why is this an expected order in the modern periodic table?

$$\text{mass number} \longrightarrow {}^9_4\text{Be} \longleftarrow \text{atomic number}$$

neutrons = 9 – 4 = 5

protons = 4

electrons = 4

D how to calculate the number of subatomic particles in an atom from its full chemical symbol

128	127
Te	**I**
tellurium	iodine
52	53

E Tellurium has a greater relative atomic mass than iodine, but is placed first in the periodic table.

Checkpoint

How confidently can you answer the Progression questions?

Foundation

F1 Describe the typical properties of metal elements and non-metal elements.

Strengthen

S1 Explain why the order of some elements had to be swapped in Mendeleev's periodic table.

S2 Why is this not a problem in the modern periodic table?

Key points

- Metals have different properties from non-metals. Metals are placed on the left of the periodic table and non-metals on the right.
- When elements react, their atoms join with other atoms to form compounds.
- The numbers of subatomic particles in atoms explain some features of the periodic table. The numbers can be calculated using mass number and atomic number.

C1e Ionic bonding

ELC C1A.15, C1A.16, C1A.17, C1A.18 **GCSE** C1.21, C1.22, C1.24, C1.27, C1.33

Progression questions

- What are ions?
- How do ionic compounds form?
- How do we explain the physical properties of ionic compounds?

A The Cave of Crystals in Mexico contains huge crystals. Why do they have regular shapes?

Forming ions

An **ion** is an atom or group of atoms with a positive or negative charge. Ions form when atoms lose or gain electrons:

- metal atoms lose electrons to form positively charged ions, called **cations**
- non-metal atoms gain electrons to form negatively charged ions, called **anions**.

> **1** What is an ion?
>
> **2** How do metal atoms form positively charged ions?

Ions form when a metal reacts with a non-metal to produce a compound.

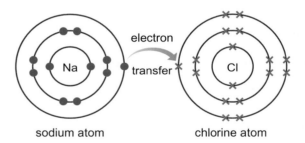

B The electron in the outer shell of a sodium atom transfers to the outer shell of a chlorine atom.

The transfer of electrons forms sodium ions, Na^+, and chloride ions, Cl^-. Diagram C shows a **dot and cross diagram** for these ions. Electrons are shown as dots or crosses. This is so you can tell where they have come from.

3 Look at diagram C. How does the diagram show that one of the electrons in the chloride ion has come from a sodium atom?

C Sodium ions and chloride ions have full outer shells of electrons. This makes them chemically stable.

90

Ionic compounds

Sodium chloride is an example of an **ionic compound**. It contains positively charged sodium ions and negatively charged chloride ions. The ions form a giant **lattice structure** of very many ions in a regular arrangement. Diagram D shows part of the giant lattice structure for sodium chloride.

> **4** State why the structure of sodium chloride is called a giant lattice structure.

Properties of ionic compounds

Ionic bonds are strong **electrostatic forces** of attraction between oppositely charged ions. They hold the ions together in the lattice. When an ionic compound melts or boils, a lot of energy is needed to overcome these strong ionic bonds, so ionic compounds have high melting and boiling points.

Ionic compound	Melting point (°C)	Boiling point (°C)
sodium chloride, NaCl	801	1413
potassium bromide, KBr	734	1435

E Potassium bromide has a similar structure to sodium chloride. Both these ionic compounds have high melting and boiling points.

> **5** What is an ionic bond?

Many ionic compounds are soluble in water. For example, sodium chloride dissolves in water to form sodium chloride solution. The ions separate from one another during dissolving, and mix completely with the water molecules.

An ionic compound will conduct electricity if its ions are free to move about. Ionic compounds conduct electricity when they are molten (liquid) and when they are in **aqueous solution** (dissolved in water). However, they do not conduct electricity when they are solid. This is because their ions are held in the lattice structure by strong ionic bonds, so cannot move.

> **6** When can ionic compounds conduct electricity?

Key points

- Ions are charged particles. They form when atoms lose or gain electrons to achieve a full outer shell.
- The oppositely charged ions in ionic compounds are strongly attracted to each other. This gives them a regular arrangement called a giant lattice structure.
- Ionic compounds have high melting and boiling points. They conduct electricity when they are liquid or dissolved in water but not when they are solid.

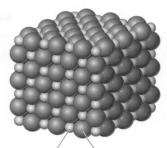

Na⁺ (a sodium ion)   Cl⁻ (a chloride ion)

D Sodium chloride has a cube-shaped lattice structure. This regular shape is why crystals have regular shapes too.

Checkpoint

How confidently can you answer the Progression questions?

Foundation

F1 Potassium bromide forms in a similar way to sodium chloride. Describe its structure and properties.

Strengthen

S1 Use labelled diagrams to explain the physical properties of sodium chloride.

C1f Covalent bonding

ELC C1A.19, C1A.20, C1A.21, C1A.22, C1A.27 **GCSE** C1.28, C1.29, C1.30, C1.31, C1.34, C1.39

Progression questions

- What are covalent bonds?
- How do simple molecules form?
- How do we explain the physical properties of simple molecular compounds?

A Bubbles of carbon dioxide form in an iced cola drink. Why is carbon dioxide still a gas at a low temperature?

Forming covalent bonds

A **covalent bond** is a shared pair of electrons. It forms when a pair of electrons is shared between two non-metal atoms. For example, a hydrogen atom has one electron. It can fill its outer shell by sharing with another hydrogen atom. A hydrogen **molecule**, H_2, forms when two hydrogen atoms share their electrons.

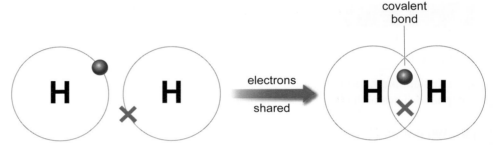

B A hydrogen molecule is two hydrogen atoms joined by a covalent bond.

Substance	Dot and cross diagram
hydrogen chloride, HCl	H ⊙× Cl
water, H_2O	H ⊙× O ×⊙ H
methane, CH_4	H ×⊙ C ⊙× H (with H above and below)

C Each covalent bond is shown as a dot and a cross in dot and cross diagrams.

1 What is a covalent bond?

2 How does a covalent bond form?

Molecules

Covalent bonding usually results in the formation of simple molecules. These are molecules with only a few atoms in them, like the two atoms in a hydrogen molecule. Atoms and simple molecules have similar typical sizes. They are very tiny, around 0.1 nm across.

3 What is a simple molecule?

Dot and cross diagrams

You can use dot and cross diagrams to show the covalent bonds in simple molecules. Electrons from each atom are shown as dots or crosses. You only need to show the outer electrons (see table C).

4 Use the diagrams in table C to help you answer these questions.

a Count the total number of electrons in the outer shells of the Cl, O and C atoms in the HCl, H_2O and CH_4 molecules. What do you notice?

b Chlorine is in group 7. How many covalent bonds do its atoms form in hydrogen chloride molecules?

c Oxygen is in group 6. How many covalent bonds do its atoms form in water molecules?

d Carbon is in group 4. How many covalent bonds do its atoms form in methane molecules?

Properties of simple molecular substances

Covalent bonds within molecules are very strong. However, the forces *between* molecules are weak. When a simple molecular substance melts or boils, these weak **intermolecular forces** are overcome, not the strong covalent bonds. Only a little energy is needed to do this, so simple molecular substances have low melting and boiling points.

5 Name the forces that are overcome when a simple molecular substance melts or boils.

Carbon dioxide and water are both simple molecular substances. Carbon dioxide has even weaker intermolecular forces than water, so it remains as a gas when water is chilled with ice.

Simple molecular substances do not conduct electricity. This is because simple molecules have no overall electric charge. There are no charged particles to carry the charge and form an electric current.

6 Why do simple molecular substances not conduct electricity?

Simple polymers

Poly(ethene) is an example of a simple **polymer**. These compounds consist of large molecules containing chains of carbon atoms. Atoms of other elements are joined to the chain by covalent bonds.

7 Name the element that forms chains in poly(ethene).

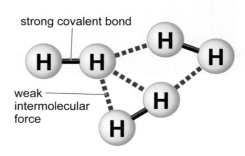

D weak intermolecular forces between hydrogen molecules, H_2

Key points

- A covalent bond is a pair of electrons shared between two non-metal atoms.
- Covalent bonding usually creates simple molecular substances. However, it can result in the formation of giant molecules.
- Simple molecular substances have low melting and boiling points because they have weak intermolecular forces. They do not conduct electricity.

Checkpoint

How confidently can you answer the Progression questions?

Foundation

F1 Use a labelled diagram to show the structure and bonding in a methane molecule.

F2 Describe the properties of methane.

Strengthen

S1 Explain the physical properties of hydrogen. You may use labelled diagrams to help you.

C1g Giant covalent substances

ELC C1A.23, C1A.24, C1A.25, C1A.26 **GCSE** C1.35, C1.36, C1.37, C1.38

Progression questions

- What are giant covalent substances?
- How do we explain the properties of diamond, graphite and fullerenes?
- What are the uses of diamond and graphite?

A What does a diamond have in common with a pencil tip?

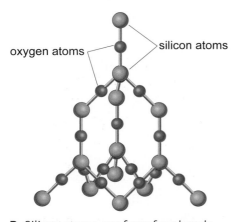

B Silicon atoms can form four bonds. Oxygen atoms can form two bonds. This allows them to join to form a giant covalent structure.

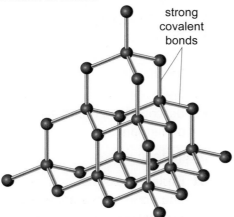

C Diamond contains very many carbon atoms joined to form a network.

Giant covalent compounds

Sand is mostly silica, a compound of silicon and oxygen. The atoms in silica are joined together by strong covalent bonds to form a three-dimensional network. Silica has a **giant covalent** structure. Each molecule contains very many atoms joined by covalent bonds.

> **1** Describe the way in which atoms in silica are joined together.

Silica has the typical properties of a giant covalent substance:

- it has high melting and boiling points, so it is solid at room temperature
- it is a poor **electrical conductor**
- it is **insoluble** in water, so it does not dissolve.

Diamond and graphite

Diamond and graphite are different forms of the element carbon. They are both giant covalent substances. Each carbon atom in diamond is joined to four other carbon atoms by covalent bonds. They form a network of atoms like the network in silica.

Diamond is very hard because its network of atoms is held together by many strong covalent bonds. Diamond is used in cutting tools.

> **2** Why is diamond very hard?

In graphite each carbon atom is joined by covalent bonds to three other atoms, rather than four. This gives layers of atoms. These layers are only held together by weak forces.

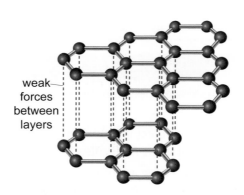

D Graphite consists of layers of carbon atoms.

Graphite is slippery because its layers can slide over each other. This makes graphite useful as a **lubricant**. It also lets graphite pencil tips make black lines on paper.

3 Why is graphite slippery?

Graphite conducts electricity because it has **delocalised electrons** that can move through the structure. Graphite is used to make **electrodes** because it is a good electrical conductor.

4 Why does graphite conduct electricity?

Graphene and fullerenes

A **graphene** molecule is a single layer of graphite. It is very strong because its atoms are joined by many strong covalent bonds. **Fullerenes** are like graphene sheets rolled into tubes or hollow balls. Graphene and fullerenes conduct electricity because they have delocalised electrons.

5 What is a graphene molecule?

Fullerene tubes are called nanotubes. Graphene and nanotubes have high melting and boiling points, like other giant covalent substances.

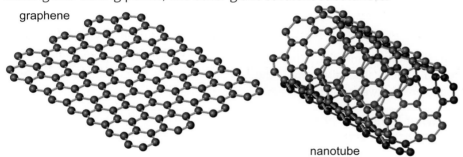

E graphene and a nanotube

Fullerene balls are called buckyballs. They are simple covalent molecules rather than giant covalent molecules. For example, C_{60} molecules have 60 carbon atoms joined by strong covalent bonds. Weak intermolecular forces attract C_{60} molecules to each other. Little energy is needed to overcome these forces, so C_{60} has low melting and boiling points.

6 Why does C_{60} have a low melting point?

Key points

- Giant covalent substances have high melting and boiling points. They do not usually conduct electricity. They are insoluble in water.
- Diamond, graphite, graphene and fullerenes are different forms of carbon with different structures.
- Diamond is used in cutting tools. Graphite is used in electrodes and as a lubricant.

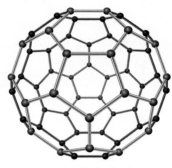

F C_{60} consists of a ball of carbon atoms.

Checkpoint

How confidently can you answer the Progression questions?

Foundation

F1 What are the similarities and differences between diamond and graphite?

Strengthen

S1 Describe how the structure and bonding in graphene and fullerenes cause different properties.

C1h Metallic bonding and bonding summary

ELC C1A.28 **GCSE** C1.32, C1.40

Progression questions

- What are metals like?
- How do we explain the physical properties of metals?
- How can we tell what type of bonding a substance contains?

A Why can plumbers bend copper pipes without the copper shattering?

2 Why is copper metal a good electrical conductor?

Metallic structure and bonding

The atoms in a solid metal have a regular arrangement. They form metal ions surrounded by a 'sea' of **delocalised electrons** from their outer shells. **Metallic bonding** is the strong force of attraction between positive metal ions and negative delocalised electrons. Metals have high melting and boiling points because a lot of energy is needed to overcome these forces.

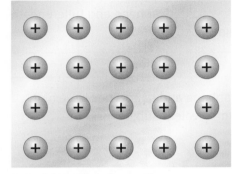

B In this model of metallic structure, the 'sea' of delocalised electrons is the shaded area between the positive ions.

1 What is metallic bonding?

Properties of metals

Metals are good electrical conductors. This is because their delocalised electrons move and carry electric charge through the metal.

Metals are **malleable**, so they can be bent or hammered into shape without shattering. When a force is applied to a metal, layers of metal ions can slide over each other. The delocalised electrons hold the ions together.

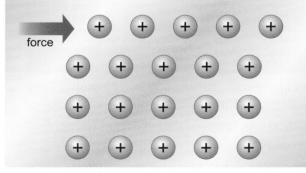

C Layers of metal ions in the regular structure slide over each other when a force is applied.

3 Describe what happens when a force is applied to a metal.

96

Different types of substance

Elements and compounds can be classified into four types, depending on their structure and bonding. Table D shows typical properties of each type.

	Type of substance			
	Ionic	Simple molecular	Giant covalent	Metallic
Melting point and boiling point	high	low	high	high
Solubility in water	usually good	usually poor	insoluble	insoluble
Conducts electricity when solid?	✗	✗	✗	✓
Conducts electricity when liquid?	✓	✗	✗	✓
Conducts electricity when dissolved	✓	✗	does not dissolve	does not dissolve

D Some substances do not have these typical properties. For example, mercury is a liquid metal and graphite is a giant covalent substance that conducts electricity.

Explaining properties

The melting and boiling points of a substance depend on how much energy is needed to overcome the forces between its particles. Melting and boiling points are high if strong ionic bonds, covalent bonds or metallic bonds must be overcome. Simple molecular substances have low melting and boiling points because weak intermolecular forces need little energy to overcome.

A substance dissolves if its particles are more strongly attracted to water molecules than they are to each other. Ions are attracted strongly to water molecules, so ionic compounds usually dissolve. Atoms in giant covalent structures and metals are more strongly attracted to each other, so they do not dissolve.

> **6** Why can sugar dissolve in water?

A substance conducts electricity if it has charged particles that are free to move. Simple molecular substances and giant covalent substances are not charged, so they cannot conduct electricity. Metals and graphite conduct electricity because they have delocalised electrons.

Ionic compounds contain ions, which are charged particles. Ions cannot move when the compound is solid. However, they can move if the compound is liquid or dissolved in water.

> **7** Table salt is an ionic compound. Give the conditions in which it can conduct electricity.

Key points

- Metals are good electrical conductors and are malleable.
- Substances exist as ionic compounds, simple molecular substances, giant covalent substances or metals.
- Structure and bonding can explain the properties of substances.

> **4** Name the type of substance that conducts electricity when it is liquid but not when it is solid.
>
> **5** Why do simple molecular substances have low melting points and boiling points?

E Candle wax is a simple molecular substance that melts easily.

Checkpoint

How confidently can you answer the Progression questions?

Foundation

F1 Give the physical properties of metals that rely upon free electrons.

Strengthen

S1 Summarise the key differences between substances containing ionic bonds, covalent bonds and metallic bonds.

States of matter

1 Sodium is a metal that melts at 98 °C. Describe how the movement and arrangement of sodium atoms change when sodium is heated from 93 °C to 103 °C. **(2 marks)**

....

Student answer

The sodium atoms change from just vibrating in fixed positions to moving around each other [A].

[A] This is a correct statement about how the movement of atoms changes when a solid melts to form a liquid.

....

Verdict

This is a poor answer. Two marks are available but the answer only describes one change. It could also state that the arrangement of the atoms changes from regular to random.

Covalent bonding

2 A water molecule can be shown as H–O–H. The symbol – shows a covalent bond.

The electronic configuration of hydrogen is 1 and the electronic configuration of oxygen is 2.6.

Draw the dot-and-cross diagram for a molecule of water. Show outer electrons only. **(2 marks)**

....

Student answer

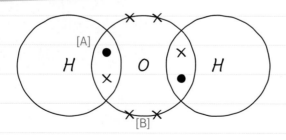

[A] A shared pair of electrons, a covalent bond, is shown as a dot and a cross.

[B] The unpaired electrons in the outer shell of the oxygen atom are shown.

....

Verdict

This is a good answer. The outer electrons in all three atoms are shown correctly. Electrons in hydrogen atoms are shown as dots. Electrons in oxygen atoms are shown as crosses. However, the dots and crosses could be used the opposite way around, as long as each covalent bond is shown as a dot and a cross.

C2 Separating mixtures

Materials sent for recycling are a mixture of many different substances. These include metals, polymers and glass. Old cars and other metal items are often sent to a scrapyard. The different materials are separated so they can be recycled. A huge electromagnet lifts steel pieces away from the mixture. This works because steel has a different physical property to the other substances. Steel is magnetic but the other substances are not.

In this unit you will learn how to separate materials from one another using their different physical properties.

The learning journey

Previously you will have learnt at KS3:

- how mixtures differ from pure substances
- how to separate some mixtures using filtration, distillation and chromatography.

In this unit you will learn:

- about separating insoluble substances from a mixture using filtration
- how a solute is separated from a solution using crystallisation
- about separating a solvent from a solution using simple distillation
- how a liquid is separated from a mixture of liquids using fractional distillation
- how to separate and identify coloured substances using chromatography
- about how compounds are broken down by electrolysis.

C2a Separating mixtures

ELC C1B.1, C1B.2, C1B.5 **GCSE** C2.5, C2.7, C2.12

Progression questions

- How can crystallisation be used to separate mixtures?
- How can filtration be used to separate mixtures?
- How is drinking water produced?

A Is 'pure' orange juice really a pure substance?

B laboratory apparatus used for crystallisation

A **mixture** contains two or more substances that are not chemically combined. Orange juice is a mixture because it contains water, pieces of orange and dissolved substances that are not chemically joined together.

> **1** Why is orange juice a mixture?

In everyday use, the word '**pure**' describes something with nothing else added to it. When a carton says 'pure' orange juice, it means its contents are just orange juice. However, in chemistry a pure substance contains only one element or compound.

> **2** What does the word 'pure' mean to a chemist?

Crystallisation

A **solution** forms when a substance dissolves in a liquid. For example, salt dissolves in water to form salt solution. In this mixture, salt is the **solute** and water is the **solvent**. You can separate a solute from a solvent by **crystallisation**.

> **3** Sodium chloride dissolves in water to form sodium chloride solution. Name the solute in this mixture.

Diagram B shows how crystallisation can be done. The solution is heated using a boiling water bath. Crystals start to form as the solvent evaporates. You get bigger and better shaped crystals if you heat slowly, and stop heating before all the solvent has evaporated. Crystallisation also works if you leave the solution on a windowsill, but this takes longer.

> **4** Crystallisation is carried out on sodium chloride solution. Name the substance that forms the crystals.

Filtration

If a substance is **insoluble** in water, it does not dissolve. **Filtration** is used to separate insoluble substances from a mixture. For example, sand is insoluble so it can be separated from water by filtration. Filter paper has tiny holes in it. The holes are large enough to let water and dissolved substances through, but too small for insoluble particles to go through.

When a mixture of sodium chloride solution and sand is filtered:

- Sodium chloride solution goes through the filter paper and forms a **filtrate**.
- Sand does not go through. It forms a **residue**.

Diagram C shows how filtration can be done.

C laboratory apparatus used for filtration

> **5** Explain why sodium chloride solution passes through filter paper but sand does not.

Making water drinkable

If water is safe to drink, we say that it is **potable**. In the UK, drinking water comes from rivers, lakes or underground rocks containing groundwater. Water must be treated to make it potable.

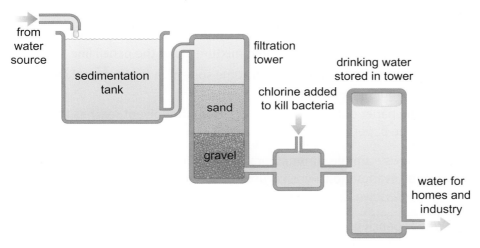

D the main stages in making water safe to drink

During water treatment:

- Grit and other smaller insoluble particles settle out by **sedimentation**.
- Very small insoluble particles are removed by filtration.
- Chlorine is added to kill harmful bacteria. This is called **chlorination**.

> **6** Describe what happens in the chlorination stage of water treatment.

Key points

- Crystallisation is used to produce solid crystals of a soluble substance from its solution.
- Filtration is used to separate an insoluble substance from a mixture.
- Water is treated to make it safe to drink using sedimentation, filtration and chlorination.

Checkpoint

How confidently can you answer the Progression questions?

Foundation

F1 Describe how you would separate sand and salt from a mixture of the two substances.

F2 Draw a flow chart to describe how fresh water is made safe to drink.

Strengthen

S1 Describe how you could produce copper sulfate crystals from a mixture of copper oxide powder and copper sulfate solution.

C2b Chromatography

ELC C1B.2, C1B.4 **GCSE** C2.7, C2.9, C2.10

Progression questions

- How can chromatography be used to separate mixtures?
- What are the differences between mixtures and pure substances on a chromatogram?
- How do you calculate an R_f value?

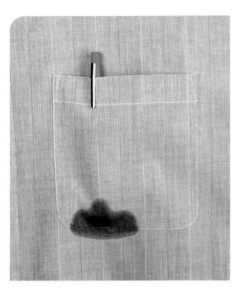

A Why does an ink stain spread and separate?

B paper chromatography of felt-tip pen inks

Ink and food often contain mixtures of coloured substances. These substances are separated and identified using **paper chromatography**.

> **1** Name the method used to separate and identify different coloured substances.

Paper chromatography

To carry out paper chromatography:

a Draw a pencil line near the bottom of a piece of chromatography paper.

b Add a small spot of each coloured mixture along the pencil line.

c Put the paper in a container with some solvent in it. Let the solvent move through the paper.

d Take the paper out of the container before the solvent reaches the top. Leave the paper to dry.

Photo B shows a simple chromatography experiment. A lid stops the solvent escaping by evaporation. Pencil is used at step **a** because pencil is insoluble. It does not dissolve, spread out and interfere with the results, unlike ink.

> **2** Why is pencil used in step **a** of the chromatography method, rather than ink?

Analysing chromatograms

Paper chromatography results are called a **chromatogram**. Diagram C shows the results of an investigation into the food colours in sweets. E133 is a pure dye because it gives one spot. E104 is a mixture of two dyes because it gives two spots. The orange sweet contains E110 because both the sweet and the dye sample give an orange spot that travels the same distance.

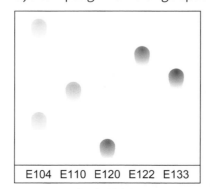

E104	E110	E120	E122	E133

food colours

orange	green	brown	blue	yellow	violet	pink

different coloured sweets

C chromatograms for five food colours and different coloured sweets

3 One of the food colours in diagram C is called E120. Is E120 a single substance or a mixture? State how you know.

4 Name the two food colours found in the violet-coloured sweets.

5 Brown sweets contain a food colour that is not found in yellow sweets. Name this food colour.

Explaining paper chromatography

Paper chromatography works because the coloured substances are attracted to two different 'phases':

- the paper contains the **stationary phase**, which does not move
- the **mobile phase** is the solvent, which travels through the paper.

Some substances are attracted more strongly to the stationary phase. They move slowly, so they do not travel very far up the paper. Other substances are attracted more strongly to the mobile phase. They move quickly and so travel further.

6 What is the mobile phase in paper chromatography?

R_f **values** allow different substances to be compared on a chromatogram, or the same substance on different chromatograms.

$$R_f = \frac{\text{distance travelled by a substance}}{\text{distance travelled by the solvent}}$$

R_f values vary from 0 (the substance does not move) to 1 (the substance moves as far as the solvent does). A given substance has the same R_f value when the same paper and solvent are used.

7 Two green substances have different R_f values. Explain how you know that they are different.

Key points

- Coloured substances can be separated using paper chromatography. This involves a stationary phase (paper) and a mobile phase (solvent).
- A chromatogram can be used to show whether a substance is pure or not. It can also be used to identify substances by comparing them with known substances.
- The use of R_f values improves the analysis and identification of substances.

Checkpoint

How confidently can you answer the Progression questions?

Foundation

F1 The police have taken four different black ballpoint pens from suspects. Describe how paper chromatography could be used to find out if one of the pens could have been used at a crime scene.

Strengthen

S1 Explain how determining R_f values improves the analysis and identification of substances by paper chromatography.

C2c Purifying mixtures

ELC C1B.2, C1B.3 **GCSE** C2.7, C2.8, C2.12

Progression questions

- How can simple distillation be used to separate mixtures?
- How can seawater be made safe to drink?
- How can fractional distillation be used to separate mixtures?

A Seawater is too salty to drink. How can we get fresh water from seawater?

Simple distillation

Simple **distillation** separates a solvent from a solution.

> 1 Name the method used to separate a solvent from a solution.

Simple distillation can produce pure water from salt solution:

- Salt solution is heated in a flask.
- Water **evaporates** and water **vapour** leaves the salt solution.
- Water vapour travels into a condenser.
- The condenser cools the water vapour. It **condenses** to form distilled water.

> 2 Name the change of state that happens in the flask during heating.

Simple distillation may be used to produce potable water (drinking water) from seawater. A lot of energy is needed to heat the seawater. This limits it to countries with little fresh water, but with a coastline and cheap energy resources.

> 3 Drinking water can be produced from seawater using simple distillation.
>   **a** Give two features of countries where this is carried out.
>   **b** Give a reason that explains your answer to part **a**.

Fractional distillation

Fractional distillation separates a liquid from a mixture of liquids. It works because different liquids have different **boiling points**. For example, the boiling point of ethanol (alcohol) is 78 °C and the boiling point of water is 100 °C. Ethanol turns into a vapour more easily than water does.

> 4 Name the physical property of different liquids that fractional distillation relies on.

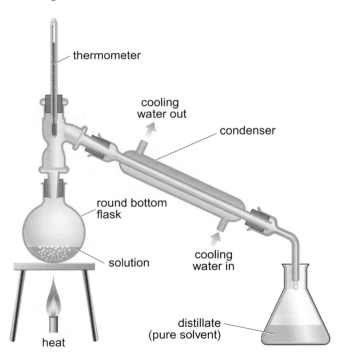

B laboratory apparatus used for simple distillation

When ethanol is separated from a mixture of ethanol and water:

- The mixture is heated in a flask. Ethanol and water vapours leave the mixture.
- The vapours cool as they rise through the **fractionating column**.
- Water vapour condenses to form a liquid that drips back into the flask.
- Ethanol vapour reaches the condenser because it has a lower boiling point than water.
- The condenser cools the vapour. It condenses to form concentrated liquid ethanol.

> **5** A mixture of ethanol and water is separated by fractional distillation. Why does ethanol vapour reach the condenser first?

- The top of the column eventually becomes hot enough for water vapour to reach the condenser.
- At this stage you get dilute ethanol and then just water.

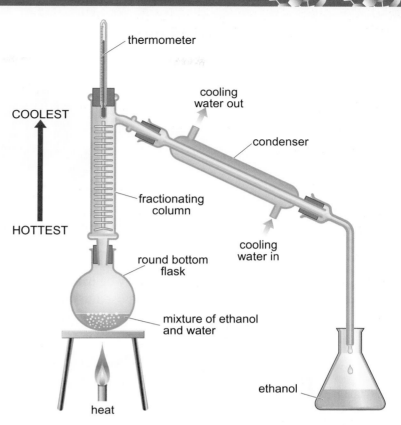

C laboratory apparatus used for fractional distillation

> **6** A mixture of ethanol and water is being separated by fractional distillation. At what stage will you get concentrated ethanol?

> **7** A black ink contains two coloured dyes, dissolved in a mixture of two liquids. Name the method used to:
>
> **a** get one of the liquids from the ink
>
> **b** separate the two dyes in the ink.

Choosing a separation method

The physical properties of the substances in a mixture can help you decide how to separate them.

Type of mixture	Separation method
solution of a solute dissolved in a solvent	crystallisation to get the solute
	simple distillation to get the solvent
insoluble substance in a liquid	filtration
coloured substances in solution	paper chromatography
mixture of liquids	fractional distillation

D different separation methods

Key points

- Simple distillation is used to separate a solvent from a solution.
- Drinking water can be produced from seawater by simple distillation.
- Fractional distillation is used to separate a liquid from a mixture of liquids.

Checkpoint

How confidently can you answer the Progression questions?

Foundation

F1 Describe how distillation is done. Use labelled diagrams to help you.

Strengthen

S1 What are the advantages and disadvantages of producing potable water from seawater by distillation?

A Ink is a mixture of coloured substances dissolved in a liquid solvent.

Forensic scientists analyse substances found at crime scenes. Their results may be used in a court. Simple distillation and paper chromatography can be used to analyse different inks. These methods can show if two samples are likely to contain the same ink or two different inks.

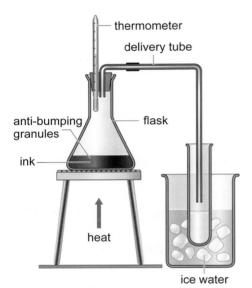

B separating ink using simple distillation

Method

Simple distillation

Wear eye protection.

A Set up your apparatus so that the ink is in a flask. You must have a piece of apparatus to collect and condense the vapours produced when the ink is heated. Diagram B shows some typical apparatus but yours may be different.

B Heat the flask of ink using a Bunsen burner. Make sure the ink simmers gently and does not boil over into the delivery tube.

C Continue heating until you have collected a few cm³ of distillate (distilled solvent).

D Record the maximum temperature reached.

Paper chromatography

E Draw a pencil line on a piece of chromatography paper. It should be about 2 cm from the bottom.

F Add a small spot of ink to the pencil line.

G Add water to a boiling tube, beaker or other container to a depth of about 1 cm.

H Put the paper into the container. Make sure the paper is supported so that it does not slump when it becomes damp. Allow the water to travel through the paper.

I Take the paper out before the water reaches the top. Immediately mark the height it reached using a pencil. Leave the paper to dry.

J Record the colour of each spot.

K Measure and record the distance travelled by each spot, and the water, from the pencil line.

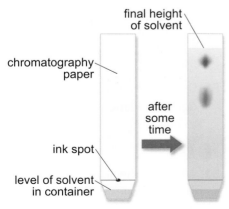

C separating coloured substances using paper chromatography

Exam-style questions

1 Look at diagram B to help you answer these questions.

 a Explain why a Bunsen burner is used in the apparatus. *(2 marks)*

 b Explain why a beaker of iced water is used in the apparatus. *(2 marks)*

2 A student carries out simple distillation on a sample of blue ink.

 a Predict how the appearance of the ink changes. *(1 mark)*

 b Give a reason that explains your answer to part **a**. *(2 marks)*

3 A coloured dye is dissolved in propanol to make an ink.

 a Identify the solute in the ink. *(1 mark)*

 b Identify the solvent in the ink. *(1 mark)*

 c Describe how a pure solvent is separated from a solution by simple distillation. *(3 marks)*

4 Propanone is a flammable solvent that irritates the eyes and skin. A student carries out paper chromatography of ink using propanone as the mobile phase.

 a Identify the mobile phase in her experiment. *(1 mark)*

 b Identify the part that contains the stationary phase. *(1 mark)*

 c The student draws a pencil line so she knows where to place the ink spots. Explain why she should not draw this line with an ink pen instead. *(2 marks)*

 d The level of the propanone should be below the ink spot on the paper at the start. Give a reason for this. *(1 mark)*

 e Explain one precaution to control the risk of harm in her experiment. *(2 marks)*

5 A student uses paper chromatography to analyse four samples of ink (X, A, B and C). Diagram D shows his results. Describe what the results tell you about ink sample X. *(2 marks)*

6 A student uses paper chromatography to analyse the dyes present in a sample of ink. She adds a sample of the ink and four dyes (1, 2, 3 and 4) to the paper. Table E shows her results.

 a Explain whether the dyes are pure substances. *(2 marks)*

 b A mixture of dyes 1 and 4 appears as a single green spot in a paper chromatogram. Suggest an explanation for this. *(2 marks)*

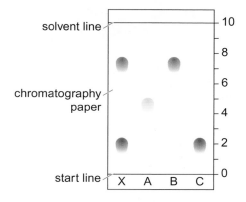

D chromatogram for question 5

Dye	Spot colour	Distance travelled (mm)
1	yellow	10
2	red	35
3	green	67
4	blue	12

E results for question 6

C2d Electrolysis

ELC C1B.6, C1B.7, C1B.8 **GCSE** C3.22, C3.23, C3.24, C3.25, C3.25e, C3.26

Progression questions

- What is an electrolyte?
- What happens during electrolysis?
- What products form during electrolysis of molten compounds and solutions?

A Chlorine is used to kill harmful bacteria in swimming pools. How can it be made using electricity?

Electrolytes and electrodes

Electrolysis is when electrical energy from a **direct current (d.c.)** supply **decomposes** an **electrolyte**. An electrolyte is an **ionic compound** that is molten (liquid) or dissolved in water.

> **1** What is electrolysis?
>
> **2** What is an electrolyte?

To carry out electrolysis you need:

- an electrolyte in a container
- a d.c. supply, such as a battery or power pack
- two **electrodes** to conduct electricity through the electrolyte.

Electrodes are made from an inert (unreactive) substance with a high melting point. Platinum metal is best but graphite or copper are cheaper. An electrode is connected to each terminal of the d.c. supply:

- the **cathode** is the negatively charged electrode
- the **anode** is the positively charged electrode.

> **3** Give the meanings of the terms cathode and anode.

During electrolysis:

- Positively charged **ions** (**cations**) move to the negative cathode.
- Negatively charged ions (**anions**) move to the positive anode.

Hydrogen and metals form cations, so are given off at the cathode. Non-metals (other than hydrogen) form anions, so are given off at the anode.

Molten compounds

Diagram B shows what happens during electrolysis of molten lead bromide.

Lead ions move to the cathode and form lead metal. Bromide ions move to the anode and form bromine gas.

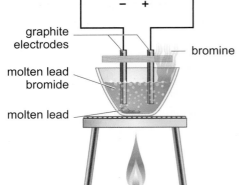

B electrolysis of molten lead bromide (bromine and lead vapour are both toxic)

> **4** Sodium metal and chlorine gas form during the electrolysis of molten sodium chloride.
>
> **a** Name the electrode where sodium will form.
>
> **b** Give a reason for your answer to part **a**.

Water

Water conducts electricity when it is acidified with sulfuric acid. During the electrolysis of acidified water, hydrogen ions move to the cathode and form hydrogen gas. Hydroxide ions move to the anode and form oxygen. Diagram C shows the electrolysis of acidified water.

> **5** Name the product formed at each electrode during the electrolysis of acidified water.

Copper chloride solution

During the electrolysis of copper chloride solution, copper ions move to the cathode and form copper metal. Chloride ions move to the anode and form chlorine gas. Photo D shows the simple apparatus that can be used in the electrolysis of solutions.

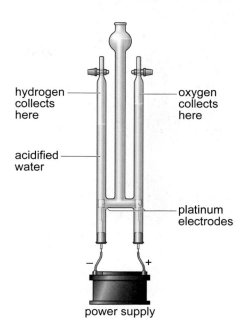

C The gases formed during electrolysis can be collected.

D Copper and bubbles of chlorine form during the electrolysis of copper chloride solution.

> **6** Name two electrolytes that produce chlorine during electrolysis.

Key points

- Electrolysis is when electrical energy from a d.c. supply decomposes electrolytes.
- An electrolyte is an ionic compound in the molten state or dissolved in water.
- During electrolysis, hydrogen or metals form at the cathode. Non-metals other than hydrogen form at the anode.

Checkpoint

How confidently can you answer the Progression questions?

Foundation

F1 Name the products formed at each electrode during the electrolysis of molten zinc chloride. How do you know this?

Strengthen

S1 Explain why the electrolysis of molten potassium hydroxide produces potassium and oxygen at the electrodes.

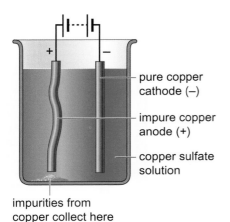

A The mass of the anode decreases as the mass of the cathode increases.

Electrolysis is used to purify copper so that it is suitable for use in electrical cables. Electrolysis is also used in the chemical industry to produce useful gases including hydrogen, oxygen and chlorine.

Method

With copper electrodes

Wear eye protection.

A Label one piece of copper foil 'anode' and the other piece 'cathode'. Measure and record the masses of these two electrodes.

B Set up a container of copper sulfate solution. Connect the two electrodes to a power pack and ammeter. Put them in the container. Photo B shows suitable apparatus.

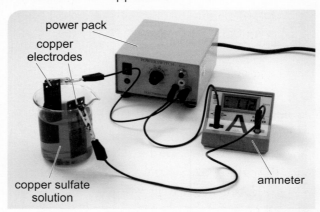

B investigating electrolysis with copper electrodes and a copper sulfate electrolyte

C Turn the power pack on. Adjust it to obtain a current of about 0.2 A. Record the current.

D Leave the experiment running for 20 minutes. Make sure the current stays constant. Turn the power pack off and remove the electrodes from the solution.

E Gently wash the electrodes with distilled water. In a fume cupboard, dip them into propanone. Lift them out and allow the propanone to evaporate.

F Measure and record the new masses of the dry electrodes.

G Repeat the experiment using different currents, as directed by your teacher.

With graphite electrodes

Wear eye protection.

H Set up the circuit as shown in diagram C.

I Turn the power pack on. Observe and record what happens at each electrode.

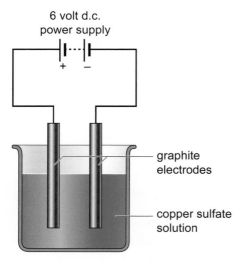

C electrolysis circuit using graphite electrodes

Exam-style questions

1 Bubbles form on one of the graphite electrodes during the electrolysis of copper sulfate solution.

   a Name the gas formed. State whether it forms at the anode or the cathode. *(2 marks)*

   b Name the other product formed. *(1 mark)*

2 Look at the method for electrolysis using copper electrodes.

   a Other than using a fume cupboard, give one precaution necessary to control the risk of harm in this experiment. Give a reason for your answer. *(2 marks)*

   b Explain why the two electrodes must be labelled at step A. *(2 marks)*

   c Suggest an explanation for why the electrodes are washed at step E. *(2 marks)*

3 Electrolysis of copper sulfate solution with copper electrodes is carried out using four different currents. Table D shows the results obtained.

   a Calculate the change in mass of the anode at each current. The results at 0.2 A have been completed for you. *(1 mark)*

   b Describe the effect of increasing the current on the change in mass of the anode. *(1 mark)*

   c Calculate the change in mass of the cathode at each current. The results at 0.2 A have been completed for you. *(1 mark)*

   d Describe the effect of increasing the current on the change in mass of the cathode. *(1 mark)*

   e Compare your answers to parts **b** and **d**. Describe what you notice. *(1 mark)*

   f Look at the changes in mass at each current. The change in mass of the anode differs from the change in mass of the cathode. Suggest an explanation for why this is. *(2 marks)*

Current (A)	Anode mass (g)			Cathode mass (g)		
	At start	At end	Change	At start	At end	Change
0.2	2.77	2.69	−0.08	2.51	2.58	+0.07
0.3	2.68	2.55		2.55	2.66	
0.4	2.53	2.36		2.62	2.76	
0.5	2.36	2.15		2.70	2.87	

D

Separating mixtures

A cloudy, runny mixture contains three compounds (X, Y and Z).

Compound	Boiling point (°C)	State at room temperature	Notes
X	4000	solid	not soluble in Y or Z
Y	97.4	liquid	soluble in Z
Z	78.4	liquid	soluble in Y

Devise a method to separate out X, Y and Z. Use the information in the table above and explain why you have suggested each step.

(6 marks)

Plan your answer

A 'devise' question means you need to plan or invent a procedure from what you know. So a student plan might look like this:

– separate X first by filtration – a solid that does not dissolve

– separate Y and Z by fractional distillation – two liquids with different boiling points

– explain why I chose each method

· ·

Student answer

Filter the mixture. Compound X will collect in the filter paper, but the two liquids (compounds Y and Z) will pass through [A]. This works because compound X is a solid, and it is insoluble in the two liquids [B].

[A] This describes what will happen during filtration.

[B] This explains why compound X can be separated by filtration.

Use fractional distillation next to separate compounds Y and Z from each other. This works because they have different boiling points [C]. Compound Z will distil off first because it has the lower boiling point [D], leaving compound Y behind.

[C] The physical property that fractional distillation depends on is given.

[D] This explains that compound Z will be collected first during fractional distillation.

· ·

Verdict

This is a good answer. It shows good knowledge and understanding of separation methods. However, it could also mention how compound X could be purified. After filtration, compound X will be wet with compounds Y and Z. These have low boiling points, so compound X could be dried in a warm oven.

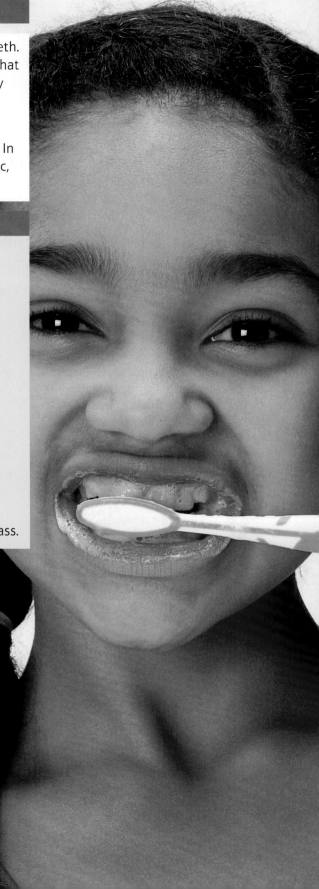

C3 Acids and metals

The food we eat produces acids in our mouths that can damage our teeth. When we brush our teeth with toothpaste, a chemical reaction occurs that neutralises the acid in our mouths. This helps to keep our teeth healthy and free from decay.

All solutions in water can be classified into three groups, according to their chemistry. These groups are acidic, alkaline and neutral solutions. In this topic we will investigate the main reactions and properties of acidic, alkaline and neutral solutions.

The learning journey

Previously you will have learnt at KS3:

- about solubility, solutes, solvents and solutions
- how common international hazard symbols are used
- about common acids, alkalis and neutral solutions
- about the use of indicators to test for acids and alkalis
- about simple neutralisation reactions.

In this unit you will learn:

- about the pH scale and how different indicators are used
- the difference between acids, alkalis and bases
- what happens during neutralisation reactions
- how a soluble salt can be prepared in the laboratory
- about the reactions and reactivity of metals
- about extracting and recycling metals
- how to carry out calculations involving mass and relative formula mass.

C3a Acids and alkalis

ELC C1B.9, C1B.10 **GCSE** C3.2, C3.3

Progression questions

- Why are hazard symbols useful?
- How do acids and alkalis affect common indicators?
- What do the different numbers on the pH scale tell us?

A The international hazard symbols on these household products warn that they are flammable, corrosive and harmful to the environment. Which symbol is which?

1 **a** Why are hazard symbols useful?

b Suggest an advantage of using hazard symbols, which are the same in all countries.

c Choose one of the bottles in photo A and suggest a suitable safety precaution to take when using this substance.

Solutions in water are either **acidic**, **alkaline** or **neutral**. Some can be dangerous, even some neutral solutions. Every year, thousands of children in the UK are harmed by household cleaning products. International hazard symbols on all chemicals are useful as they warn people of the possible dangers, and can be understood in all countries.

Hazard symbols help us to decide what safety precautions to take when using substances. For example, if an acid solution is labelled **corrosive** then we need to handle it with care and wear gloves and eye protection.

The pH scale

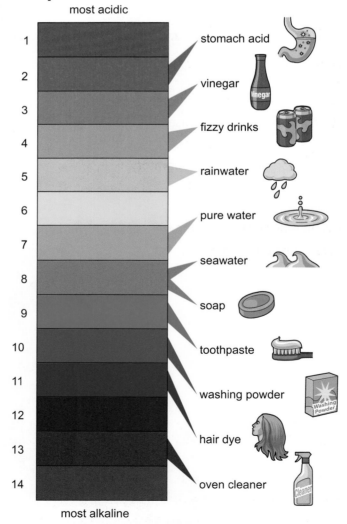

B the pH scale and universal indicator colours

114

The acidity or alkalinity of a solution is measured on the **pH scale** (diagram B). Most solutions are between 0 and 14 on the scale. Acids have a pH below 7. The lower the pH, the more acidic the solution. Alkalis have a pH above 7. The higher the pH, the more alkaline the solution. Solutions that have a pH of 7 are neutral.

Indicator	Litmus	Methyl orange	Phenolphthalein
colour in alkaline solutions	blue	yellow	pink
colour in acidic solutions	red	red	colourless

C indicator colours in acids and alkalis

> **2** Use the information in diagram B to answer these questions.
>
> **a** Name three alkaline substances.
>
> **b** Place the following solutions in order from least acidic to most acidic: stomach acid, vinegar, fizzy drinks, seawater, rainwater.

Indicators

Substances that change colour depending on the pH of a solution are called **indicators**. The different colours of three common indicators are shown in table C.

> **3** Explain why litmus can be used as an indicator.

The **universal indicator** in photo D contains a mixture of indicators. It gives a range of colours depending on the pH of the substance being tested. The range of colours of universal indicator is shown in diagram B.

D Universal indicator gives an approximate pH value.

> **4 a** Use diagram B to estimate the pH of the solution being tested in photo D.
>
> **b** Look at table C. What colour would the solution in photo D turn:
> **i** litmus **ii** methyl orange **iii** phenolphthalein.
>
> **5** Describe how universal indicator is different from other indicators.

Checkpoint

How confidently can you answer the Progression questions?

Foundation

F1 Describe why we use hazard symbols on the containers of some household chemicals.

F2 Describe what indicators can show.

Strengthen

S1 Describe what the different numbers on the pH scale tell us about a solution.

Key points

- Hazard symbols warn us that a substance may be dangerous. They remind us to use the right safety precautions.
- Indicators change colour depending on the pH.
- Acid pH is below 7, alkali pH is above 7 and neutral pH equals 7.

C3b Neutralisation

ELC C1B.11, C1B.12, C1B.13 **GCSE** C3.9, C3.10, C3.11, C3.12, C3.13, C3.16

Progression questions

- How can you neutralise an acid?
- What are bases and alkalis?
- What is formed during a neutralisation reaction?

A How do indigestion remedies work?

During **neutralisation** reactions, **acids** react with **bases** to form a **salt** and water.

$$acid + base \rightarrow salt + water$$

Many neutralisation reactions occur in everyday life. Indigestion remedies contain bases to neutralise excess stomach acid. 'Milk of magnesia' contains magnesium hydroxide, which **neutralises** hydrochloric acid in the stomach to form the salt magnesium chloride and water.

$$magnesium\ hydroxide + hydrochloric\ acid \rightarrow magnesium\ chloride + water$$

A base is any substance that reacts with acids to form a salt and water only. Metal oxides and metal hydroxides are examples of bases.

---

1. What happens during neutralisation reactions?
2. What is a base?

Soluble bases are called **alkalis**. They dissolve in water to form alkaline solutions. They will also neutralise acids to form a salt and water only.

$$acid + alkali \rightarrow salt + water$$

---

3. Explain why all alkalis are bases, but not all bases are alkalis.

Table B and diagram C describe how salts are named from the acid and base they are formed from.

Acid	Salt formed
hydrochloric acid	chloride
sulfuric acid	sulfate
nitric acid	nitrate

B salts formed from acids

---

4. Name the salt formed from:
   a hydrochloric acid and calcium oxide
   b nitric acid and sodium hydroxide.

Titrations

Photo D shows a **titration**. This involves adding measured volumes of acid to exactly neutralise the alkali in the flask. The solution produced only contains the salt, as all the acid and alkali have been used up. Titrations can be used to prepare samples of soluble salts.

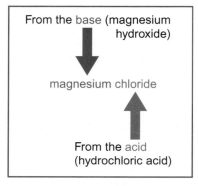

From the base (magnesium hydroxide)

magnesium chloride

From the acid (hydrochloric acid)

C how to name a salt

Reactions of acids with metal carbonates

Acids can also be neutralised by metal carbonates. This reaction forms a salt, water and carbon dioxide gas. The test for carbon dioxide is that it turns limewater milky, as shown in photo E.

acid + metal carbonate → salt + water + carbon dioxide

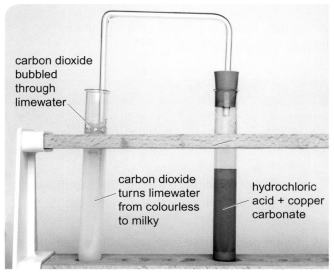

hydrochloric acid + copper carbonate
→ copper chloride + water + carbon dioxide

E the reaction of an acid and a carbonate

---

6 a Name the products when zinc carbonate neutralises nitric acid.

   b How can you tell when the reaction is finished?

Reactions of acids with metals

Metals neutralise acids to form a salt and hydrogen gas. The test for hydrogen gas is that it burns with a squeaky 'pop' when lit.

acid + metal → salt + hydrogen

---

7 Iron metal neutralises sulfuric acid to form iron sulfate.

   a What else will be formed during the reaction?

   b What kind of substance is iron sulfate?

   c Write a word equation for the reaction.

Key points

Neutralisation reactions:

- acid + base (metal oxide or hydroxide) → salt + water
- acid + alkali (soluble base) → salt + water
- acid + metal carbonate → salt + water + carbon dioxide
- acid + metal → salt + hydrogen

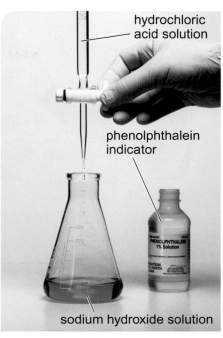

hydrochloric acid + sodium hydroxide
→ sodium chloride + water

D An indicator colour change shows when neutralisation has occurred. This solution is now alkaline.

---

5 How do we know when the acid is neutralised during a titration?

Checkpoint

How confidently can you answer the Progression questions?

Foundation

F1 Name four types of substance that can neutralise hydrochloric acid.

Strengthen

S1 a Name the products of the reaction between sodium carbonate and sulfuric acid.

   b Describe how you could test for the gas produced.

A measuring pH

The pH of a solution is how acidic or alkaline it is. The lower the pH the more acidic a solution and the higher the pH the more alkaline a solution. Neutral solutions are pH 7. Acids can be neutralised by bases to form a salt and water. Bases include metal oxides and metal hydroxides. Soluble bases are called alkalis.

The method below measures the change in pH that occurs as the base calcium hydroxide is added to hydrochloric acid.

Method

Wear eye protection.

A Use a measuring cylinder to measure out 50 cm³ of dilute hydrochloric acid. Pour this into a beaker.

B Put a piece of universal indicator paper onto a white tile. Dip the end of a glass rod into the liquid then tap it onto the universal indicator paper.

C Leave the universal indicator paper for 30 seconds. Then match the colour to a pH on a pH colour chart. Record this pH.

D Rinse the glass rod with water.

E Use an electronic balance to measure out 0.3 g of calcium hydroxide powder onto a piece of paper or a 'weighing boat'.

F Add the calcium hydroxide powder to the beaker of dilute hydrochloric acid and stir.

G Measure and record the new pH of the mixture. Use the same method as given in steps B to D.

H Repeat steps E to G seven times. This should mean that you add a total of 2.4 g of calcium hydroxide powder to the dilute hydrochloric acid.

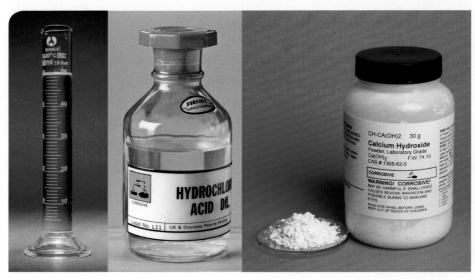

B investigating pH and neutralisation

Exam-style questions

1 Name the salt formed when hydrochloric acid reacts with calcium hydroxide. *(1 mark)*

2 State the type of reaction that occurs between hydrochloric acid and calcium hydroxide. *(1 mark)*

3 Explain why calcium hydroxide can be described as a base. *(2 marks)*

4 Calcium oxide and calcium hydroxide neutralise hydrochloric acid in a similar way. Diagram C shows part of the labels found on bottles of these chemicals.
Explain why calcium hydroxide is used in this investigation rather than calcium oxide. *(3 marks)*

5 Suggest two reasons why eye protection must be worn during this investigation. *(2 marks)*

6 A student investigates the change in pH when calcium hydroxide powder is added to a measured volume of dilute nitric acid.

   a Apart from the volume of acid state two other measurements that the student will have to make. *(2 marks)*

   b State the dependent variable in his experiment. *(1 mark)*

7 A student carried out an experiment using dilute hydrochloric acid and magnesium oxide powder. She wanted to find the mass of powder that needs to be added to 75 cm³ of hydrochloric acid to give a neutral solution. She added 0.5 g of magnesium oxide powder at a time and measured the pH of the solution after each addition. She used a pH meter to measure the pH. Table D shows her results.

   a Describe how the pH changes as the magnesium oxide is added. *(1 mark)*

   b Predict the mass of magnesium oxide needed to give a neutral solution. *(1 mark)*

   c Suggest one way in which the student could improve her experiment to get a more accurate estimate. She must use the same apparatus and solutions. *(1 mark)*

   d Explain whether indicator paper or a pH meter would give more useful results. *(2 marks)*

calcium oxide CaO $M_r = 56.0774$	calcium hydroxide Ca(OH)$_2$ $M_r = 74.093$

C chemical labels for question 4

Mass of magnesium oxide added (g)	pH of reaction mixture
0.0	0.3
0.5	0.6
1.0	2.8
1.5	12.3
2.0	12.5

D results for question 7

C3c Making salts

ELC C1B.14 **GCSE** C3.15, C3.19, C3.20, C3.21

Progression questions

- How can we prepare soluble and insoluble salts?
- What are the rules for solubility of common substances in water?
- How can you predict if a precipitate will form when solutions are mixed?

Step 1
Add excess
tin oxide...

... to
hydrochloric
acid.

gentle heating
(e.g. using a
water bath)

Step 2
Gently warm the
mixture to speed
up the reaction.

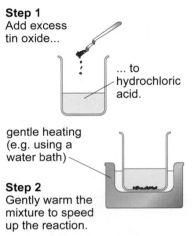

Step 3
Filter to remove
the unreacted
solid from the
solution.

tin
oxide

tin
chloride
solution

tin
chloride solution

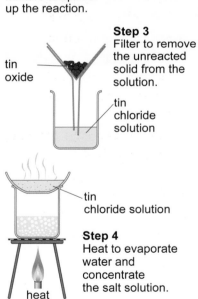

Step 4
Heat to evaporate
water and
concentrate
the salt solution.

heat

Step 5
Leave to evaporate
water slowly for
crystallisation to occur.

tin
chloride solid

B preparing tin chloride

Many useful salts can be made by neutralisation. For example Epsom salts (magnesium sulfate) can be used as a foot soak to cure sprains, bruises, fungal infections and even smelly feet.

A How could you make Epsom salts by neutralisation?

> 1 Name the type of reaction that makes salts like Epsom salts.
>
> 2 Name the acid used to make magnesium sulfate.

Preparing soluble salts

Some **soluble salts** can be prepared by neutralising an **acid** with an **insoluble base**. Diagram B outlines the steps involved in preparing tin chloride. Note that:

- excess base is added to make sure all acid is used up
- **filtration** is used to separate the unreacted solid base from the solution
- the solid salt is obtained by letting the water **evaporate** so **crystallisation** occurs.

> 3 The salt cobalt nitrate can be made using the base cobalt oxide.
>
>   a Name the acid needed.
>
>   b Why is excess cobalt oxide added?
>
>   c Why is the mixture filtered?

Preparing insoluble salts

Insoluble salts can be prepared by a **precipitation** reaction. As shown in photo C, this involves mixing two solutions of soluble salts to form an insoluble **precipitate**.

Solubility rules shown in table D can be used to predict when a precipitate will form. For example, if lead nitrate and sodium iodide solutions are mixed, two new salts are formed. These salts are sodium nitrate and lead iodide. The rules tell us that sodium nitrate is soluble and stays in solution, while lead iodide is insoluble and forms a precipitate.

Solubility rules		Exceptions
1	All common sodium, potassium and ammonium salts are soluble.	(no exceptions)
2	All nitrates are soluble.	(no exceptions)
3	Most common chlorides are soluble.	(except silver and lead)
4	Most common sulfates are soluble.	(except calcium, barium and lead)
5	Most common hydroxides and carbonates are insoluble.	(except sodium, potassium and ammonium)

D solubility rules

To prepare a pure, dry sample of an insoluble salt:
- Mix the two solutions that form the insoluble salt.
- Filter the mixture.
- Pour a little distilled water over the precipitate.
- Remove the filter paper and dry the precipitate.

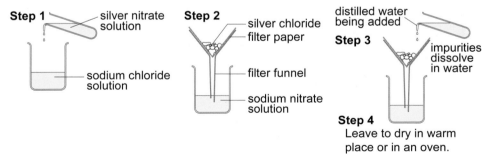

Step 1 silver nitrate solution / sodium chloride solution

Step 2 silver chloride / filter paper / filter funnel / sodium nitrate solution

Step 3 distilled water being added / impurities dissolve in water

Step 4 Leave to dry in warm place or in an oven.

E preparing an insoluble salt

C The yellow precipitate is the salt lead iodide.

4 Which of the following substances are soluble and which are insoluble in water? lead nitrate, calcium sulfate, potassium bromide, silver chloride, calcium carbonate

5 Name a metal whose salts are mostly insoluble.

6 a Name the insoluble salt formed in diagram E.

   b Name the salt left in solution.

7 a Explain why distilled water is poured over the precipitate.

   b Suggest two ways of drying the precipitate.

Checkpoint

How confidently can you answer the Progression questions?

Foundation

F1 Draw a flow chart to explain the steps involved in preparing a soluble salt from an acid and an insoluble base.

Strengthen

S1 Describe how to prepare a pure, dry sample of insoluble lead sulfate from two named solutions.

Key points

- Soluble salts can be made by neutralising an acid with an insoluble base.
- Solubility rules can be used to identify a precipitate.
- Insoluble salts can be prepared by mixing two solutions to form a precipitate.

Salts can be formed by neutralising the correct acid and base. The general neutralisation reaction is:

$$acid + base \rightarrow salt + water$$

Soluble salts can be prepared by neutralising the correct acid with an insoluble base. For example, the soluble salt copper sulfate can be prepared by neutralising sulfuric acid with insoluble copper oxide.

$$sulfuric\ acid + copper\ oxide \rightarrow copper\ sulfate + water$$

The method below describes how to prepare crystals of the salt copper sulfate.

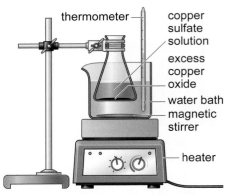

A Heating the acid makes the reaction between sulfuric acid and copper oxide faster.

B Filtration separates the excess solid copper oxide from the copper sulfate solution.

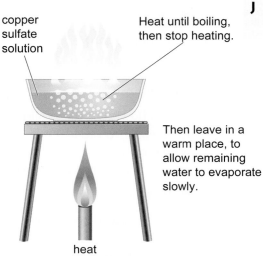

C Evaporation of the water leaves pure crystals of the solid salt.

Method

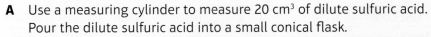

Wear eye protection.

A Use a measuring cylinder to measure 20 cm³ of dilute sulfuric acid. Pour the dilute sulfuric acid into a small conical flask.

B Warm the conical flask of sulfuric acid in a water bath set at 60 °C. Use a thermometer to check the temperature.

C Add a spatula of copper oxide powder to the acid and stir.

D If all the copper oxide reacts so none is left, add a little more.

E Stop adding copper oxide when it no longer reacts (the solution remains cloudy black).

F Filter the mixture to separate the excess solid from the solution.

G Transfer the solution to an evaporating basin.

H Heat the evaporating basin until the liquid boils. Once the liquid boils, stop heating.

I Leave the solution in the basin to cool before moving it.

J Pour the solution into a Petri dish. Leave it to allow the water to evaporate.

D Crystals of copper sulfate form when the water evaporates. Large crystals will form if the water evaporates slowly.

Exam-style questions

1 Copy and complete the sentence below.
   Copper sulfate is described as a _____ because it is formed
   by a _____ reaction between an _____
   and a base. *(3 marks)*

2 State why the sulfuric acid is heated in step B. *(1 mark)*

3 Explain why the copper oxide gets stuck in the filter paper while
   the copper sulfate goes through it. *(2 marks)*

4 Explain how you know a chemical reaction has occurred when you
   carry out step C. *(2 marks)*

5 State how you know when all the acid has been used up. *(1 mark)*

6 State why it is important that the copper oxide is in excess in
   step E. *(1 mark)*

7 Apart from taking care when heating solutions, describe one other
   safety precaution that should be taken during this experiment
   and explain why it is necessary. *(2 marks)*

8 Nickel chloride is a soluble salt. It can be made by reacting
   insoluble nickel oxide with hydrochloric acid.

   a Write a word equation for this reaction. *(1 mark)*

   b Briefly describe the four main stages involved in preparing a
   pure sample of solid nickel chloride crystals. *(4 marks)*

9 Two class groups prepared some zinc chloride. One group
   produced lots of very small crystals. The other group produced
   larger crystals.

   Suggest a possible reason for the groups producing
   different-sized crystals. *(2 marks)*

Progression questions

- How can we find out how reactive a metal is?
- What are metal ores and where do we find them?
- Why are different metals produced in different ways?

A If you are very lucky you might find a piece of gold in river gravel. Why are chemical reactions needed to obtain aluminium and iron?

potassium
sodium
calcium
magnesium
aluminium
zinc
iron
(hydrogen)
copper
silver
gold

increasing reactivity →

B Hydrogen is not a metal. It is shown in this reactivity series to help you make predictions about reactions.

---

3 State which metal, copper or iron, will react with dilute hydrochloric acid. Give a reason for your answer. Use diagram B to help you.

Gold is very **unreactive**. It does not react with water or dilute acids. Other metals are more reactive. They react with water or dilute acids to produce hydrogen bubbles. The faster this happens, the more reactive the metal is.

---

1 Name the gas produced when a metal reacts with water or dilute acids.

Reactivity series

The **reactivity series** is a list of metals in order of reactivity (diagram B).

---

2 Use diagram B to name three metals that are more reactive than copper, but less reactive than magnesium.

A metal usually reacts with water or dilute acids if it is more reactive than hydrogen. Gold is less reactive than hydrogen, so it does not react with water or dilute acids.

Displacement reactions

A **displacement reaction** happens between a reactive metal and a compound of a less reactive metal.

For example, zinc metal reacts with copper sulfate solution (see photo C):

zinc + copper sulfate → zinc sulfate + copper

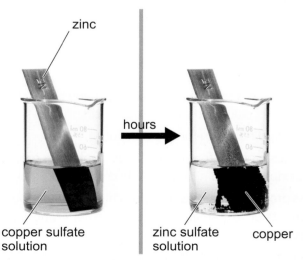

zinc

hours →

copper sulfate solution

zinc sulfate solution

copper

C Zinc gradually becomes coated with copper. The blue colour fades as copper sulfate solution is replaced by colourless zinc sulfate solution.

Zinc is more reactive than copper, so zinc can displace copper from copper compounds. Copper is not reactive enough to displace zinc from zinc compounds.

> **4** You can use the reactivity series to predict if a displacement reaction happens.
>
> **a** Use diagram B to name the more reactive metal, magnesium or zinc.
>
> **b** Predict whether magnesium metal will react with zinc sulfate solution. Explain your answer.

Extracting metals

Metals and their compounds are found in the Earth's crust. Unreactive metals are found as the uncombined elements. However, most metals must be extracted from **ores**. An ore is a rock that contains enough of a metal to make extracting the metal profitable.

> **5** State what is meant by an ore.

All metals could be extracted from their ores using **electrolysis**. However, large amounts of electricity are expensive. If a metal is less reactive than carbon, it is cheaper to extract the metal by heating its ore with carbon (diagram D).

> **6** Why must aluminium be extracted from aluminium ore using electrolysis?

Iron is extracted by heating iron ore (iron oxide) with carbon. Carbon is more reactive than iron, so it can displace iron from its compounds:

$$\text{carbon} + \text{iron oxide} \rightarrow \text{carbon dioxide} + \text{iron}$$

> **7** Explain why copper can be extracted by heating copper ore with carbon.

potassium sodium calcium magnesium aluminium	electrolysis
(carbon)	
zinc iron copper	heating with carbon
silver gold	found uncombined

D Different metals are extracted in different ways. Carbon is not a metal. It is shown here so you can tell if a metal is less reactive than carbon.

Checkpoint

How confidently can you answer the Progression questions?

Foundation

F1 Describe how you can use dilute hydrochloric acid to place two metals in order of reactivity.

Strengthen

S1 Explain why iron is extracted from iron ore by heating with carbon, but aluminium is extracted by electrolysis.

Key points

- You can place metals in a reactivity series by seeing how they react with water, dilute acids or salt solutions.
- Unreactive metals like gold are found in the Earth's crust as uncombined elements. Most other metals must be extracted from ores.
- Metals that are more reactive than carbon are extracted using electrolysis. Other metals can be extracted by heating their ores with carbon.

- What are some uses of aluminium, copper, gold and steel?
- Why are different metals used for different purposes?
- What are the advantages of recycling metals?

A What are the advantages of recycling metals such as the aluminium in these drinks cans?

Metal	Cost (£/kg)
aluminium	1
copper	3
gold	27 500
steel	0.35

B the approximate cost of four metals

1 Give a reason why aluminium is used for aircraft parts.

2 Give the properties of copper that make it suitable for water pipes.

3 Give one use of gold. State the property of gold that makes it suitable for this use.

Properties and uses of metals

The uses of a metal depend on its cost and properties. These include **density**, strength, resistance to **corrosion**, and whether it conducts electricity.

Aluminium has a low density, so it is used for aircraft parts. The low density helps to keep the aircraft as lightweight as possible. Aluminium is also used for overhead electrical cables. Copper is a better conductor, but aluminium is cheaper and resists corrosion better.

Copper is **malleable** (easily bent into shape) and does not react with water. It is also a very good conductor of electricity. It is used for water pipes and electrical wiring.

Gold is very resistant to corrosion. Gold stays shiny, so it is used in jewellery. This property means that gold is preferred for some electrical uses, even though copper is cheaper and conducts electricity better. Gold is used in tiny amounts to connect memory chips in computers.

Steel is the most widely used metal. It does not resist corrosion, so it rusts easily. However, steel is malleable and strong. It is used to make cars, bridges, ships and the frameworks for buildings.

4 Steel is widely used even though it rusts. Suggest a reason, other than its strength, that explains why. Use table B to help you.

Metal recycling

A lot of what we throw away contains valuable metals. These can be collected, sorted, melted down and reused. Recycling uses far less energy than extracting metals from their ores. This has an economic benefit because it reduces costs.

> **5** Describe an economic benefit of recycling metals.

Ores are **finite resources** because they form very slowly or are no longer being made. Mining ores damages the landscape and produces noise, dust and other **pollution**. Recycling provides environmental benefits. It reduces the need for mining and conserves the remaining ores.

> **6** Describe one environmental benefit of recycling metals.

Life cycle assessments

The effects of a product on the environment over its lifetime are analysed using a **life cycle assessment (LCA)**. An LCA needs information about each of the stages in diagram D. This includes use of energy, transport and storage, and release of waste materials. The aim is to find ways to reduce the effect of a product on the environment.

C This river is polluted by waste substances from mining metal ores.

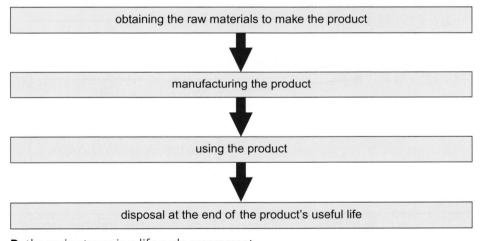

obtaining the raw materials to make the product
↓
manufacturing the product
↓
using the product
↓
disposal at the end of the product's useful life

D the main stages in a life cycle assessment

> **7** Describe what a life cycle assessment involves.

Key points

- Different metals have different uses. These uses are related to their properties.
- Recycling has economic and environmental benefits. It also conserves valuable raw materials.
- A life cycle assessment looks at the effect of a product on the environment over the whole of its lifetime.

Checkpoint

How confidently can you answer the Progression questions?

Foundation

F1 Give one use for each of these metals: aluminium, copper, gold and steel.

F2 Give a reason why each metal is suitable for the use you gave in question F1.

Strengthen

S1 Describe the advantages of recycling metals.

C3f Calculations involving masses

GCSE C1.43, C1.44, C1.45a, C1.47

Progression questions

- What is the law of conservation of mass?
- How do we calculate the relative formula mass of a substance?
- How do we find the formula for a substance using experiments and calculations?

A When you put a piece of flat-pack furniture together, what happens to the total mass of all the parts from the box?

No atoms are created or destroyed in a chemical reaction. Atoms in reactants join in different ways to form products. The total mass of substances stays the same. This is the **law of conservation of mass**.

1	What happens to the total mass of substances in a chemical reaction?

Relative formula mass

The **relative atomic mass** (A_r) of an element tells you the mass of its atoms compared with atoms of other elements. You can find the **relative formula mass** (M_r) of a substance by adding together the relative atomic masses of all the atoms in its formula.

Worked example W1

Calculate the relative formula mass of methane, CH_4 (relative atomic masses: C = 12, H = 1).

$(1 \times C) + (4 \times H)$ ●————————→ Count the atoms of each element in the formula.

$(1 \times 12) + (4 \times 1)$ ●

$= 12 + 4$ ●

$= 16$

Write relative atomic masses in place of symbols.

Use the values to calculate the relative formula mass.

2	Calculate the relative formula mass of ammonia, NH_3 (relative atomic masses: N = 14, H = 1).

Finding a formula

You can find the formulae of a simple compound using an experiment. For example, you can find the formula of magnesium chloride by reacting magnesium with dilute hydrochloric acid. You need to:

- measure the mass of magnesium used
- measure the mass of magnesium chloride made.

Worked example W2 shows how to find the formula with this information.

B magnesium reacting with dilute hydrochloric acid

3	Give one way in which photo B shows that a reaction is happening.

Worked example W2

0.96 g of magnesium reacts with hydrochloric acid to form 3.80 g of magnesium chloride:

magnesium + hydrochloric acid → magnesium chloride + hydrogen

Find the formula of magnesium chloride (relative atomic masses: Mg = 24, Cl = 35.5).

mass of chlorine that reacts with magnesium = mass of magnesium chloride – mass of magnesium

= 3.80 g – 0.96 g

= 2.84 g

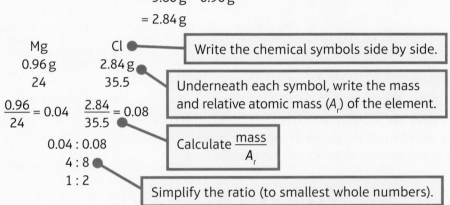

Write the chemical symbols side by side.

Underneath each symbol, write the mass and relative atomic mass (A_r) of the element.

Calculate $\dfrac{mass}{A_r}$

Simplify the ratio (to smallest whole numbers).

The ratio shows 1 magnesium atom to 2 chlorine atoms.
The formula is $MgCl_2$.

---

4 1.2 g of magnesium reacts with oxygen to form 2.0 g of magnesium oxide.

   a Calculate the mass of oxygen that reacts with magnesium.

   b Follow the steps shown in Worked example W2 to calculate the formula for magnesium oxide (relative atomic masses: Mg = 24, O = 16).

A formula found by experiment is an **empirical formula**. It is the simplest whole number ratio of the atoms of each element in a substance. The formula for ethane is C_2H_6. You can simplify this formula if you divide both numbers by 2. So the empirical formula for ethane is CH_3.

---

5 The formula for a gas is N_2O_4. Give its empirical formula.

Key points

- The total mass stays the same in chemical reactions. This is the law of conservation of mass.
- You find a relative formula mass (M_r) by adding the A_r values for all the atoms in a formula.
- An empirical formula is the simplest whole number ratio of the atoms of each element in a substance.

Checkpoint

How confidently can you answer the Progression questions?

Foundation

F1 Calculate the relative formula mass of ethane, C_2H_6 (relative atomic masses: C = 12, H = 1).

Strengthen

S1 0.5 g hydrogen reacts with oxygen to form 4.5 g of water.

   a Calculate the mass of oxygen that reacts with hydrogen.

   b Calculate the empirical formula for water (relative atomic masses: H = 1, O = 16).

Extracting metals

1 Iron is produced when iron oxide is heated with carbon.

Complete the word equation for the reaction.

iron oxide + carbon → .... + ...   (2 marks)

Student answer

iron oxide + carbon → *iron* + ... [A]   [A] The second empty space has not been completed.

Verdict

This is a poor answer. It only shows one product, which is the product given in the question. It is better to try to work out the name of the other product as well. Looking at the reactants, this is carbon monoxide or carbon dioxide here.

Making an insoluble salt

2 Silver nitrate solution reacts with sodium chloride solution. Silver chloride forms as an insoluble solid. A student uses this method to make some silver chloride:

- pour 50 cm^3 of silver nitrate solution into a beaker
- add drops of sodium chloride solution until the mixture turns cloudy
- let the silver chloride settle to the bottom of the beaker, then pour off the liquid.

Only a little silver chloride is obtained this way. Explain two ways of improving this method so that more silver chloride is obtained from 50 cm^3 of silver nitrate solution.   (4 marks)

Student answer

Add excess sodium chloride solution instead of just a few drops [A]. *More silver nitrate will react, so more silver chloride will be made* [B]. *Instead of just letting the precipitate settle, filter the reaction mixture* [C]. *This will reduce the amount of silver chloride lost during separation from the reaction mixture* [D].

[A] This describes the first improvement.
[B] The reason for suggesting the first improvement is given.
[C] This describes the second improvement.

[D] The reason for suggesting the second improvement is given.

Verdict

This is a good answer. Two relevant improvements are given, and both are explained clearly.

C4 Elements and chemical reactions

When we think of fireworks we remember amazing displays of light, sound and movement. However, what we are actually watching are chemical reactions. The energy released by these reactions makes rockets fly into the air, bangers explode and shells produce starbursts of bright light. To use chemical reactions we need to understand the properties of the elements and how energy is involved.

In this unit you will look at how chemical reactions can be controlled. You will learn about the energy changes that can occur during reactions. You will also learn about the properties of some of the most important elements in the periodic table.

The learning journey

Previously you will have learnt at KS3:

- about elements, compounds and the periodic table
- what happens during chemical reactions.

In this unit you will learn:

- about the properties and reactions of the elements in groups 1, 7 and 0 of the periodic table
- how the speed of a reaction can be changed
- about the energy changes that occur during chemical reactions
- about reversible chemical reactions.

C4a Group 1

ELC C2A.1, C2A.2, C2A.3, C2A.4 **GCSE** C6.1, C6.2, C6.3, C6.4

Progression questions

- Where are the alkali metals found in the periodic table?
- What are the properties of some alkali metals?
- How can we predict the properties of other alkali metals?

A Foods rich in potassium compounds are essential for health. What are the properties of potassium?

The **periodic table** shows elements arranged by their **physical** and **chemical properties**. Elements with similar properties are placed in the same vertical column or **group**. The periodic table in diagram B shows some of these groups. The elements in group 1 of the periodic table are called the **alkali metals**.

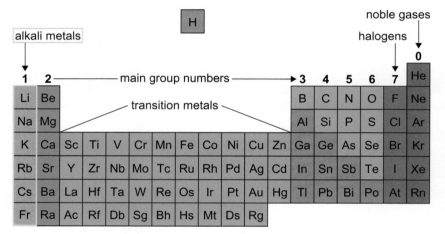

B The alkali metals are found on the far left of the periodic table. The halogens (group 7) and noble gases (group 0) are found on the right.

1 In which group of the periodic table would you find the alkali metals?
2 Why are potassium and sodium placed in the same group of the periodic table?

Physical properties of alkali metals

The first three alkali metals are lithium, sodium and potassium. They look similar and have similar physical properties. Like other metals they are: **malleable**, good **conductors of heat** and **electricity**, and shiny (when cut or polished). Unlike other metals they have relatively low melting points and are soft and easy to cut

3 a Give two physical properties of alkali metals that are typical of most metals.
  b Give two physical properties of alkali metals that make them different from other metals.

Chemical properties of alkali metals

The alkali metals are very reactive. They are stored in bottles of oil to keep out air and water, which would otherwise react with them. The reactions of three alkali metals with water are shown in photo C and described in table D. In all these reactions, a metal hydroxide (an alkali) and hydrogen gas are formed.

alkali metal + water → alkali metal hydroxide + hydrogen

For example, when lithium reacts with water:

lithium + water → lithium hydroxide + hydrogen

The reactivity of the alkali metals increases down the group. Lithium is the least reactive alkali metal.

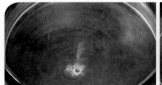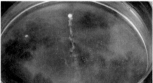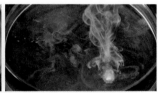

C The alkali metals react strongly with water (left to right: lithium, sodium, potassium).

Alkali metal reacting with water	Observation	Trend in reactivity
lithium	bubbles fiercely on the surface	reactivity increases down the group
sodium	melts into a ball and fizzes around the surface	
potassium	bursts into flames and flies around the surface	

D describing the reactions of the first three alkali metals with water

> **6** Rubidium is the fourth alkali metal. Predict how the reactivity of rubidium will compare with that of potassium.

Key points

- The alkali metals are found in group 1 of the periodic table.
- Alkali metals are soft and have relatively low melting points.
- Alkali metals are very reactive. They all react strongly with water to give a metal hydroxide and hydrogen.
- The reactivity of the alkali metals increases down the group.

> **4** Why are alkali metals stored under oil?
>
> **5** Name the products of the reactions of water with:
>
>   **a** sodium
>
>   **b** potassium

Checkpoint

How confidently can you answer the Progression questions?

Foundation

F1 State five common physical properties of lithium, sodium and potassium.

Strengthen

S1 Describe the reactions of lithium, sodium and potassium with water. State the order of reactivity.

S2 Complete the general equation:
alkali metal + water →

C4b Group 7

ELC C2A.1, C2A.5, C2A.6, C2A.7, C2A.8 **GCSE** C6.1, C6.6, C6.7, C6.8, C6.9, C6.10

Progression questions

- What pattern is there in the physical properties of the halogens?
- How can we test for chlorine gas?
- What happens when the halogens react with metals and with hydrogen?

A What halogen is used in swimming pools to kill germs?

The **halogens** are found in group 7 of the periodic table. They include the elements chlorine, bromine and iodine.

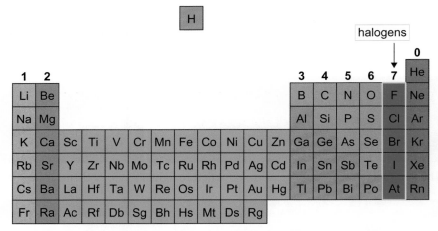

B The halogens are on the right hand side of the periodic table.

Chlorine first turns damp blue litmus paper red and then **bleaches** it white (photo C). This is used as the test for chlorine.

> 1   Name the group in the periodic table that chlorine belongs to.
> 2   Describe the test for chlorine gas.

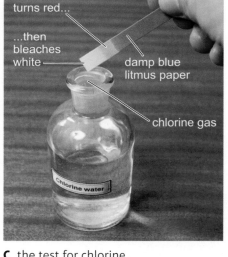

C the test for chlorine

Physical properties

The halogens, shown in photo D, are all typical non-metals. They have low melting and boiling points and are poor conductors of heat and electricity.

D chlorine, bromine and iodine

The melting and boiling points increase down group 7. The melting and boiling points of three of the halogens are shown in table E.

Halogen	Melting point (°C)	Boiling point (°C)	Appearance at room temperature
chlorine	−101	−34	light green gas
bromine	−7	59	brown liquid
iodine	114	184	dark purple solid

E The melting points and boiling points of the halogens increase down the group.

Reactions with metals

The halogens all react with metals to form solid metal **halides**:

$$metal + halogen \rightarrow metal\ halide$$

For example, sodium reacts with chlorine to give sodium chloride:

$$sodium + chlorine \rightarrow sodium\ chloride$$

> **5** Name the product formed when:
> **a** calcium metal burns in fluorine
> **b** astatine reacts with sodium.

Reactions with hydrogen

The halogens also all react with hydrogen to form hydrogen halides:

$$hydrogen + halogen \rightarrow hydrogen\ halide$$

For example, hydrogen and chlorine mixtures explode to form hydrogen chloride:

$$hydrogen + chlorine \rightarrow hydrogen\ chloride$$

> **6** Write a word equation for the reaction between hydrogen and bromine.

Hydrogen halides dissolve in water to form **acidic** solutions. For example, hydrogen chloride dissolves in water to produce hydrochloric acid.

Key points

- The halogens are found in group 7 of the periodic table. Iodine is a dark purple solid, bromine is a brown liquid and chlorine is a pale green gas.
- The melting and boiling points of halogens increase as you move down group 7.
- The halogens react with metals to give metal halides.
- The halogens react with hydrogen to give hydrogen halides, which dissolve in water to form acidic solutions.

> **3** Describe what happens to the melting points and boiling points of the halogens as you move down group 7.
>
> **4** Look at photo D and table E.
> **a** Fluorine is above chlorine in group 7. Predict if fluorine is likely to be a solid, liquid or gas?
> **b** Astatine is below iodine in group 7. Predict if the melting point of astatine is likely to be higher or lower than the melting point of iodine.

Checkpoint

How confidently can you answer the Progression questions?

Foundation

F1 a Describe the appearance of bromine, chlorine and iodine.
b Describe the trend in melting points and boiling points down group 7.

Strengthen

S1 Write word equations for the reactions of:
a fluorine with zinc
b fluorine with hydrogen.

C4c Group 0

ELC C2A.1, C2A.9, C2A.10 **GCSE** C6.1, C6.14, C6.15, C6.16

Progression questions

- Why are the noble gases unreactive?
- What are some uses of the noble gases?
- What is the pattern in the physical properties of the noble gases?

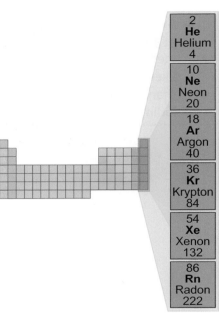

2	**He** Helium 4
10	**Ne** Neon 20
18	**Ar** Argon 40
36	**Kr** Krypton 84
54	**Xe** Xenon 132
86	**Rn** Radon 222

B the atomic numbers, names, symbols and relative atomic masses of the noble gases

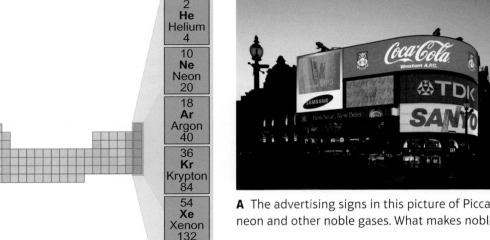

A The advertising signs in this picture of Piccadilly Circus contain neon and other noble gases. What makes noble gases special?

The **noble gases** are found in group 0 of the periodic table. They include neon, helium, argon and krypton. These elements are all:

- colourless gases with very low melting and boiling points
- **inert**, which means they do not react easily with anything.

---

1 Name four noble gases.

2 What do noble gases look like?

3 State what is meant by the term inert.

---

4 Where in the periodic table are the noble gases found?

D helium-filled balloons

Table C shows some uses of the group 0 elements linked to their properties.

Noble gas	Use	Reason
helium	balloons	not flammable and low density, so the balloons float
neon	advertising signs	unreactive and glows when electricity is passed through it
argon	light bulbs	unreactive, so thin metal filament in bulbs will not react

C some uses of group 0 elements linked to their properties

---

5 **a** Explain why helium gas is used for weather balloons.

b Explain why argon is used in light bulbs.

Explaining reactivity

The noble gases are very unreactive, as they have stable arrangements of electrons. The **electronic configurations** of noble gases are shown in diagram E. All noble gases have a full outer shell of electrons. During reactions elements gain, lose or share electrons to get a stable electronic configuration. Noble gases do not need to react, as their atoms are already stable.

> **6** Explain why the noble gases are all unreactive.

Patterns in properties

There are patterns in the physical properties of the noble gases. For example, their melting points, boiling points and densities are all low. However, these properties all increase as you move down group 0.

helium
2

He

Helium has two electrons. The first shell can only contain a maximum of two electrons. Helium has a full outer shell.

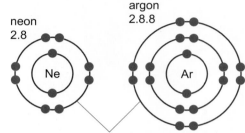

neon
2.8

Ne

argon
2.8.8

Ar

Neon and argon both have full outer electron shells with eight electrons.

E Noble gases have a full outer shell of electrons.

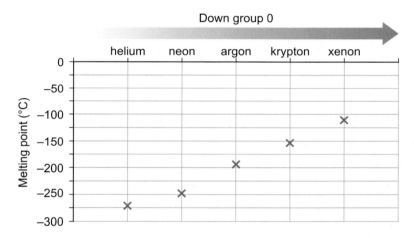

F Melting points increase down group 0.

> **7** Look at graph F.
>
>   **a** Describe the trend in melting point down group 0.
>
>   **b** Suggest a possible melting point for the sixth noble gas, radon.
>
> **8** Potassium has one more electron than argon. Explain the difference in reactivity between these two elements in terms of their electron arrangements.

Key points

- The noble gases are found in group 0 of the periodic table. They are useful because they are all stable and unreactive.
- The noble gases are inert because they all have full outer shells of electrons.
- The melting points, boiling points and densities of the group 0 elements all increase down the group.

Checkpoint

How confidently can you answer the Progression questions?

Foundation

F1 What are the main properties of the noble gas elements?

F2 Choose one noble gas.

  a State a use for this noble gas.

  b Describe how its properties make it suitable for the use.

Strengthen

S1 Explain how the electronic configurations of the noble gases affect their properties.

C4d Energy changes

ELC C2A.11, C2A.12, C2A.13 GCSE C7.9, C7.10, C7.11

Progression questions

- What are exothermic reactions?
- What are endothermic reactions?
- How can heat changes be investigated?

A Where does the heat energy in a fire come from?

Combustion

We heat our homes and cook our food by burning fuels like coal, oil and natural gas. Burning, or **combustion**, is a chemical reaction that always gives out heat energy. During combustion, a fuel combines with the oxygen in the air to form new substances and release energy. Reactions that give out heat energy are known as **exothermic** reactions. These reactions make the surroundings warmer, so the temperature of the substances around the reaction increases.

> 1 What happens to the surroundings during an exothermic reaction?
>
> 2 Explain why combustion reactions are described as being exothermic.

Dissolving

Some reactions can take in heat energy from the surroundings. Those that take in energy are known as **endothermic** reactions. These make the surroundings colder. Diagram B shows the energy change when the **salt** ammonium chloride dissolves in water. This particular salt takes in energy as it dissolves, and causes the temperature of the solution to fall.

Dissolving can be an exothermic or endothermic change depending on the particular salt involved.

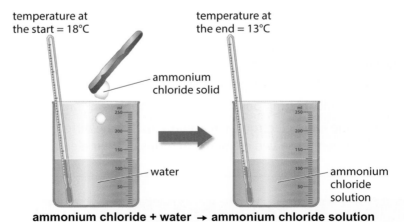

temperature at the start = 18°C

temperature at the end = 13°C

ammonium chloride solid

water

ammonium chloride solution

ammonium chloride + water → ammonium chloride solution

B Some salts take in energy when they dissolve.

Neutralisation

> 3 Name a type of chemical change that can be either exothermic or endothermic.

All chemical reactions involve some kind of energy change. Diagram C shows how the energy change can be measured during the **neutralisation** reaction involving sodium hydroxide and hydrochloric acid. This is another example of an exothermic reaction. Heat energy is given out and the temperature of the solution increases.

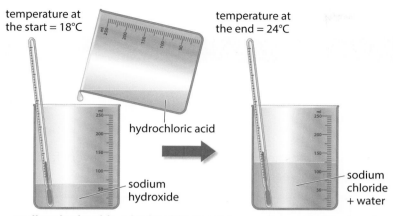

temperature at the start = 18°C

temperature at the end = 24°C

hydrochloric acid

sodium hydroxide

sodium chloride + water

sodium hydroxide + hydrochloric acid → sodium chloride + water

C measuring energy changes in a neutralisation reaction

Displacement

Displacement reactions happen when a more reactive element takes the place of (displaces) a less reactive element in a compound. For example:

zinc + copper sulfate → zinc sulfate + copper

Like combustion and neutralisation reactions, displacement reactions are also always exothermic. This means that they increase the temperature of the solution.

> **5** A displacement reaction occurs between chlorine and sodium bromide. The products formed are sodium chloride and bromine. During this reaction, the temperature of the solution rises.
>
> **a** Write a word equation for this reaction.
>
> **b** Is this an endothermic or exothermic reaction? Explain your answer.

Precipitation

Photo D shows a **precipitation reaction**. A solid insoluble product is formed from two solutions. Precipitation reactions are usually exothermic. The energy change depends on the substances involved.

> **6** In photo D, the temperature changed from 18 °C to 21 °C. What does this tell you about the reaction?

Key points

- Exothermic reactions give out heat energy and warm the surroundings, so the temperature of the substances around the reaction increases.
- Endothermic reactions take in heat energy and cool the surroundings, so the temperature of the substances around the reaction decreases.
- Combustion, neutralisation and displacement reactions are exothermic. Salts dissolving in water may be exothermic or endothermic reactions.

> **4 a** State whether the reactions shown in diagrams B and C are exothermic or endothermic.
>
> **b** What happens to the temperature of the surroundings during an endothermic reaction?

D During this precipitation reaction, the temperature changes from 18 °C to 21 °C.

Checkpoint

How confidently can you answer the Progression questions?

Foundation

F1 Describe exothermic and endothermic reactions in terms of energy transfer and changes in temperature.

Strengthen

S1 You need to work out whether a reaction in a solution is exothermic or endothermic. Describe how you could carry out an experiment to find out.

C4e Rates of reaction

ELC 2A.14, 2A.15, 2A.16 **GCSE** C7.3, C7.4, C7.5

Progression questions

- What has to happen for a reaction to occur?
- How do changes in temperature, concentration and surface area affect reaction rates?
- How can we measure and compare rates of reaction?

A What makes some chemical reactions happen so quickly?

Fierce fires and explosions are examples of very fast chemical reactions.

> **1** Name an example of a very fast chemical reaction.

To understand why reactions take place at different speeds, we need to understand how chemical reactions occur. During a reaction, the reactants come together to form new substances – the products. For example, hydrogen and chlorine react to form hydrogen chloride.

hydrogen + chlorine → hydrogen chloride

Diagram B shows the molecules in a mixture of hydrogen and chlorine. For a reaction to occur, the reactant molecules have to collide or 'bump' together with enough energy, called the **activation energy**. This energy is needed to break bonds in the reactants, so that the atoms can be rearranged to form the products.

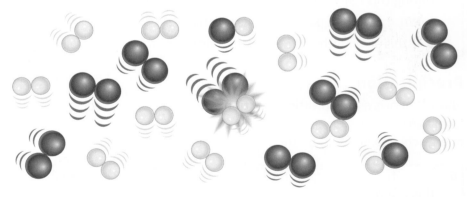

B A reaction can only occur if the molecules have enough energy to react when they collide.

> **2** **a** What two things must happen before hydrogen and chlorine can react?
>
> **b** What is the activation energy needed for?

> **3** What changes to the collisions and energy of the reactant molecules will increase the rate of reaction?

The speed, or **rate**, of a chemical reaction can be increased if the conditions are changed so that the reactant molecules:

- collide more often
- have more energy.

Concentration and reaction rate

Change: Increasing the **concentration** of reactants increases the rate of reaction.

Explanation: There are more reacting particles in the same volume, so more collisions occur.

low concentration   higher concentration

C

Surface area and reaction rate

Change: Increasing the surface area, by decreasing the size of solid pieces, increases the rate of reaction.

Explanation: There is more surface for collisions to occur on, so more collisions occur.

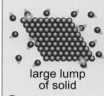 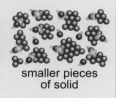

large lump of solid   smaller pieces of solid

D

Temperature and reaction rate

Change: Increasing the temperature increases the rate of reaction.

Explanation: The reactant particles speed up and have more energy. The particles therefore collide more often, and more of them have enough energy to react when they collide.

lower temperature   higher temperature

E

Comparing reaction rates

We can compare reaction rates by measuring changes that take place during a reaction. In the reaction between marble chips and hydrochloric acid in diagram F, carbon dioxide gas escapes as the acid is used up. We could follow this reaction by measuring changes in the acid concentration, volume of gas produced or mass of reactants.

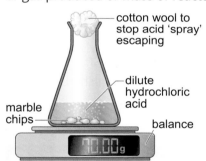

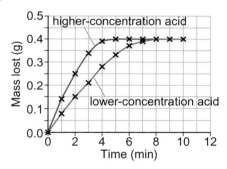

F comparing reaction rates by measuring changes in the mass of reactants

The graph shows that the higher concentration loses mass more quickly, losing 0.40 g of mass in 5 minutes, while the lower concentration takes 8 minutes. This confirms that reactions are faster at higher concentrations.

---

7 Explain how a loss of mass can occur during a chemical reaction.

8 Explain how the graph in diagram C shows that more concentrated acids react faster.

Key points

- Reactions occur when reacting particles collide with enough energy.
- Temperature, concentration and surface area all change reaction rates.
- Reaction rates can be compared by measuring changes in concentration, mass, or volume of gas produced with time.

---

4 Which burns most quickly in air: wood chips, wood dust or wood shavings?

5 Explain why concentrated bleach cleans faster than dilute bleach.

6 State two reasons why increasing the temperature makes a reaction faster.

Checkpoint

How confidently can you answer the Progression questions?

Foundation

F1 Describe three ways of speeding up a chemical reaction.

Strengthen

S1 Use ideas about collisions and energy to explain how the rate of a reaction can be changed by changes in three different conditions.

In this practical you will investigate rates of reaction using two different methods. The method chosen depends on the changes that occur during the reaction, and how easily these changes can be measured.

You are going to investigate the reaction between hydrochloric acid and marble chips and how the surface area of the marble chips affects the reaction rate. You will compare reaction rates by measuring the volume of carbon dioxide gas produced as the reaction happens.

You are also going to investigate the effect of temperature on the rate of reaction between sodium thiosulfate and hydrochloric acid. You will compare reaction rates by measuring the time taken for a colour change to occur, as shown in photo C.

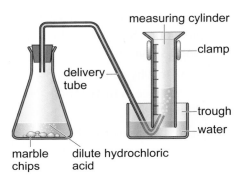

A investigating rates of reaction by measuring the volume of gas produced

Method

Comparing reaction rates by measuring volumes of gases

A Set up the apparatus as shown in diagram A.

B Wear eye protection. Measure $40\,cm^3$ of dilute hydrochloric acid into the conical flask.

C Measure 5 g of large marble chips.

D Add the marble chips to the flask.

E Immediately stopper the flask and start the stop clock.

F Record the volume of gas produced every 30 seconds.

G Carry on recording the volumes until the reaction has finished.

H Repeat steps D to G using 5 g of smaller marble chips.

Exam-style questions

1 a State what is being investigated in this practical. *(2 marks)*

   b Name two variables that would need to be controlled (kept the same). *(2 marks)*

2 a Explain why you must immediately stopper the flask in step E. *(1 mark)*

   b State the apparatus you would use to measure:

     i the mass of marble chips   **ii** the volume of acid. *(2 marks)*

3 Look at graph B.

   a State the time when the reaction is complete. Explain your answer. *(2 marks)*

   b Sketch graph B and add the curve that would be produced by smaller marble chips. *(2 marks)*

B investigating large marble chips

Method

Comparing reaction rates by observing a colour change

A Place 50 cm³ of sodium thiosulfate solution into a 250 cm³ conical flask.

B Measure 5 cm³ of dilute hydrochloric acid into a test tube.

C Clamp the conical flask in place in a water bath at a set temperature (between 20 and 50 °C). Place the test tube in a rack in the same water bath.

D Record the temperature of the water bath.

E After 5 minutes, remove the flask and place it on a piece of paper marked with a cross.

F Add the acid to the thiosulfate in the flask and start the stop clock.

G Looking down from above, stop the clock when you cannot see the cross.

H Record this time and the final (and mean) temperature of the mixture.

I Repeat at three or four other temperatures between 20 and 50 °C.

C We can follow the rate of this reaction by measuring the time taken for the cross to disappear.

Exam-style questions

4 **a** State what is being investigated in this practical. *(2 marks)*

   b State why the initial and final temperatures are measured. *(1 mark)*

5 Some results are shown in table D.

Mean temperature (°C)	Time for cross to disappear (s)
30	165
40	81
50	42
60	21

D

   a State why the cross disappears. *(1 mark)*

   b Explain what these results tell us about the effect of temperature changes on reaction rates. *(2 marks)*

C4f Reversible reactions

ELC 2A.17, 2A.18 GCSE C4.13, C4.14, C7.6, C7.8

Progression questions

- What happens in a reversible reaction?
- What happens when a dynamic equilibrium is established in a reaction?
- What are catalysts and enzymes?

A Why will the toys never be cleared away?

As fast as the mother puts the toys in the box, the child takes them out again. As long as they both keep going at the same rate, the toys will never be cleared away. We call this a state of **equilibrium**, a stable situation where opposite actions are balanced. The number of toys in the box and on the floor stays the same.

Some chemical reactions can also be in a state of equilibrium. This happens in **reversible reactions**, where the products can react to reform the reactants. Photo B shows a reversible reaction. In the equation, a double arrow, ⇌, shows that both the forward and backward reactions happen at the same time.

forward reaction

ammonium chloride ⇌ ammonia + hydrogen chloride

backward reaction

As the reaction proceeds, the forward reaction gets slower as the backward reaction gets faster, until the rate of the forward and backward reactions is the same. Like the toys going in and out of the toy box, the reaction has reached a state of equilibrium. This is called a **dynamic equilibrium**, because both reactions keep going, but the amount of reactants and products stays the same.

Dynamic equilibrium only occurs in **closed systems**, where there is no loss of reactants or products. In photo B, removing the bung would create an **open system**. The gases could escape, so equilibrium would not be achieved.

---

1 Describe what is meant by a state of equilibrium.

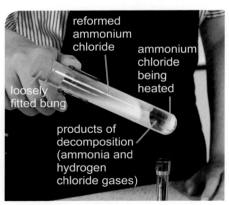

reformed ammonium chloride

ammonium chloride being heated

loosely fitted bung

products of decomposition (ammonia and hydrogen chloride gases)

B Heating ammonium chloride is a reversible reaction.

2 Write a word equation for the backward reaction in photo B and in the above equation.

3 When in equilibrium, which reaction is faster: forward or backward?

4 What is happening when a reaction reaches a dynamic equilibrium?

5 When calcium carbonate is heated in an open test tube, it decomposes to form calcium oxide and carbon dioxide.

    a Write a word equation to represent this change as a reversible reaction.

    b Explain why equilibrium will not be achieved in this case.

The manufacture of ammonia

Ammonia is an important industrial chemical used to make fertilisers and explosives. It is manufactured by a reversible reaction between nitrogen from the air and hydrogen from natural gas.

nitrogen + hydrogen ⇌ ammonia

The amount of reactants and products at equilibrium can be altered by changing the reaction conditions. In industrial reversible processes, the conditions are usually chosen to make as much product as quickly as possible.

6 For the equilibrium in the manufacture of ammonia:

    a Write separate word equations for the forward and the backward reactions.

    b What happens to the amount of ammonia in the mixture after equilibrium is reached?

Catalysts and enzymes

Both **catalysts** and **enzymes** (biological catalysts) can speed up chemical reactions without being permanently changed. They are often used in industry, because they allow the products to be formed more quickly, or at lower temperatures. This makes industrial reactions more profitable, especially as the catalysts and enzymes do not need to be replaced often, because they are not used up in the process.

7 Describe how catalysts and enzymes are similar.

C An enzyme in yeast helps change sugar (glucose) into alcohol when making beer and other alcoholic drinks.

Checkpoint

How confidently can you answer the Progression questions?

Foundation

F1 Describe what the sign ⇌ in a chemical equation tells you about the reaction.

Strengthen

S1 Explain, by referring to reaction rates, how the formation of ammonia reaches a dynamic equilibrium.

Key points

- In a reversible reaction, the products can reform the reactants.
- A dynamic equilibrium is produced when the forward and backward reactions occur at the same rate, so the amount of reactants and products stays the same.
- Catalysts and enzymes speed up chemical reactions without being used up.

Groups in the periodic table

1 All alkali metals react with water. For example, when a small piece of lithium is added to water it fizzes gently on the surface, until all the metal has reacted.

State two similarities and two differences between the reactions of lithium with water and potassium with water.

(4 marks)

Student answer

Similarities: Both lithium and potassium float on the surface of the water [A] and both metals are stored under oil to keep out air [B].

Differences: Potassium bursts into flames when it reacts with water. Lithium just produces bubbles of gas in water [C].

[A] This is a correct similarity. However the answer should have given two similarities. For example, both metals move around and fizz. Both metals also react to form hydrogen and an alkaline solution.

[B] Although a correct statement, this part of the answer gains no marks as it does not answer the question asked.

[C] Only one mark is awarded, as these two statements describe only one difference. A further difference should have been that the potassium moves faster or explodes.

Verdict

This is a poor answer as it does not answer the question fully. The question asks for two similarities and two differences in the reactions of the two metals with water. The answer gives one similarity that is not about how the metals react with water. The answer also only gives one difference when the question asks for two differences.

Rates of reaction

2 A group of students investigated how temperature affects the rate of the reaction between hydrochloric acid and magnesium. Their results showed that a temperature increase of 10 °C roughly doubled the rate of the reaction.

Explain why an increase in temperature increases the rate of reaction. Refer to particles in your answer. **(4 marks)**

Student answer

Increasing the temperature increases the energy of the reacting particles [A]. This means the particles have more speed and so they move about faster [B]. This causes an increase in reaction rate, as more collisions occur [C].

[A] This correctly describes how temperature affects the energy of the particles and is awarded one mark.

[B] Two points are made here about the speed and the movement of the particles. Both are correct, but they are really the same point, so only one mark is awarded.

[C] The statement linking the speed of the particles to the number of collisions gains one mark. A further mark would be awarded for explaining how the increase in energy means that more particles have enough energy to react when they collide.

Verdict

This is a good answer, which would gain three out of four marks. It shows a good understanding of the effect of temperature on reaction rate. Note that repeating the same point, using different words, did not gain or lose a mark. However it can make you think you have given enough points to gain the total marks for a question.

C5 Fuels and the Earth's atmosphere

Crude oil gives us valuable raw materials. With these, we can make a huge range of products, including polythene and other polymers. However, crude oil is mostly used to provide fuels.

This jet fighter carries over 8 tonnes of kerosene, a liquid fuel produced from crude oil. The kerosene is mixed with air and burnt in the engines, pushing the aircraft to speeds over 600 m/s. Fuels from crude oil produce carbon dioxide when they burn. Carbon dioxide is one of the gases thought to be changing our atmosphere and climate.

The learning journey

Previously you will have learnt at KS3:

- that mixtures may be separated using fractional distillation
- about fuels and energy resources
- about the production of carbon dioxide by human activity and the impact on climate.

In this unit you will learn:

- about the hydrocarbons found in crude oil
- how crude oil is separated into useful fractions
- about the problems caused by some atmospheric pollutants
- about the advantages and disadvantages of different fuels for cars
- how and why cracking of oil fractions is carried out
- how the Earth's atmosphere has changed in the past and how it is still changing
- more about the causes and effects of climate change.

C5a Hydrocarbons

ELC C2B.1, C2B.2, C2B.3, C2B.4 **GCSE** C8.1, C8.2, C8.3, C8.4, C8.5

Progression questions

- What are hydrocarbons?
- Why is crude oil so useful?
- How do we get useful substances from crude oil?

A An airliner's fuel tanks contain about 100 000 litres of kerosene. Where does all this fuel come from?

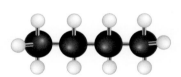

B These two hydrocarbons are 'alkanes', the main type of hydrocarbon found in crude oil. The carbon atoms are shown as black and the hydrogen atoms as white.

Crude oil

Crude oil is formed over millions of years from the remains of microscopic animals and plants. It is an important source of:

- fuels for cars, aircraft, trains, ships and power stations
- **feedstock** (raw materials) for the petrochemical industry.

Petrochemicals are substances made from crude oil, such as poly(ethene) and other **polymers**.

> 1   Name the substance that is the source of fuel for aircraft.

Oil wells form when oil is trapped under layers of rock. The oil is reached by drilling through this rock. Crude oil is a **finite resource** because it forms extremely slowly or is no longer being made.

> 2   Why is crude oil described as a finite resource?

Crude oil is a complex mixture of **hydrocarbons**. Hydrocarbons are compounds that only contain carbon and hydrogen atoms. The carbon atoms in hydrocarbon molecules are joined together in chains and rings. Diagram B shows two examples of these molecules.

> 3   Give the meaning of the term 'hydrocarbon'.

Separating crude oil

Crude oil is separated into simpler mixtures of hydrocarbons using **fractional distillation**. This works because the different hydrocarbons have different boiling points. Separation is carried out in a tall metal tower called a **fractionating column**. The column is hottest at the bottom and coolest at the top.

> 4   Describe how the temperature changes inside a fractionating column.

Crude oil is heated strongly. It is piped into the bottom of the fractionating column, where:

- hydrocarbon vapours rise through the column and cool down
- vapours **condense** to form liquids when they get to a part of the column below their boiling point
- the liquid hydrocarbon falls into a tray and is piped away.

Some hydrocarbons have very low boiling points, so they do not condense in the column. Instead they leave at the top as a mixture of gases. Bitumen has the highest boiling point and is solid at room temperature. It leaves at the bottom of the column as a hot liquid.

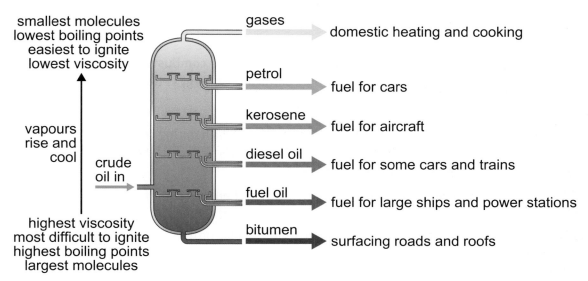

smallest molecules
lowest boiling points
easiest to ignite
lowest viscosity

vapours
rise and
cool

crude
oil in

highest viscosity
most difficult to ignite
highest boiling points
largest molecules

gases → domestic heating and cooking

petrol → fuel for cars

kerosene → fuel for aircraft

diesel oil → fuel for some cars and trains

fuel oil → fuel for large ships and power stations

bitumen → surfacing roads and roofs

C The molecules have fewer carbon and hydrogen atoms as you go up the column.

The separated hydrocarbons are called **fractions** because they are only a part of the crude oil. They have different uses because they have different properties. For example, petrol is easier to ignite (set on fire) than fuel oil. It has a lower **viscosity** so it is runnier. This makes petrol more suitable as a fuel for cars.

5   Give one use for the gases fraction, and one use for the bitumen fraction.
6   Kerosene has smaller molecules than diesel oil. Give three other differences between the properties of these two fractions. Use diagram C to help you.

Key points

- Crude oil is a mixture of hydrocarbons. Hydrocarbons are compounds of hydrogen and carbon only.
- Crude oil is separated into useful mixtures called fractions using fractional distillation.
- Crude oil is an important source of fuels and starting materials for making substances such as polymers.

Checkpoint

How confidently can you answer the Progression questions?

Foundation

F1 Describe how crude oil is separated into useful substances.

F2 Make a table to show the names and uses of the fractions from crude oil.

Strengthen

S1 Explain how fractional distillation of crude oil works.

S2 Describe the differences between crude oil fractions.

C5b Combustion

ELC C2B.5, C2B.6, C2B.7, C2B.8 **GCSE** C8.7, C8.8, C8.9, C8.10

Progression questions

- What happens during the combustion of hydrocarbon fuels?
- Why is carbon monoxide dangerous?
- What problems does incomplete combustion cause?

A Energy is given out as the propane fuel in this gas cylinder burns. What else is given out when hydrocarbon fuels burn?

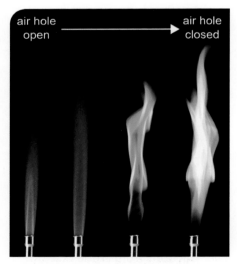

B When a Bunsen burner air hole is open, lots of air mixes with the hydrocarbon fuel. Complete combustion happens, giving a very hot blue flame. Incomplete combustion happens when the air hole is closed, giving a cooler orange flame.

Burning is a type of chemical reaction called **combustion**. Fuels react with oxygen in the air during combustion. Energy is transferred to the surroundings, mainly by heating and light.

> 1 Name the gas in air that fuels react with during combustion.

Complete combustion

Complete combustion happens when there is a plentiful supply of oxygen or air. When oxygen reacts with a hydrocarbon fuel:

- carbon atoms and oxygen atoms join to form carbon dioxide, CO_2
- hydrogen atoms and oxygen atoms join to form water, H_2O.

These equations model the complete combustion of propane, a hydrocarbon fuel:

$$\text{propane} + \text{oxygen} \rightarrow \text{carbon dioxide} + \text{water}$$
$$C_3H_8 + 5O_2 \rightarrow 3CO_2 + 4H_2O$$

> 2 Name the two substances produced during the complete combustion of a hydrocarbon fuel.

Incomplete combustion

Incomplete combustion happens when the supply of oxygen or air is poor. During incomplete combustion of a hydrocarbon fuel:

- water is produced
- **carbon monoxide** gas and carbon particles are produced.

The flame from the burning fuel heats the carbon particles, making them glow orange (see photo B).

> 3 Look at the photo of the propane fire (photo A). State whether complete or incomplete combustion is happening. Give a reason for your answer.

Problems with incomplete combustion

Less energy is given out during incomplete combustion than during complete combustion. So appliances such as heaters and boilers use more fuel unless they have plenty of air. Carbon particles form black soot (see photo C). Soot can cause breathing problems, and it can block pipes and chimneys that carry waste gases away.

C Soot from the metal chimney has blackened the brick chimney on the right.

> **4** Gauze mats are often used with Bunsen burners. Explain why the mats might have a black substance on them after use.

Carbon monoxide, CO, is a **toxic** gas. It joins with **haemoglobin** in the body's **red blood cells** and reduces the amount of oxygen that these cells can carry. Carbon monoxide poisoning causes people to feel sleepy. In severe cases it can make people fall unconscious or even die.

> **5** Explain why carbon monoxide is dangerous.

Key points

- Complete combustion of hydrocarbons gives out energy, and produces carbon dioxide and water.
- Incomplete combustion of hydrocarbons produces carbon monoxide and carbon.
- Incomplete combustion causes problems because carbon monoxide is a toxic gas, and carbon particles form soot.

Checkpoint

How confidently can you answer the Progression questions?

Foundation

F1 Name the products formed by incomplete combustion, but not by complete combustion.

F2 Name the product *always* formed by both types of combustion of hydrocarbon fuels.

Strengthen

S1 Explain why burning hydrocarbon fuels in a lack of oxygen causes problems.

C5c Fuel pollution

ELC C2B.9, C2B.10, C2B.11 GCSE C8.11, C8.12, C8.13

Progression questions

- Why do fuels give out pollutants when they are used?
- How does acid rain form?
- What problems does acid rain cause?

A Why is this cyclist wearing a mask on his way to work in the city?

2 Write a word equation for the reaction that produces oxides of nitrogen.

3 Give one problem caused by oxides of nitrogen such as nitrogen dioxide.

A **pollutant** is a substance that harms living organisms when it is released into the environment. Hydrocarbon fuels produce pollutants. These pollutants include sulfur dioxide and oxides of nitrogen. Some people wear 'anti-smog masks' on the streets of cities to avoid breathing in pollutants.

1 What is a pollutant?

Oxides of nitrogen

Most vehicles use hydrocarbon fuels. The fuel is mixed with air in the engines and burnt. This makes the engines very hot. Nitrogen and oxygen in the air react together at the high temperatures inside the engines. Pollutant gases called **oxides of nitrogen** form. For example, nitrogen dioxide is a toxic oxide of nitrogen that can cause breathing problems.

B In sunlight, oxides of nitrogen react with other pollutants to form a harmful, hazy smog.

Sulfur dioxide

Hydrocarbon fuels naturally contain **impurities**. Impurities are small amounts of unwanted substances mixed with the fuel. These impurities may include sulfur compounds. When the fuel is burnt, the sulfur reacts with oxygen to produce sulfur dioxide.

4 Give a reason why hydrocarbon fuels may produce sulfur dioxide when they are burnt.

Sulfur dioxide gas escapes into the air through exhaust pipes and chimneys. Sulfur dioxide dissolves in rain water to form **acid rain**. Acid rain is more **acidic** than normal rain. Acid rain causes many environmental problems.

Limestone and marble are rocks used in buildings. The calcium carbonate in these rocks reacts with acid rain. This causes **weathering** to happen faster than normal, so the stonework wears away. Acid rain also reacts with steel and other metals used in buildings, weakening their structure.

> **6** Describe two effects of acid rain on buildings.

Acid rain makes lakes and rivers acidic. Fish eggs do not hatch in acidic water, and the gills of fish produce a sticky mucus. The mucus makes it difficult for the fish to get enough oxygen from the water, so they suffocate and die. Acidic water may also kill water plants and insects. Acid rain increases the acidity of soil, which makes it difficult for crop plants to grow well.

D Acid rain has killed trees in this forest.

> **7** The petrol and diesel sold in filling stations is described as 'low sulfur'. Suggest a reason that explains why oil refineries remove most of the sulfur compounds from these fuels.

Key points

- Oxides of nitrogen are pollutants produced when nitrogen and oxygen react together in hot engines.
- Sulfur dioxide is produced from sulfur impurities in some hydrocarbon fuels.
- Sulfur dioxide dissolves in rain water to form acid rain. Acid rain damages buildings and harms living things.

> **5** Describe how sulfur dioxide forms acid rain.

C This stonework has been damaged by acid rain.

Checkpoint

How confidently can you answer the Progression questions?

Foundation

F1 Describe three problems that acid rain causes for living things.

Strengthen

S1 Explain how some harmful oxides are produced when hydrocarbon fuels are used in cars.

C5d Cracking

ELC C2B.12, C2B.13, C2B.14, C2B.15 GCSE C8.14, C8.15, C8.16, C8.17

Progression questions

- Why are fuels from crude oil and natural gas described as non-renewable?
- Why do oil refineries carry out cracking?
- What are the advantages and disadvantages of hydrogen and petrol as fuels for cars?

A Fuel tankers regularly deliver petrol and diesel oil to filling stations. On average, each person in the UK uses almost 4 litres of fuels from crude oil every day. Why might this eventually have to stop?

Fossil fuels are obtained from crude oil or natural gas. They include petrol, kerosene and diesel oil from crude oil, and methane in natural gas. Fossil fuels are **non-renewable**. We are using them faster than they are being formed. They will run out one day if we carry on using them.

> **1** Name two non-renewable fossil fuels.

Making crude oil more useful

Fractional distillation separates crude oil into different fractions. Fuel oil and bitumen are the fractions with the largest hydrocarbon molecules. They are difficult to **ignite** (set alight), and are not runny enough to use in cars, aircraft and trains. These larger hydrocarbon molecules can be broken down into the smaller, more useful hydrocarbon molecules found in other fractions by a process called **cracking** (diagram B).

> **2** Name the process used to break down larger hydrocarbon molecules into smaller molecules.

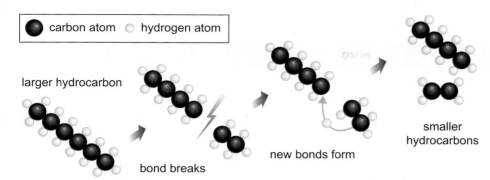

carbon atom ○ hydrogen atom

larger hydrocarbon

bond breaks

new bonds form

smaller hydrocarbons

B In cracking, hot vapour from a crude oil fraction is passed over a hot catalyst. This causes some bonds to break and new ones to form.

Reasons for cracking

The **supply** of a fraction is how much of it is produced. The **demand** for a fraction is how much of it can be sold. Fractional distillation produces more of some fractions than can be sold. Cracking lets an oil refinery match its supply with demand. It also produces hydrocarbons that are useful for making plastics such as polythene.

3   Describe what is meant by the supply and demand of a fraction.

Hydrogen and petrol

Petrol is a liquid at room temperature, which makes it easier to store than a gas. Petrol produces carbon dioxide and other waste products when it is used. Carbon dioxide is a **greenhouse gas** linked to **climate change**. As petrol is non-renewable, it will run out one day if we carry on using it.

4   Give two disadvantages of petrol as a fuel.

Hydrogen can be used instead of petrol as a fuel for some cars. Hydrogen is a **by-product** of cracking, and it can also be produced by passing electricity through water. Like petrol, hydrogen is easily ignited and its combustion releases large amounts of energy. However, the only waste product is water vapour. Hydrogen is a gas at room temperature. This makes it difficult to store in large amounts unless it is compressed using high pressure, or cooled until it becomes liquid.

5   Describe how large amounts of hydrogen can be stored.

Checkpoint

How confidently can you answer the Progression questions?

Foundation

F1 Give two reasons why cracking is needed.

F2 Give one advantage and one disadvantage of hydrogen as a fuel for cars.

Strengthen

S1 Use a labelled diagram to explain how cracking works.

Key points

- Methane, petrol, kerosene and diesel oil are non-renewable fossil fuels.
- Cracking breaks down larger hydrocarbon molecules into smaller, more useful hydrocarbons. This helps to match supply with demand.
- Hydrogen can be used instead of petrol as a fuel for some cars.

C5e Early Earth

ELC C2B.16, C2B.17, C2B.18, C2B.19, C2B.20, C2B.21 **GCSE** C8.18, C8.19, C8.20, C8.21, C2.22, C8.23

Progression questions

- How did the Earth's early atmosphere form?
- What was the composition of the early atmosphere?
- How did the Earth's atmosphere change to become the one we have today?

A What did rain and the oceans have to do with the Earth's early atmosphere?

The Earth is about 4.5 billion years old. Scientists believe that there were many volcanoes when our planet was young. **Volcanic activity** produced the gases that formed the Earth's early **atmosphere**.

> **1** What produced the gases that formed the Earth's early atmosphere?

The early atmosphere

Scientists use data about volcanoes today to work out what the early Earth's atmosphere may have contained. The amounts of each gas produced by modern volcanoes vary. However, carbon dioxide and water vapour are the most common gases they produce. There are smaller amounts of other gases but almost no oxygen. This means it is likely that the Earth's early atmosphere contained:

- a large amount of carbon dioxide
- water vapour
- little or no oxygen
- small amounts of other gases.

> **2** Name two gases that scientists think were present in large amounts in the Earth's early atmosphere.

The oceans and carbon dioxide

The Earth gradually cooled after it formed. About 3.8 billion years ago it became cool enough for water vapour to condense. Water vapour in the atmosphere became liquid water. The water fell as rain and formed the oceans.

Carbon dioxide from the atmosphere dissolved in the oceans as they formed. This caused a decrease in the amount of carbon dioxide in the Earth's atmosphere. Today the Earth's atmosphere only contains about 0.04% carbon dioxide.

> **3** Describe how the oceans formed as the Earth cooled down.
>
> **4** Describe how the formation of oceans caused a decrease in the amount of carbon dioxide in the Earth's atmosphere.

Oxygen

Primitive plants evolved about 3 billion years ago. They carried out **photosynthesis** to make their own food. This word equation shows the overall reaction involved:

$$\text{carbon dioxide} + \text{water} \rightarrow \text{glucose} + \text{oxygen}$$

These primitive plants used carbon dioxide from the atmosphere. They also released oxygen, so the amount of oxygen in the atmosphere gradually increased (diagram B).

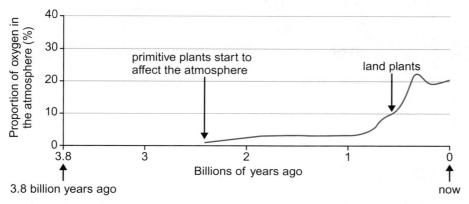

B The amount of oxygen in the atmosphere has changed over billions of years.

For a long time, photosynthesis did not affect the amount of oxygen in the atmosphere. One reason was that iron in rocks reacted with oxygen to form layers of iron oxide (photo C). Once the iron had been used up, the amount of oxygen in the atmosphere began to rise.

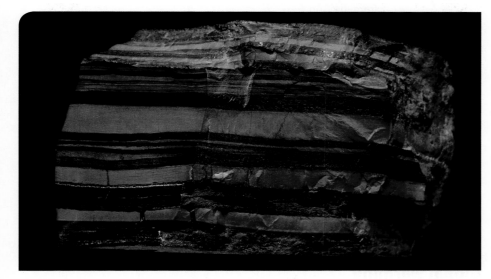

C This ancient rock has layers of orange-red iron oxide.

There is a simple way to test for the presence of oxygen. Light a wooden splint, then gently blow it out. A glowing splint relights in a test tube of oxygen.

7   Describe the chemical test for oxygen.

Key points

- Gases from volcanic activity formed the early atmosphere. The early atmosphere contained a large amount of carbon dioxide, water vapour, little or no oxygen, and small amounts of other gases.
- Condensation of water vapour formed the oceans. Carbon dioxide dissolved in the oceans, causing its level in the atmosphere to decrease.
- Oxygen levels gradually increased because of photosynthesis by plants.

5   Estimate, using diagram B, the proportion of oxygen in today's atmosphere.

6   Explain why rocks like the one in photo C are evidence that oxygen was produced billions of years ago.

Checkpoint

How confidently can you answer the Progression questions?

Foundation

F1 Describe the main differences between the Earth's early atmosphere and its atmosphere today.

Strengthen

S1 Give reasons why the levels of carbon dioxide and oxygen in the atmosphere changed over time.

C5f Today's atmosphere

ELC C2B.22, C2B.23, C2B.24 **GCSE** C8.24, C8.25, C8.26

Progression questions

- What is the greenhouse effect?
- What are the potential effects of climate change?
- What is the evidence that climate change is caused by human activities?

A What has this flooded road got to do with fossil fuels and farming?

---

1 Name three greenhouse gases.

2 Give the result of the greenhouse effect on the Earth's surface temperature.

The greenhouse effect

Energy from the Sun heats up the Earth's surface. The warm surface transfers energy towards space by **infrared** radiation. Greenhouse gases in the atmosphere absorb this energy, then release it again in all directions. This warms the atmosphere and helps to keep the Earth's surface warm. Greenhouse gases include carbon dioxide, methane and water vapour. The warming process is called the **greenhouse effect** (diagram B).

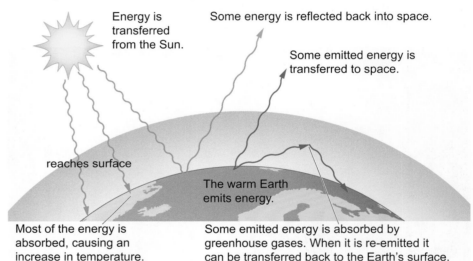

Energy is transferred from the Sun.

Some energy is reflected back into space.

Some emitted energy is transferred to space.

reaches surface

The warm Earth emits energy.

Most of the energy is absorbed, causing an increase in temperature.

Some emitted energy is absorbed by greenhouse gases. When it is re-emitted it can be transferred back to the Earth's surface.

B If there were no greenhouse gases, the Earth would be much colder than it is.

Global warming

There is a strong **correlation** between carbon dioxide levels and the Earth's surface temperature. Diagram C shows how these have changed over the last 220 000 years. These results, and laboratory experiments, support the idea that increasing levels of carbon dioxide *cause* temperature increases.

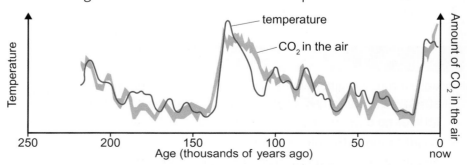

temperature

CO_2 in the air

C Scientists analyse air trapped in ancient ice in the Antarctic to work out what conditions were like in the past.

---

3 Describe, using diagram C, how the Earth's temperature has changed as carbon dioxide levels have changed.

Table D shows human activities that release greenhouse gases into the atmosphere.

> **4** Give one way in which human activities release:
>   **a** carbon dioxide   **b** methane.

Carbon dioxide is being released into the atmosphere faster than natural processes can remove it. This means carbon dioxide levels are increasing. Most scientists who study the Earth and its atmosphere agree that this is causing **global warming**, an increase in mean worldwide temperature.

> **5** Give the meaning of 'global warming'.

Climate change

There are potential effects of global warming on **climate**. This **climate change** may cause some areas to become drier, leading to drought and famine. Other areas may have more rainfall, causing flooding with damage to property and crops. A warmer atmosphere stores more energy, causing more powerful winds and storms.

E Higher temperatures cause glaciers and polar ice to melt.

Scientists have collected evidence about human activities and climate change. For example, between 1966 and 2016:

- fossil fuel use increased more than three times
- carbon dioxide levels increased from 0.032% to 0.040%
- the Earth's average surface temperature increased by nearly 1 °C.

> **7** Explain how these changes between 1966 and 2016 provide evidence that human activities are leading to climate change.

Key points

- Carbon dioxide, methane and water vapour are greenhouse gases. They are involved in the greenhouse effect, which keeps the Earth warm.
- Human activities lead to increased levels of greenhouse gases.
- Increased levels of greenhouse gases are linked to changes in climate.

Greenhouse gas	Released by
carbon dioxide	burning fossil fuels, e.g. • coal • natural gas • fuels from crude oil
methane	livestock (cattle) farming rice farming

D some sources of two greenhouse gases

> **6** Describe two potential effects of climate change.

Checkpoint

How confidently can you answer the Progression questions?

Foundation

F1 Make a flow chart to show how the greenhouse effect works.

Strengthen

S1 Describe the evidence to support the idea that increasing levels of greenhouse gases have caused increased average global temperatures.

Fuels for cars

Petrol and diesel oil are the fuels used in most car engines, but some cars use hydrogen instead.

Discuss the advantages and disadvantages of using hydrogen, rather than petrol, as a fuel for cars.   **(6 marks)**

Plan your answer

A 'discuss' question means you need to look at different aspects of an issue. Unlike an 'evaluate' question, it does not need a conclusion. So a student plan might look like this:

− advantage − how hydrogen is made

− advantage − burning petrol makes harmful substances; burning hydrogen doesn't

− disadvantage − hydrogen is difficult to store

Student answer

Hydrogen can be made by the electrolysis of water. We have lots of water so it will not run out. On the other hand [A], petrol is a non-renewable fossil fuel [B].

Water is the only product when hydrogen burns. However, petrol produces carbon dioxide as well as water. Carbon dioxide is a greenhouse gas [C].

Hydrogen is difficult to store. It must be stored under pressure. This needs strong fuel tanks, which make the car heavier [D]. Also, far fewer filling stations sell hydrogen than petrol.

[A] Words and phrases like 'on the other hand' and 'however' are useful when you are comparing two things.

[B] Non-renewable fuels will run out one day if we keep using them.

[C] The answer could add that greenhouse gases are linked to climate change.

[D] Hydrogen can also be stored as a very cold liquid. This part of the answer explains the disadvantages of how hydrogen must be transported and stored.

Verdict

This is a good answer. It shows good scientific knowledge and understanding. However, it could also explain that incomplete combustion happens in petrol engines. This is a disadvantage because it wastes petrol and produces carbon monoxide, which is a toxic gas.

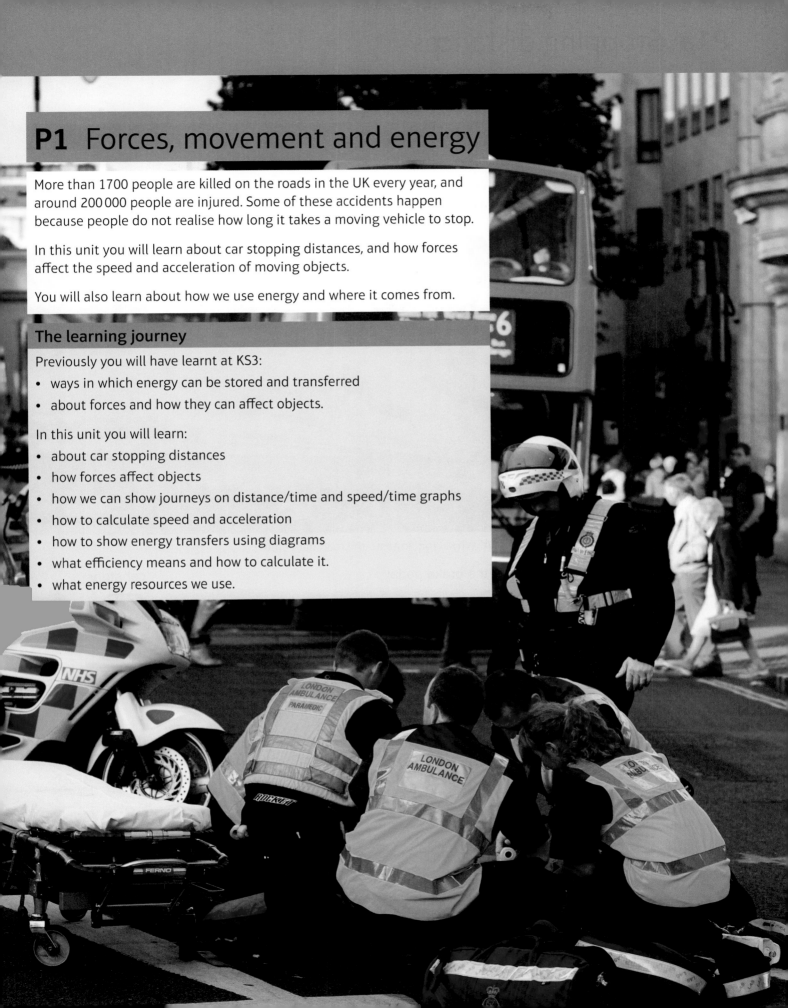

P1 Forces, movement and energy

More than 1700 people are killed on the roads in the UK every year, and around 200 000 people are injured. Some of these accidents happen because people do not realise how long it takes a moving vehicle to stop.

In this unit you will learn about car stopping distances, and how forces affect the speed and acceleration of moving objects.

You will also learn about how we use energy and where it comes from.

The learning journey

Previously you will have learnt at KS3:
- ways in which energy can be stored and transferred
- about forces and how they can affect objects.

In this unit you will learn:
- about car stopping distances
- how forces affect objects
- how we can show journeys on distance/time and speed/time graphs
- how to calculate speed and acceleration
- how to show energy transfers using diagrams
- what efficiency means and how to calculate it.
- what energy resources we use.

P1a Stopping distances

ELC P1A.13, P1A.14, P1A.15 **GCSE** P2.28, P2.29, P2.30

Progression questions

- What does stopping distance mean?
- What can affect a driver's reaction time?
- What affects the braking distance of a car?

It can take a long time for a car to stop if a child suddenly runs into the road. The driver needs to **react** to seeing the child, and then put their foot on the brake. A car moving at 30 mph travels 23 m while it is coming to a stop.

- The **thinking distance** is the distance the car travels while the driver is reacting.
- The **braking distance** is the distance the car travels while the brakes are slowing it down.
- The overall **stopping distance** = thinking distance + braking distance.

A Why is running into the road dangerous?

 driver sees the child   driver presses the brake pedal

 car stops

thinking distance (12 m)   braking distance (24 m)

stopping distance (36 m)

B thinking distance, braking distance and stopping distance for a car travelling at 40 mph

1 **a** State what the thinking distance is.
   b State what the braking distance is.
   c State what the stopping distance is.

2 When a lorry stops the thinking distance is 30 m and the braking distance is 90 m. Calculate the stopping distance.

Worked example

A car is travelling at 40 mph. When it stops, the thinking distance is 12 m and the braking distance is 24 m.

Calculate the stopping distance.

stopping distance = thinking distance + braking distance

$$= \quad 12\text{ m} \quad + \quad 24\text{ m}$$

stopping distance = 36 m

Factors affecting thinking distance

The thinking distance depends on how fast the driver realises that they need to stop. This time is the driver's **reaction time**.

A driver's reaction time is longer if:

- they have been drinking alcohol or taking certain medicines
- they are distracted by talking on the phone or looking at a map.

A longer reaction time gives a longer thinking distance.

The thinking distance is also longer if the car is moving faster, as the car travels further while the driver is thinking.

> **3** List two things that can make a driver's reaction time longer.

Factors affecting braking distance

Lots of **factors** can affect the braking distance of a vehicle.

heavy vehicle (high mass)

worn brakes or tyres

high speed

slippery road (wet or icy)

C factors that increase braking distance

> **4** A lorry and a car are both travelling at the same speed. Explain why the lorry has a longer stopping distance than the car.
>
> **5** A driver fits new tyres to her car. Explain how this will affect the stopping distance.

Key points

- stopping distance = thinking distance + braking distance
- The stopping distance is longer if the driver has been drinking or is distracted, if the road is slippery, if the car is heavy or going fast, and if the brakes or tyres are worn.

Checkpoint

How confidently can you answer the Progression questions?

Foundation

F1 What can increase a driver's reaction time?

F2 List three factors that can affect the stopping distance of a vehicle.

Strengthen

S1 List the factors that affect the stopping distance of a vehicle.

S2 State whether each factor identified in **S1** affects the thinking distance or the braking distance, and how they affect this distance.

P1b Balanced and unbalanced forces

ELC P1A.9, P1A.10, P1A.11 **GCSE** P2.14

Progression questions

- What are the forces on moving objects?
- What are balanced and unbalanced forces?
- What can unbalanced forces do?

Forces are pushes or pulls. You push the pedals round on a bicycle to make it move.

There are some forces on a bicycle that you cannot see. There is **friction** in the wheels, which slows the bicycle down. If you are moving fast you can feel wind on your face. This causes **air resistance**, which also slows you down.

> **1** Name two forces.

Balanced forces

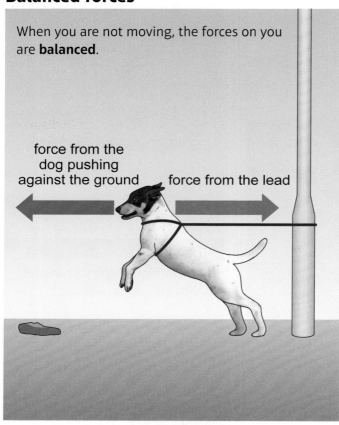

When you are not moving, the forces on you are **balanced**.

force from the dog pushing against the ground

force from the lead

Forces are also balanced when you are moving at a steady speed. The forward forces and the backward forces are the same size. They cancel each other out.

friction and air resistance

force from the pedals

A Balanced forces do not change the speed.

> **2** Look at diagram A. How do the arrows show that the forces are balanced in both pictures?

We can use arrows to show forces. The length of the arrow shows how strong the force is.

Unbalanced forces

If all the forces on an object do not cancel out, the forces are **unbalanced**.

Unbalanced forces can:

- change the shape of something
- change the speed of something (make it speed up or slow down)
- change the direction in which something is moving.

> **3** You squash a piece of chewing gum. Are the forces on the gum balanced or unbalanced?

B The weight of the people has caused an unbalanced force on the mud. The shape of the mud has changed.

If the forward force is greater than the backward force, the **resultant** (overall) force is forwards and the bicycle will go faster.

If the backward force is greater than the forward force, the resultant (overall) force is backwards and the bicycle will slow down.

friction   force from the pedals
speeding up

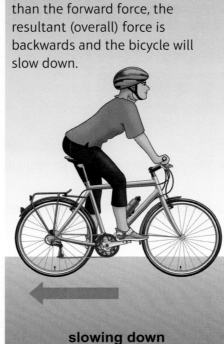

slowing down

C Unbalanced forces change the speed of an object.

> **5** Sally is pedalling with a force of 20 N. The friction and air resistance forces are 25 N.
>
> **a** Is the resultant force forwards or backwards?
>
> **b** Explain what happens to her speed.
>
> **c** What is the resultant (overall) force?

Key points

- Forces are balanced when an object is not moving, or is moving at a constant speed.
- Unbalanced forces can change the shape, speed or direction of movement of an object.

> **4** Look at the cyclists in diagram C. What will happen if they start to pedal harder?

Checkpoint

How confidently can you answer the Progression questions?

Foundation

F1 How do balanced forces affect the speed of a bicycle?

F2 Write down two things that unbalanced forces can do to an object.

Strengthen

S1 Describe the resultant force when the forces on an object are:

   a balanced

   b unbalanced.

S2 Describe how balanced and unbalanced forces can affect objects.

P1c Measuring quantities

ELC P1A.1 **GCSE** P1.1, P1.2, P2.1, P2.2, P2.3, P2.4

Progression questions

- What are the standard units we use for measuring?
- How do we describe forces?
- What are vector and scalar quantities?

Semi-skimmed milk

1 litre e

Consume within 3 days of opening and by date shown.

Best before :

nutrition	
Typical values	**per 100 ml**
Energy	**204 kJ**

A Why is it important to use standard units for measurement?

The bottle in photo A contains 1 litre of milk. A litre is a **unit** used for measuring the **volume** of something. Every measurement has a number and a unit.

> **1** What two things must every measurement have?

The label in photo A also shows that each 100 millilitres (ml) of milk provides 204 kilojoules (kJ) of **energy**. Litres and kilojoules are units used by many countries in the world. Scientists also use standard units. Table B shows some of the standard units we use in science.

2 What is the standard unit for measuring:

  a length

  b time

  c energy?

Measurement	Standard unit	Other units
length or distance	metre (m)	millimetre (mm), centimetre (cm), kilometre (km)
mass	kilogram (kg)	gram (g)
time	second (s)	minute (min), hour (h)
force	newton (N)	
energy	joule (J)	kilojoule (kJ)
temperature	degrees Celsius (°C)	
area	metres squared (m^2)	centimetres squared (cm^2)
volume	metres cubed (m^3)	centimetres cubed (cm^3)

B standard units used in science

Sometimes we need to use bigger or smaller units. We can multiply or divide the standard units to give us units of the right size. We show this using a **prefix** with the unit.

Prefix	Meaning	Example
kilo	× 1000	1 kilometre = 1000 metres
centi	÷ 100	1 centimetre = $\frac{1}{100}$ metres
milli	÷ 1000	1 millimetre = $\frac{1}{1000}$ metres (1 metre = 1000 millimetres)

C prefixes used with standard units

D The units for measuring this ladybird would be millimetres and milligrams.

> **3 a** How many metres (m) are there in a kilometre (km)?
>
> **b** How many milligrams (mg) are there in a gram (g)?

Forces and directions

When you measure a **force**, it is important to give its direction as well as its size. **Weight** is a force caused by gravity acting on the **mass** of an object. Weight always acts downwards. **Friction** is a force that always acts in the opposite direction to the movement of an object, or to the direction in which an object is trying to move.

Vectors and scalars

Quantities like forces that have a direction as well as a size are called **vector quantities**.

Mass is the amount of matter in something. Quantities like mass, energy and time that do not have a direction are called **scalar quantities**. Length, temperature, area and volume are also scalar quantities.

> **5** Write down three quantities that are scalars.

Key points

- Scientists use standard units for measuring quantities, such as metres and kilograms.
- Forces are vector quantities and have a direction as well as a size. Scalar quantities only have a size.
- Friction acts in the opposite direction to the movement of an object.

E We use arrows to represent vector quantities, such as force.

> **4** You are pushing a supermarket trolley forwards. In which direction is friction acting?

Checkpoint

How confidently can you answer the Progression questions?

Foundation

F1 Draw someone pushing a pushchair. Add labelled arrows to show the pushing force and the friction.

F2 List four standard units that scientists use.

Strengthen

S1 Describe the difference between a millimetre and a kilometre.

S2 Describe the difference between a vector quantity and a scalar quantity.

P1d Journeys

ELC P1A.3, P1A.6, P1A.7, P1A.8 **GCSE** P2.7, P2.10, P2.12

Progression questions

- What are the typical speeds we might move at during a day?
- What can a distance/time graph tell us about a journey?
- What can a speed/time graph tell us about a journey?

A How does your speed change during your journey to school?

The **speed** of an object tells us how quickly it travels a certain distance. Common units for speed are **metres per second (m/s)**, kilometres per hour (km/h) and miles per hour (mph). The standard scientific unit for speed is metres per second.

> **1** What is the standard scientific unit for speed?

Graph B shows some typical speeds.

> **2** Look at graph B. Write these things down in order of speed, starting with the fastest one: ferry, train, bicycle, aeroplane

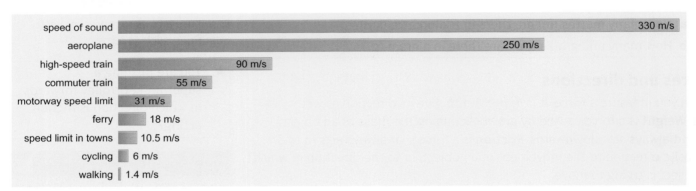

speed of sound — 330 m/s
aeroplane — 250 m/s
high-speed train — 90 m/s
commuter train — 55 m/s
motorway speed limit — 31 m/s
ferry — 18 m/s
speed limit in towns — 10.5 m/s
cycling — 6 m/s
walking — 1.4 m/s

B some typical speeds

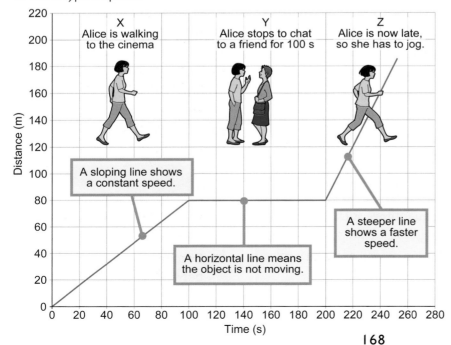

X Alice is walking to the cinema

Y Alice stops to chat to a friend for 100 s

Z Alice is now late, so she has to jog.

A sloping line shows a constant speed.

A horizontal line means the object is not moving.

A steeper line shows a faster speed.

C a distance/time graph for Alice's walk

Distance/time graphs

We can show a journey on a **distance/time graph**. The **gradient** (slope) of a line on a distance/time graph shows the speed.

> **3** Look at graph C. How can you tell from the line of the graph that Alice is moving fastest in part Z of the graph?

Speed/time graphs

We can also show journeys on a **speed/time graph**.

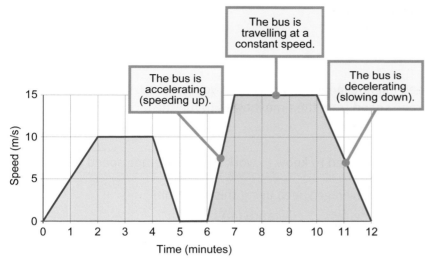

D a speed/time graph for part of a bus journey

On a speed/time graph:

- a horizontal line means the object is travelling at constant speed
- a sloping line shows that the object is **accelerating** (changing speed)
- the steeper the line, the greater the acceleration
- if the line slopes up to the right, the object is getting faster
- if the line slopes down to the right, the object is **decelerating** (slowing down).

The area under the graph shows the distance the object has travelled. In graph D, the bus travelled further between 6 and 12 minutes than it did between 0 and 5 minutes, because the pink area is larger than the blue area.

---

4 Look at the first part of the bus journey in graph D. Write down the time when the bus first starts to:

   a travel at a constant speed

   b decelerate.

5 The bus starts to accelerate at 0 minutes and at 6 minutes. Explain which is the greater acceleration.

Key points

- The gradient of a line on a distance/time graph shows the speed.
- The gradient of a line on a speed/time graph shows the acceleration. The area under the graph shows the distance travelled.

Checkpoint

How confidently can you answer the Progression questions?

Foundation

F1 Write down two things that a distance/time graph can tell you.

F2 Write down three things that a speed/time graph can tell you.

Strengthen

S1 Explain what a distance/time graph can tell you.

S2 Explain what a speed/time graph can tell you.

P1e Calculating speed and acceleration

ELC P1A.2, P1A.4, P1A.5 **GCSE** P2.6, P2.8, P2.13

Progression questions

- How can we measure speed?
- How do we calculate average speed?
- How do we calculate acceleration?

A How can you measure the speed in a race?

Your speed might change during a race if you get tired. We can work out the **average speed** from the time it takes to run the race and the length of the race.

> **1** What do you need to know to work out the average speed for a race?

We can calculate average speed using this equation:

$$\text{average speed (m/s)} = \frac{\text{distance (m)}}{\text{time (s)}}$$

Worked example W1

Jinny runs the 100 m race in 16 s. Calculate her average speed.

$$\text{average speed (m/s)} = \frac{\text{distance (m)}}{\text{time (s)}}$$

Write out the equation.

$$= \frac{100 \text{ m}}{1 \text{ s}}$$

Substitute the numbers from the question.

$$= 6.25 \text{ m/s}$$

Work out the answer. Remember the units.

> **2** Danny runs a 200 m race in 40 s. Calculate his average speed.

Acceleration

An acceleration is a change in speed. A large acceleration happens when the speed changes by a large amount, or when the speed change happens in a small time.

> **3** A car accelerates from 0 m/s to 15 m/s in 10 s. A motorbike accelerates to the same speed in 5 s. Explain which has the greater acceleration.

We can calculate the change in speed using this equation:

$$\text{change in speed (m/s)} = \text{final speed (m/s)} - \text{starting speed (m/s)}$$

We can calculate acceleration using this equation:

$$\text{acceleration (m/s}^2\text{)} = \frac{\text{change in speed (m/s)}}{\text{time taken (s)}}$$

Acceleration tells us the change in speed each second, so the units are metres per second per second. This is written as m/s² (metres per second squared). If the object is slowing down, the acceleration will be negative.

Worked example W2

A cyclist accelerates from 2 m/s to 8 m/s in 4 s. Calculate her acceleration.

change in speed $= 8$ m/s $- 2$ m/s

$= 6$ m/s

acceleration (m/s²) $= \dfrac{\text{change in speed (m/s)}}{\text{time (s)}}$

$= \dfrac{6 \text{ m/s}}{4 \text{ s}}$

$= 1.5 \text{ m/s}^2$

Remember that the change in speed is the final speed minus the starting speed.

C What is making these boys accelerate downwards?

Gravity makes things accelerate downwards. We say that a falling object is in **free fall**. The acceleration in free fall is 10 m/s². It is given the symbol g.

> **4** A car speeds up from 10 m/s to 20 m/s in 5 s. Calculate its acceleration.
>
> **5** Sam drops a bottle of water out of a window. The bottle takes 0.8 s to reach the ground. It is moving at 8 m/s when it hits the ground. Calculate the acceleration of the bottle. (*Hint*: the starting speed $= 0$ m/s.)

Key points

- We calculate average speed using the equation
  $$\text{average speed} = \frac{\text{distance}}{\text{time}}$$
- We calculate acceleration using the equation
  $$\text{acceleration} = \frac{\text{change in speed}}{\text{time taken}}$$

B The car decelerates as it approaches the red traffic lights. A deceleration is a negative acceleration.

Checkpoint

How confidently can you answer the Progression questions?

Foundation

F1 Jamal walks 1500 m to school. It takes him 1250 s. Calculate his average speed.

F2 A cyclist takes 5 s to change his speed by 10 m/s. Calculate his acceleration.

Strengthen

S1 A car is travelling at 40 m/s when the driver applies the brakes. It stops in 8 s. Calculate the acceleration. (*Hint*: your answer should be a negative number, showing that the car is decelerating.)

P1f Mass, weight and acceleration

ELC P1A.12 GCSE P2.15, P2.16, P2.17, P2.18

Progression questions

- How do we weigh objects?
- How can we calculate the weight of an object from its mass?
- How can we calculate the force that is accelerating an object?

A Bathroom scales like these measure your weight. They should have a scale marked in newtons, but in everyday life people talk about their weight in kilograms.

Mass is the amount of matter in something. It is measured in kilograms. The **weight** of something is the size of the force of **gravity** pulling it towards the Earth. As weight is a force, its units are newtons.

> **1** **a** What is mass?
>
>   **b** What is weight?

B In science, we can find the weight of an object using a force meter. This scientist is weighing a dormouse.

Calculating weight

The weight of an object depends on its mass, and on the strength of gravity. On Earth, gravity pulls on every kilogram of mass with a force of 10 N.

We can calculate weight using this equation:

$$\text{weight (N)} = \text{mass (kg)} \times 10 \text{ N/kg}$$

> **2** Ben has a mass of 55 kg. Calculate his weight.
>
> **3** A house mouse has a mass of 30 g. Calculate its weight.

Worked example W1

The dormouse in photo B has a mass of 20 g (0.02 kg). Calculate its weight.

weight (N) = mass (kg) × 10 N/kg

           = 0.02 kg × 10 N/kg

           = 0.2 N

> The mass must always be in kilograms.

Force, mass and acceleration

An unbalanced force changes the speed of an object. This means it accelerates it. The size of the force needed to accelerate an object depends on the mass of the object and the acceleration.

- The greater the mass, the greater the force needed.
- The greater the acceleration, the greater the force needed.

C The motorcycle can accelerate much faster than the van because it has a much smaller mass.

We can calculate the force needed using this equation:

$$\text{force (N)} = \text{mass (kg)} \times \text{acceleration (m/s}^2)$$

Worked example W2

A car has a mass of 2000 kg. It accelerates at 3 m/s². Calculate the force provided by its engine.

force (N) = mass (kg) × acceleration (m/s²)

= 2000 kg × 3 m/s²

= 6000 N

---

4 A car has a mass of 1200 kg. Calculate the force needed to make the car accelerate at 3 m/s².

5 A cyclist and her bicycle have a mass of 70 kg. She accelerates at 0.5 m/s². Calculate the force she is putting on the pedals.

Key points

- Mass is the amount of matter in an object. Weight is the force of gravity pulling on the object.
- We calculate weight using the equation weight = mass × 10 N/kg.
- We calculate the force needed to accelerate an object using the equation force = mass × acceleration.

Checkpoint

How confidently can you answer the Progression questions?

Foundation

F1 What is the difference between mass and weight?

F2 A bottle of lemonade has a mass of 1.5 kg. Calculate its weight.

Strengthen

S1 A hamster has a mass of 150 g. Calculate its weight.

S2 A motorcycle and rider has a mass of 250 kg. It accelerates at 5 m/s². Calculate the force from the engine.

Unbalanced forces on an object can make the object change its speed. A change in speed in a certain time is an **acceleration**.

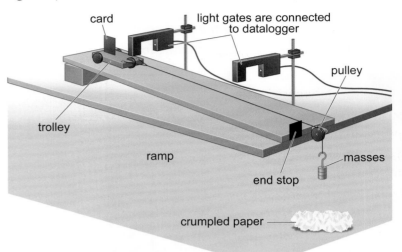

A apparatus for investigating acceleration

Method

A Prop up one end of the ramp. Place a trolley on the ramp. Change the slope of the ramp until the trolley just starts to move on its own. Use the same slope for the whole investigation.

When the trolley runs down the ramp, there will be friction in the wheels that will try to slow it down. Gravity trying to pull the trolley down the ramp cancels out this friction.

B Set up the light gates and the pulley and string as shown in diagram A.

C Stick a piece of card to the top of the trolley. Leave enough space to stand some masses on the top of the trolley.

D Measure the length of the card and write it down.

E Measure the mass of the trolley and write it down.

F Put a mass on the end of the string. You will keep this mass the same for all your tests. Your teacher will tell you what mass to use.

G Make sure the datalogger is switched on. Release the trolley from the top of the ramp.

H Write down the speed of the trolley (from the datalogger) as it passes through each light gate. Also write down the time it takes for the trolley to go from one light gate to the other.

I Put a mass on top of the trolley. Keep the masses on the end of the string the same as they were before. Repeat steps G and H.

J Repeat steps G and H for other masses on top of the trolley. You will have to decide what masses to use, how many different masses you are going to test, and whether you need to repeat any of your tests.

Exam-style questions

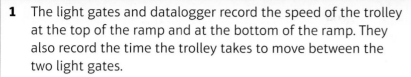

1   The light gates and datalogger record the speed of the trolley at the top of the ramp and at the bottom of the ramp. They also record the time the trolley takes to move between the two light gates.

Describe how this information can be used to calculate the acceleration. *(2 marks)*

2   Explain the difference between mass and weight. *(2 marks)*

3   Explain one way in which you would stay safe while doing the experiment. *(2 marks)*

4   Make a list of the apparatus you need to carry out the method. *(2 marks)*

5   Explain why a light gate is needed at the top of the ramp as well as at the bottom. *(1 mark)*

6   Use the results shown in graph B to draw a conclusion for this investigation. *(1 mark)*

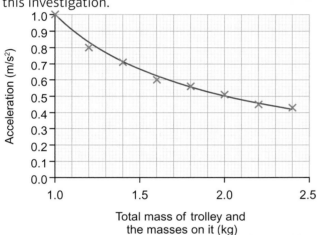

B   results for question 6

P1g Energy transfers

ELC P1A.16, P1A.17, P1A.18 **GCSE** P3.3, P3.4, P3.5, P3.6

Progression questions

- How is energy transferred between different stores?
- How can we represent energy transfers in diagrams?
- What happens to the total amount of energy when energy is transferred?

A How does your body store and transfer energy?

1   Describe how fuels such as petrol store energy.

Everything that happens needs energy. Energy is transferred and stored in different ways. Energy stored in food is often called **chemical energy**. Batteries and fuels such as petrol and natural gas also store chemical energy.

Energy can also be stored in hot objects (**thermal energy**), in moving objects (**kinetic energy**) and in stretched elastic or springs (**strain energy** or **elastic potential energy**). If you lift something up, you are storing energy as **gravitational potential energy**. Energy is also stored inside atoms (called **atomic energy** or **nuclear energy**).

2   Write down six different ways in which energy can be stored.

Energy can be transferred between different stores. When you use an electric kettle to heat water, energy is transferred to the kettle **by electricity**. The electricity makes the element inside the kettle hot. Energy is then transferred to the water in the kettle **by heating**.

A moving car is a store of kinetic energy. When it slows down, **friction** in the brakes heats up the brakes. The store of kinetic energy is transferred to a store of thermal energy **by forces**. Energy can also be transferred **by light** and **by sound**.

3   Write down five different ways in which energy can be transferred.

We can show energy transfers using diagrams.

energy stored in moving car (kinetic energy)	→ energy transferred by forces during braking →	energy stored in hot brakes (thermal energy)

B an energy transfer diagram for a car slowing down

C This child is throwing a ball at the tins. The moving ball has a store of kinetic energy. When the ball hits a tin, some of the kinetic energy will be transferred to the tin. Some energy is transferred to the surroundings by sound.

Conservation of energy

Energy cannot be created or destroyed. It can only be transferred from one store to another. This means that the total amount of energy is always the same. This idea is called the **law of conservation of energy**.

We can show this idea using a **Sankey diagram**. The width of the arrows represents the amount of energy in **joules (J)**.

energy transferred by electricity 12 J

5 J energy transferred by light

7 J energy transferred by heating

D This Sankey diagram shows energy transfers in a light bulb.

> **4** Look at diagram D. How can you tell without looking at the numbers that the light bulb transfers more energy by heating than by light?

Key points

- Energy can be stored in chemicals, inside atoms, in stretched materials and things in high places, and in moving and hot objects.
- Energy can be transferred by heating, sound, light, forces and electricity.
- Energy cannot be created or destroyed, so the total amount stays the same.
- We can use energy transfer diagrams to show energy transfers, and Sankey diagrams to show the amounts of energy transferred.

Checkpoint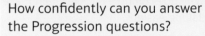

How confidently can you answer the Progression questions?

Foundation

F1 Cheryl's oven uses natural gas. She uses it to heat potatoes.

   a Describe the way in which energy is stored in the natural gas and in the hot potatoes.

   b Burning the gas transfers 500 J of energy. How much energy ends up stored in the hot potatoes and the hot oven?

Strengthen

S1 Billy heats some water on a gas camping stove. Draw an energy transfer diagram like diagram B to show the useful energy transfers.

S2 1000 J of energy is transferred to a kettle. 850 J ends up stored in the hot water in the kettle. Explain how much energy is transferred to the kettle itself and the surroundings.

P1h Wasted energy

ELC P1A.19, P1A.20, P1A.21, P1A.22, P1A.23 **GCSE** P3.7, P3.8, P3.9, P3.11

Progression questions

- How is energy wasted in energy transfers?
- How can we reduce unwanted energy transfers?
- How can we calculate efficiency?

A Why does oiling a bicycle chain make pedalling easier?

When you pedal a bicycle, friction in the chain and other moving parts makes them heat up. Some of the energy you transferred to the pedals by forces ends up as stored thermal energy. This energy is not useful because you want all the force you put on the pedals to make the bicycle move forwards. Other **resistance forces** that transfer energy to the surroundings include **air resistance** and **water resistance**.

> **1** When you cycle, some energy is transferred by friction. Explain why this is not useful energy.

Some of the thermal energy stored in hot objects always **dissipates** (spreads out) in the surroundings. This is why a hot drink soon gets cooler. When you boil a kettle, the thermal energy transferred to the kettle itself and the surroundings is wasted energy. Only the energy stored in the hot water is useful energy.

> **2** Describe how energy is wasted when you use a kettle to boil water.

Every time energy is used, some is always wasted by being transferred to the surroundings. You can reduce the amount of wasted energy in different ways.

B The thermal insulation on this flask reduces the amount of energy wasted.

- You can oil a bicycle chain to reduce the friction. This is called **lubrication**.
- You can insulate hot objects. Thermal insulation reduces the amount of energy transferred to the surroundings by heating.

Efficiency

Efficiency is a way of describing how good a machine is at transferring energy into useful forms. The efficiency of a machine is given as a percentage between 0 per cent and 100 per cent. The higher the percentage, the more efficient the machine. This is shown in diagram C.

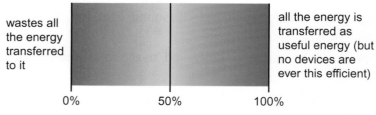

C percentage energy efficiency

D These Sankey diagrams show the energy transferred by an old-style bulb and a modern low-energy bulb.

> **3** Look at the Sankey diagrams for light bulbs in diagram D.
>   **a** Which bulb wastes the least energy?
>   **b** Which bulb is the most efficient?

You can calculate the efficiency of a machine using this equation:

$$\text{efficiency} = \frac{\text{(useful energy output)}}{\text{(total energy input)}} \times 100\%$$

Worked example

Calculate the efficiency of the old-style bulb shown in diagram D.

$$\text{efficiency} = \frac{\text{(useful energy output)}}{\text{(total energy input)}} \times 100\%$$

$$= \frac{9\,\text{J}}{100\,\text{J}} \times 100\%$$

$$= 9\%$$

> **4** Calculate the efficiency of the low-energy bulb shown in diagram D.

Key points

- Energy is transferred to the surroundings every time there is an energy transfer. Any energy transferred that is not useful is wasted energy.
- The amount of energy wasted can be reduced, for example by lubrication or by using insulation.
- An efficient machine transfers most of the energy it uses to useful energy.
- $\text{efficiency} = \dfrac{\text{(useful energy output)}}{\text{(total energy input)}} \times 100\%$

Checkpoint

How confidently can you answer the Progression questions?

Foundation

F1 Explain why an electric motor feels warm while it is working.

F2 Look at diagram D in topic P1g. Calculate the efficiency of the light bulb.

Strengthen

S1 Explain why adding oil to door hinges makes the door easier and quieter to open.

S2 A radio is supplied with 50 J of energy. It transfers 5 J of this by sound. Explain what happens to the rest of the energy and calculate the efficiency of the radio.

P1i Energy resources

ELC P1A.24, P1A.25 **GCSE** P3.13

Progression questions

- What is the difference between renewable and non-renewable energy resources?
- What non-renewable energy resources do we use?
- What renewable energy resources do we use?

A Is the fuel that powers this bus a renewable energy resource or will it run out one day?

Most cars and buses use petrol or diesel as fuel. These are fuels made from oil. Coal, oil and natural gas are formed underground over millions of years from the remains of dead plants and animals. Coal, oil and natural gas are called **fossil fuels**.

1   Write down the name used to describe coal, oil and natural gas.

Coal and natural gas are used in power stations to make electricity. The atoms of some elements such as uranium can be used as **nuclear fuel** in power stations. These are all called **non-renewable energy resources**, because they will run out one day.

2   Write down the names of four non-renewable energy resources.

Renewable resources

We also use **renewable energy resources**. These will not run out because they use things like the Sun or wind, or are made from plants.

Bio-fuel is made from plants or animal droppings. Some kinds of bio-fuel can be used in vehicles. Bio-fuel can also be used in power stations or for cooking and heating. Bio-fuels are reusable because more plants can be grown to make more fuel.

3   Write down three different uses for bio-fuels.

B Wind turbines are used to generate electricity.

Solar power uses energy from the Sun. This can be used to produce electricity or to heat water.

The wind can be used to spin **wind turbines** to generate electricity. The turbines only produce electricity when the wind is blowing.

Water can also be used to generate electricity. **Hydro-electricity** is generated using water stored in a **reservoir** in a hilly part of the country. Water runs down pipes and makes turbines spin to generate electricity. Rain keeps the reservoir full.

The **tides** make the level of the sea change every day. **Tidal power** uses the movement of water to spin turbines to generate electricity.

C the dam and reservoir for a hydro-electric power station

D Tidal currents in the sea can be used to make turbines spin.

---

4 Write down two different renewable resources that spin turbines to generate electricity.

Checkpoint

How confidently can you answer the Progression questions?

Foundation

F1 Describe two different non-renewable energy resources.

F2 Describe three different renewable energy resources.

Strengthen

S1 Explain the difference between renewable and non-renewable energy resources.

S2 Describe three different uses for energy resources.

Key points

- Fossil fuels and nuclear fuel are called non-renewable energy resources as they will run out one day.
- Renewable energy resources will not run out.
- Bio-fuel, solar power, wind power, tidal power and hydro-electricity are all renewable energy resources.

P1j Using energy resources

ELC P1A.24, P1A.26 **GCSE** P3.13, P3.14

Progression questions

- What are the advantages and disadvantages of non-renewable energy resources?
- What are the advantages and disadvantages of renewable energy resources?
- Why do we need to use a mixture of different resources?

A What are some of the problems with using fossil fuels to produce electricity?

Electricity is not an energy resource. It is only a way of transferring energy from one place to another.

Most of the electricity in the UK is generated using nuclear fuels or fossil fuels. Most vehicles use petrol or diesel made from oil. There are advantages and disadvantages of using these fuels.

Advantages
- Electricity can be generated all the time using these fuels.
- Petrol and diesel store a lot of energy in a small volume, which is good for vehicles.

Disadvantages
- Fossil fuels produce carbon dioxide and other polluting gases when they burn. Carbon dioxide is contributing to **climate change**.
- Accidents in nuclear power stations can cause dangerous pollution, and people worry about safety. Nuclear power stations also produce dangerous wastes that are expensive to dispose of safely.
- The fuels will run out one day.

> **1** Explain why petrol and diesel are used in cars and lorries.

> **2** Name a polluting gas that fossil fuels produce when they burn.

182

B Why do some people object to solar panels being used to generate electricity?

There are also advantages and disadvantages of using renewable energy resources.

Advantages
- Most renewable resources do not produce polluting gases.
- Renewable resources will not run out.

Disadvantages
- Solar power is not available at night or when the weather is very bad. Wind power is not available in calm weather. Tidal power is not available all the time.
- Wind farms, solar farms and the reservoirs for hydro-electricity take up a lot of land. Many people think they spoil the countryside. Plants grown to make bio-fuels use land that could be used for growing food.
- There are not many places in the UK suitable for building the dams needed for hydro-electricity.

Which resources do we need?

Most countries in the world are worried about climate change. We are trying to reduce the amount of carbon dioxide we put into the atmosphere. One way of doing this is to use more renewable resources to generate electricity.

However, we need electricity to be available all the time. Many renewable resources only produce electricity some of the time. In the UK we do not have enough hydro-electricity or bio-fuels to produce the electricity we need, so we still need to use fossil fuels and nuclear fuels in our power stations.

> **4** Explain why most countries are trying to use less energy from fossil fuels.

Key points

- Gases from burning fossil fuels cause pollution and contribute to climate change.
- Renewable resources are not available all the time.
- We need to use a mixture of renewable and non-renewable resources for our energy.

> **3 a** Give one advantage of renewable resources compared with non-renewable resources.
> **b** Give one disadvantage.

Checkpoint

How confidently can you answer the Progression questions?

Foundation

F1 Write down one reason why we cannot get all our energy from renewable resources.

F2 Give two disadvantages of using fossil fuels to generate electricity.

Strengthen

S1 Explain why the UK is using more renewable resources now than it did 10 years ago.

Stopping distances

1 The stopping distance of a car depends on the thinking distance and the braking distance.
Explain how the thinking distance depends on the driver's reaction time. **(2 marks)**

Student answer

The thinking distance increases when the driver's reaction time increases [A].

[A] This is correct. However, the student should also have explained that this happens because when the reaction time is longer the car travels further while the driver is thinking.

Verdict

This is a poor answer. When the question says 'explain', you need to say what happens and also *why* it happens. The student has only said what happens.

Force and acceleration

2 A car has a mass of 1500 kg. Calculate the force needed to give it an acceleration of 3 m/s². Give the units with your answer. **(4 marks)**

Student answer

force = mass × acceleration [A]

    = 1500 kg × 3 m/s² [B]

    = 4500 N [C]

[A] The student has written out the correct equation.

[B] They have substituted the numbers into the equation.

[C] They have worked out the answer and given the unit.

Verdict

This is a good answer. The student has shown their working, and remembered to include the unit.

P2 Waves and radiation

Have you noticed that dogs have cold noses? The colours in this photo show the temperature of different parts of the dog. White parts are the hottest and black parts are the coldest.

The photo was taken using infrared radiation. This is a form of radiation similar to light. We can detect infrared radiation with our skin, but not with our eyes.

In this unit you will learn about the different kinds of waves around us. You will also learn about radiation and some of its dangers.

The learning journey

Previously you will have learnt at KS3:

- how light and sound are transferred by waves
- that everything is made of atoms.

In this unit you will learn:

- how to describe waves
- how to measure and calculate the speed of waves
- about the waves in the electromagnetic spectrum and how they are used
- what atoms are made from and how to describe them
- what happens when a radioactive substance decays
- why radioactivity can be dangerous and how people are protected.

P2a Describing waves

ELC P1B.1, P1B.2 **GCSE** P4.1, P4.2, P4.3, P4.4, P4.5

Progression questions

- What do waves transfer?
- How can we describe waves?
- What is the difference between a longitudinal and a transverse wave?

A We can see waves on water. What kinds of waves are there that we cannot see?

Waves on water transfer energy. When large waves on the sea hit the land they transfer energy to the land and wear it away.

Light and sound also transfer energy by waves. When we watch something happening or listen to someone speaking, the light and sound waves are also transferring **information**.

> 1 State what sound waves are transferring when you listen to someone talking.

Describing waves

The **wavelength** of a wave is the distance from a point on one wave to a point in the same position on the next wave. Wavelength is measured in metres.

The **amplitude** of a wave is the maximum distance of a point on the wave away from the middle position. Amplitude is measured in metres. The greater the amplitude of a sound wave, the louder the sound.

> 2 Give two ways of describing waves that are measured in metres.
>
> 3 The tops of sea waves pass a stick twice every second. What is the frequency?
>
> 4 Draw a wave like the one in diagram B and label it X. Draw another wave next to it with a smaller amplitude and a shorter wavelength, and label this one Y.

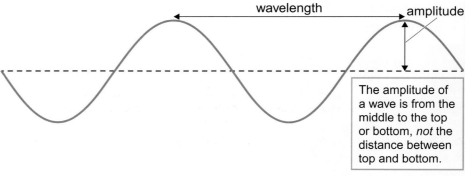

The amplitude of a wave is from the middle to the top or bottom, *not* the distance between top and bottom.

B wavelength and amplitude

Wave **frequency** is the number of waves passing a point each second. It is measured in **hertz** (**Hz**). A frequency of 1 hertz means one wave passing per second. For sound, a wave with a high frequency has a high pitch (it sounds high). For light, different frequencies of light have different colours.

Wave speed is how far a wave travels in a certain time. Waves travel at different speeds in different materials.

Transverse and longitudinal waves

Waves do not transfer **matter**. When a wave travels on water, particles in the water move up and down. They are not carried along with the wave.

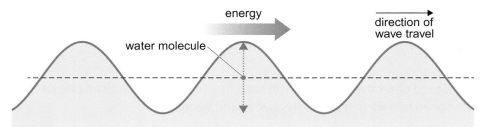

C In a transverse wave, particles move up and down at right angles to the direction the wave is moving.

Waves on the surface of water are **transverse waves**. The particles move at right angles to the direction the wave is travelling. Light waves are also transverse waves.

Sound waves are **longitudinal waves**. Particles in the material through which the wave is travelling move backwards and forwards as the wave passes.

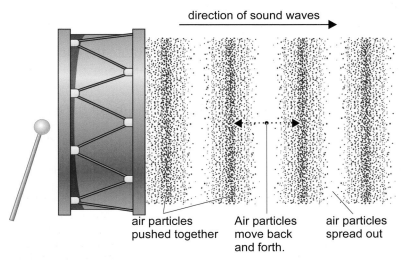

D In longitudinal waves the particles move back and forth in the same direction as the wave is travelling.

> **5** Imagine if a wave in water moved matter in the same direction as the energy. What would happen to the water in a swimming pool if you made waves at one end?

Key points

- Waves can transfer energy and information.
- Waves can be described by their wavelength, amplitude and frequency.
- Waves on water are transverse waves and sound waves are longitudinal waves.

Checkpoint

How confidently can you answer the Progression questions?

Foundation

F1 Write down two things that waves transfer. Give an example of each.

F2 Describe what these things measure:

  a frequency

  b amplitude

  c wavelength.

Strengthen

S1 Draw a transverse wave and label the amplitude and wavelength.

S2 Describe the similarities and differences between longitudinal and transverse waves.

P2b Wave speeds

ELC P1B.3 **GCSE** P4.6, P4.7

- How can we calculate the speed of a wave?
- How can we measure the speed of waves on water?
- How can we measure the speed of sound?

A Thunder is the sound made by a lightning flash. How can we calculate the speed of a sound wave?

The speed of a wave is how far it travels in a certain time. We can calculate the speed of a wave from its frequency and wavelength.

> **1** What do you need to know to calculate the speed of a wave?

Wave speed, frequency and wavelength are linked by this equation:

$$\text{wave speed (m/s)} = \text{frequency (Hz)} \times \text{wavelength (m)}$$

Worked example W1

Some waves have a wavelength of 13 m and a frequency of 0.5 Hz. Calculate their speed.

Write out the equation.

wave speed = frequency × wavelength

Substitute the numbers from the question.

= 0.5 Hz × 13 m

= 6.5 m/s

Work out the answer. Don't forget the units.

> **2** Some waves have a wavelength of 2 m and a frequency of 170 Hz. Calculate their speed.

We can also calculate the speed of a wave from the distance it travels in a certain time. This is the same equation we used for calculating the speed of moving objects (see topic P1e).

$$\text{wave speed (m/s)} = \frac{\text{distance (m)}}{\text{time (s)}}$$

Worked example W2

A wave travels 52 m in 8 s. Calculate the wave speed.

$$\text{wave speed (m/s)} = \frac{\text{distance (m)}}{\text{time (s)}}$$

$$= \frac{52 \text{ m}}{8 \text{ s}}$$

$$= 6.5 \text{ m/s}$$

> **3** Light waves travel 900 000 000 m in 3 s. Calculate their speed.

Measuring the speed of waves

One way of measuring the speed of waves on water is to measure the time it takes for a wave to travel between two fixed points such as the ladders on the jetty in diagram B. You can calculate the speed from the time and the distance between the points.

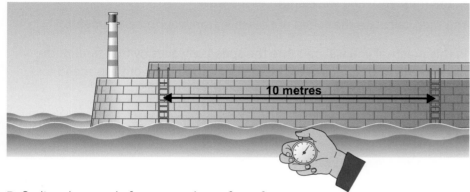

10 metres

B finding the speed of waves on the surface of water

> **4** Look at diagram B. It takes 7 s for a wave to move from one ladder to the other. Calculate the speed of the wave.

It is more difficult to measure the speed of sound, because sound waves travel much faster than waves on water. One way of measuring the speed of sound is to use echoes.

- Stand in front of a large wall and make a noise. You should hear an echo when the sound is reflected by the wall.
- Measure the time between making the sound and hearing the echo.
- Calculate the speed using the speed, time, distance equation.

> **5** You measure the time it takes for an echo to reach you. Explain what other measurement you need to take to allow you to calculate the speed of sound.

Key points

- We can calculate wave speed using the equation:
$$\text{wave speed} = \text{frequency} \times \text{wavelength}$$

- We can also calculate wave speed using the equation:
$$\text{wave speed} = \frac{\text{distance}}{\text{time}}$$

- We can measure the speed of waves by measuring their frequency and wavelength. Alternatively we can measure how long a wave takes to move a certain distance. We then use the relevant equation above to work out the speed.

Checkpoint

How confidently can you answer the Progression questions?

Foundation

F1 A sound wave in water has a frequency of 1100 Hz and a wavelength of 1.4 m. Calculate the speed of the wave.

Strengthen

S1 Look at diagram B. Explain how you could work out the speed of the waves using the equation for wave speed, frequency and wavelength.

You cannot measure speed directly. To find the speed of a wave you need to measure:

- how long the wave takes to cover a certain distance

or

- the frequency and wavelength of the wave.

You then calculate the speed of the wave from your measurements.

In this practical you will measure the speed of waves by first finding the frequency and wavelength of the waves. You will work out the speed for waves on water and the speed of sound in a metal bar.

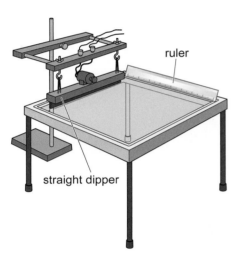

A a ripple tank

B measuring the frequency of sound in an aluminium rod

Method

Measuring waves on water

A Set up a ripple tank with a straight dipper near one of the short sides of the tank. Be ready to mop up any spills immediately.

B Fasten a ruler to one of the long sides so you can see the markings above the water level.

C Change the current to the motor until you get waves with a wavelength about half as long as the ripple tank (so you can always see two waves).

D Count how many waves are formed in 10 s and write it down.

E Divide the number of waves in step D by 10 to find the frequency of the waves.

F Look at the waves against the ruler. Use the markings on the ruler to estimate the wavelength of the waves.

G Calculate the speed of the waves using the wavelength and frequency you have measured.

Measuring waves in solids

H Suspend a metal rod horizontally using clamp stands and rubber bands.

I Set up a smartphone with a frequency app and hold it close to the rod.

J Tap one end of the rod with a hammer. Write down the highest frequency shown by the frequency app on the smartphone.

K Measure the length of the rod and write it down.

L Sound inside a metal rod has a wavelength that is twice the length of the rod. Multiply the length of the rod by 2 to find the wavelength.

M Calculate the speed of sound in the rod using the frequency and wavelength you have measured.

Exam-style questions

1 A sound wave in air travels 660 m in 2 s. Calculate the speed of the sound wave. *(2 marks)*

2 Adanna is watching waves on the sea go past two buoys. She knows the buoys are 20 m apart. Explain how she can find the speed of the waves. *(2 marks)*

3 Luke estimated the wavelength of the waves in the ripple tank using the method described in step F. Emily took a photo of the waves in the ripple tank and estimated the wavelength using the photo. Explain which method was likely to give the most accurate result. *(2 marks)*

4 You can find the speed of sound in air by making a loud sound in front of a large wall. You then time how long it is before you hear the echo.

   a Write down a list of the apparatus you need to find the speed of sound using this method. *(2 marks)*

   b Write down the equation you need to use to calculate the speed of sound from your measurements. *(1 mark)*

5 Zoe stands 20 m away from a wall and bangs two pieces of wood together. She uses a microphone and a datalogger to measure the time between the bang and the echo. The time is 0.12 s.

   a Calculate how far the sound has travelled. *(1 mark)*

   b Calculate the speed of sound in air using Zoe's measurements. *(2 marks)*

6 Gina used the method described in steps H to M to measure the frequency of sound in an aluminium rod. The rod is 0.8 m long. She recorded a peak frequency of 4000 Hz. Sound inside a metal rod has a wavelength that is twice the length of the rod.

   a Use Gina's results to calculate the speed of sound in aluminium. *(3 marks)*

   b You can also measure a distance and a time to work out the speed of a wave. Explain why Gina did not use a stopwatch to find how long it took the noise to travel down the metal rod. *(2 marks)*

P2c Electromagnetic waves

ELC P1B.4, P1B.5, P1B.6, P1B.7, P1B.8 **GCSE** P4.10, P5.7, P5.8, P5.10, P5.11, P5.12

Progression questions

- What do all electromagnetic waves have in common?
- What characteristics of electromagnetic waves are used to group them?
- What happens when a wave goes into a different material?

A The rainbow shows the colours in the visible part of the electromagnetic spectrum. What other waves are in this spectrum?

We see things when light transfers energy to our eyes. The light we can detect with our eyes is called **visible light**. It is part of a family of waves called **electromagnetic waves**. A rainbow happens when light from the Sun is split up into different colours. Scientists describe seven colours in the **visible spectrum**:

red, orange, yellow, green, blue, indigo, violet.

The other kinds of wave in the **electromagnetic spectrum** are shown in diagram B. The waves are put into groups according to their frequencies and wavelengths.

> **1** How many colours are there in the visible spectrum?

> **2** Look at diagram B. Write down the waves in the electromagnetic spectrum in order of wavelength, starting with gamma rays.
>
> **3** Write down the names of two groups of waves with higher frequencies than visible light.

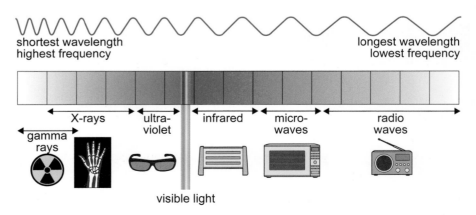

B groups of waves in the electromagnetic spectrum

Gamma rays have the highest frequencies and shortest wavelengths of all the waves in the electromagnetic spectrum. They also transfer the most energy.

Radio waves have the lowest frequencies and longest wavelengths. They transfer the least energy.

Other electromagnetic waves are **X-rays**, **ultraviolet**, **infrared** and **microwaves**.

Waves changing speed

All electromagnetic waves are transverse waves. They all transfer energy, and they all travel at the same speed in a **vacuum** (empty space). Electromagnetic waves travel more slowly through materials such as air, water or glass.

Waves change speed when they cross a boundary between one material and another. If the waves meet the boundary at an angle they change direction. This is called **refraction**.

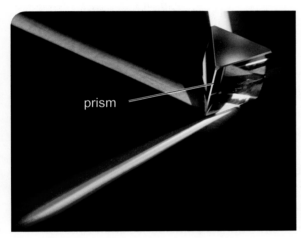

C Light is refracted when it goes through the prism. The different colours change direction by different amounts.

> **4** What is refraction?

Key points

- The electromagnetic spectrum is split into groups: gamma rays, X-rays, ultraviolet, visible light, infrared, microwaves and radio waves.
- Gamma rays have the highest frequencies, highest energies and shortest wavelengths. Radio waves have the lowest frequencies, lowest energies and longest wavelengths.
- Waves change speed when they pass into different materials. This causes refraction.
- Electromagnetic waves are all transverse waves. They all travel at the same speed in a vacuum.

Checkpoint

How confidently can you answer the Progression questions?

Foundation

F1 Name the part of the electromagnetic spectrum:

 a with the highest frequency
 b with the lowest frequency
 c that we can see with our eyes.

F2 A wave crosses a boundary between air and glass at an angle. Give two characteristics of the wave that will change as it crosses the boundary.

Strengthen

S1 a List the seven parts of the electromagnetic spectrum in order, starting with the highest frequencies.

 b Explain how the wavelength, frequency and energy change from one end of the spectrum to the other.

S2 Write down three things that all electromagnetic waves have in common.

A Light is refracted as it passes into the glass block, and again when it leaves the glass.

We can investigate refraction by marking where light rays go when they pass through different materials.

Photo A shows a ray of light shining into a glass block. The ray changes direction when it goes into the glass. It changes direction again when it leaves the glass.

We measure the angle of the light from an imaginary line at right angles to the edge of the block. This line is called the **normal line**. The angle between the normal and the light ray going towards the boundary between the two materials is called the **angle of incidence**. The angle between the normal and the light ray moving away from the boundary is called the **angle of refraction**.

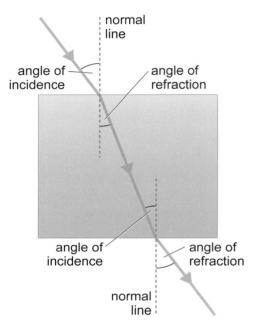

B path of a light ray

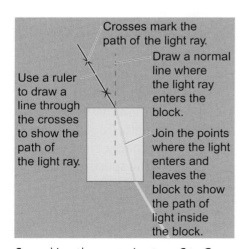

C marking the paper in steps **C** to **G**

Method

A Place a piece of plain paper on the desk. Set up the power supply, ray box and single slit so that you can shine a single ray of light across the paper on your desk.

B Place a rectangular glass block on the paper. Draw around the block.

C Shine a ray of light into your block at an angle. Use small crosses to mark where the rays of light go.

D Take the block off the paper. Use a ruler to join the crosses to show the path of the light, right up to the block. Do this for the light going into the block and the light coming out of it.

E Join the points where the light entered and left the block to show where it travelled inside the block.

F Draw lines at right angles to the edge of the block where the light enters and leaves it. Measure the angles of incidence and refraction where the light entered the block.

G Measure the angles of incidence and refraction where the light left the block.

H Put the block back on your paper in exactly the same position as before. Repeat steps C to G with the ray entering the block at different angles.

I Move the ray box so that the light ray reaches the edge of the block at right angles. Note what happens to the light as it enters and leaves the block.

Safety

Ray boxes get very hot. Take care.

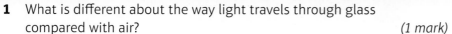

Exam-style questions

1 What is different about the way light travels through glass compared with air? *(1 mark)*

2 State what the following terms mean:

   a normal line *(1 mark)*

   b angle of incidence *(1 mark)*

   c angle of refraction *(1 mark)*

3 Table D shows a student's results from this investigation.

Air to glass		Glass to air	
angle of incidence	angle of refraction	angle of incidence	angle of refraction
10°	6°	6°	10°
20°	13°	13°	20°
30°	20°	20°	30°
40°	25°	25°	40°

D

   a Draw a diagram to show the glass block and a light ray going into the glass at an angle of incidence of 30°. *(2 marks)*

   b Draw in the refracted ray. *(1 mark)*

4 Look at table D. Copy and complete these sentences to describe what happens to the light as it enters and leaves the block. Choose words from the box. *(4 marks)*

away from   greater   less   towards

When the light enters the block the angle of refraction is _____ than the angle of incidence. This is because the light bends _____ the normal.

When the light leaves the block the angle of refraction is _____ than the angle of incidence. This is because the light bends _____ the normal.

5 **a** Light goes from air into glass with an angle of incidence of 15°. Use table D to estimate what the angle of refraction will be. *(1 mark)*

   b Light goes from glass to air. The angle of refraction is 45°. Use table D to estimate what the angle of incidence must be. *(1 mark)*

6 A different student carries out the same investigation as described above, using the same equipment. Some of their angles of refraction from glass to air are different from the ones in table D.

Suggest why some of their results are different. *(1 mark)*

P2d Using the long wavelengths

ELC P1B.10 **GCSE** P5.22

Progression questions

- What are some uses of visible light?
- What are some uses of infrared?
- What are some uses of microwaves and radio waves?

A How does a phone send texts, photos and speech?

B Light and infrared radiation can both travel along optical fibres.

We use waves in the electromagnetic spectrum every day. The uses of the waves depend on their wavelengths.

Visible light

Visible light is the part of the electromagnetic spectrum that our eyes detect. Light bulbs are designed to emit visible light. When we take a photograph, the camera detects visible light and stores the image.

> 1 How is visible light used to take photographs?

Infrared

Infrared radiation has longer wavelengths than visible light. We use infrared radiation in different ways:

- Some computers can send messages to each other using infrared radiation. This can only be done if they are in the same room. This type of **communication** is called **short range** communication.
- TV and gaming remote controls use infrared radiation.
- Phone calls and information such as TV programmes or Internet pages can be sent along **optical fibres**. An optical fibre is a very thin strand of glass that infrared radiation travels along.
- Grills and toasters transfer energy to food by infrared radiation. The food absorbs the radiation and heats up.
- **Thermal images** such as the one of the dog at the start of this unit show the amount of infrared radiation given off by different objects.
- **Security systems** set off alarms if someone breaks into a building. They often have sensors that can detect infrared radiation emitted by people.

> 2 Describe two ways in which infrared radiation can be used to send messages.

Microwaves

Microwaves are used for cooking. In a microwave oven the food absorbs microwaves and heats up.

C The potatoes on the left were baked in an oven. The ones on the right were cooked in a microwave oven.

Microwaves are also used in communications:

- Mobile phone signals are sent using microwaves.
- TV programmes and phone calls to other countries can be sent using satellites. **Satellite transmissions** use microwaves.

> **3** Name two parts of the electromagnetic spectrum that are used for cooking.

Radio waves

Radio waves are used in communications:

- They are used for transmitting radio broadcasts and TV programmes.
- Some radio communications are sent via satellites.

> **4** Name two parts of the electromagnetic spectrum that are used to transmit TV programmes.

Key points

- Visible light lets us see and is detected when cameras record images.
- Infrared is used in cooking, thermal imaging, optical fibres, remote controls and security systems.
- Microwaves are used in cooking, communications and satellite transmissions.
- Radio waves are used in broadcasting, communications and satellite transmissions.

Checkpoint

How confidently can you answer the Progression questions?

Foundation

F1 Write down two uses for each of these parts of the electromagnetic spectrum:

   a visible light

   b infrared

   c microwaves

   d radio waves.

Strengthen

S1 Draw a table or make a list of bullet points to show the uses for visible light, infrared, microwaves and radio waves.

P2e Using the short wavelengths

ELC P1B.10 **GCSE** P5.22

Progression questions

- What are some uses of ultraviolet waves?
- What are some uses of X-rays?
- What are some uses of gamma rays?

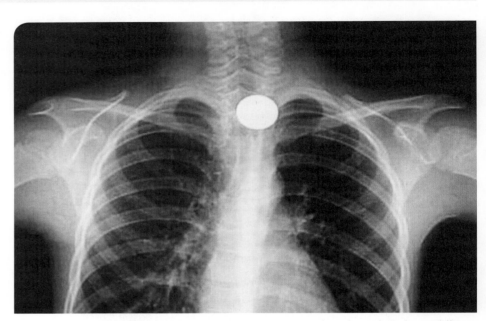

A Which part of the electromagnetic spectrum was used to show that this toddler had swallowed a coin?

Ultraviolet radiation, X-rays and gamma rays all have shorter wavelengths and higher frequencies than visible light. These parts of the electromagnetic spectrum have different uses.

Ultraviolet

The water we drink needs to be very clean. Ultraviolet light can be shone into water to **disinfect** it. The ultraviolet light kills harmful **microorganisms** in the water.

> **1** Describe how ultraviolet light is used to treat water.

Some materials absorb energy from ultraviolet radiation and then emit the energy again as visible light. This is called **fluorescence**. Many people use pens with fluorescent ink to write their postcode onto TVs or computers. You can only see these **security markings** when ultraviolet light shines on them. Police can use these markings to identify stolen goods.

Bank notes are marked with special ink that only shows up in ultraviolet light. Banks can use ultraviolet light to check that bank notes are not forgeries.

B This is a real banknote with ultraviolet light shining on it. A forged banknote does not have markings that glow.

> **2** Why might someone write their postcode on a TV or computer using a pen with fluorescent ink in it?

Ultraviolet light is also used in some light bulbs. **Fluorescent lamps** have a gas inside them. This gas produces ultraviolet radiation when electricity passes through it. The glass is coated with a fluorescent material that absorbs the ultraviolet radiation and gives out visible light.

X-rays

Doctors cannot see inside your body directly. They can make images of the inside of parts of the body using X-rays. X-rays can also be used to examine the insides of metal objects to check there are no faults in them. X-rays are also used to inspect luggage in airport security scanners.

Gamma rays

Gamma rays transfer a lot of energy, and can kill cells. Gamma rays are used:

- to **sterilise** food by killing microorganisms on it
- to sterilise instruments that surgeons will use in operations
- to kill **cancer** cells.

Gamma rays can also be used to detect cancer. A doctor injects a chemical that emits gamma rays into a patient. The chemical is designed to collect inside cancer cells. The patient is put inside a scanner that detects where in their body the gamma rays are coming from.

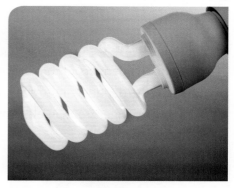

C a modern fluorescent lamp

D Microorganisms on food make it go bad or start to rot. All these strawberries are several days old, but the ones on the left were treated with gamma rays to kill microorganisms.

3 Describe two ways in which gamma rays can be used in hospitals.

4 Write down two parts of the electromagnetic spectrum that are used to kill microorganisms.

Checkpoint

How confidently can you answer the Progression questions?

Foundation

F1 Describe three uses of:
- **a** ultraviolet radiation
- **b** X-rays
- **c** gamma rays.

Strengthen

S1 Describe two parts of the electromagnetic spectrum that are used by doctors to find out what is wrong with a patient.

S2 Explain two ways in which ultraviolet light can be used to prevent crime.

Key points

- Ultraviolet radiation is used for security markings, fluorescent lamps and disinfecting water.
- X-rays are used to make images of the insides of objects, luggage and bodies.
- Gamma rays are used to sterilise food and medical equipment. They are also used to detect and treat cancer.

Progression questions

- What are the dangers of microwave and infrared radiation?
- What are the dangers of ultraviolet radiation, X-rays and gamma rays?
- How is the danger from an electromagnetic wave linked to its frequency?

A How is this mother protecting her child?

Energy transferred by electromagnetic waves is useful, but it can also be dangerous. The dangers depend on the frequencies of the waves.

Microwaves

Some frequencies of microwaves can heat water. Microwave ovens use this frequency to cook food. This heating could be dangerous to people because our bodies are mostly water. This means that microwaves could heat cells from the inside and damage or kill them.

> **1** Describe how microwaves could damage our bodies.

B This photo shows the inside of a microwave oven. The metal grid in the door reflects microwaves but the holes allow visible light through.

Mobile phones use different microwave frequencies. Scientific evidence tells us that mobile phone signals are not a health risk.

Infrared radiation

Infrared radiation is used in grills and toasters to cook food. Our skin **absorbs** infrared and we feel this as heat. Infrared radiation can burn our skin if we absorb too much of it.

> **2** Why should you be careful not to stand too close to a bonfire?

Ultraviolet radiation

Sunlight contains high-frequency ultraviolet radiation. This transfers more energy than visible radiation. Ultraviolet radiation can cause sunburn and damage **DNA**. DNA is the chemical in our cells that controls what they do. If DNA in our skin is damaged it can cause skin cancer.

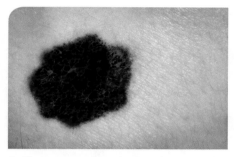

C Skin cancers like this can be caused by too much exposure to the sun.

We can help to protect our skin by staying out of the strongest sunshine. We can also cover up with clothing and hats, and use sun cream with a high SPF (sun protection factor).

The ultraviolet radiation in sunlight can also damage our eyes. We can protect our eyes by using sunglasses that absorb ultraviolet radiation.

> **3** Explain why it is a good idea to wear sunglasses in bright sunshine.
>
> **4** Look at photo A. Explain what the woman is doing to protect her child.

X-rays and gamma rays

X-rays and gamma rays have a higher frequency than ultraviolet radiation and they transfer more energy. They also pass into our bodies. If our bodies absorb too much X-ray or gamma radiation it may cause **mutations** to the DNA in our cells or damage cells in other ways. Mutations may kill cells or cause cancer.

> **5** Two different electromagnetic waves have frequencies of 10 000 Hz and 100 000 Hz. Explain which wave is likely to cause the most harm if it is absorbed by your body.

Key points

- Microwaves cause heating of body cells. Infrared radiation can cause skin burns.
- Ultraviolet radiation can damage the skin and eyes. It can lead to skin cancer.
- X-rays and gamma rays can damage cells and lead to mutations.
- Higher frequency electromagnetic waves are more dangerous than lower frequency electromagnetic waves.

Checkpoint

How confidently can you answer the Progression questions?

Foundation

F1 State one danger to your body of:

 a microwaves

 b infrared radiation

 c ultraviolet radiation

 d X-rays and gamma rays.

Strengthen

S1 Draw a table with a row for each part of the electromagnetic spectrum mentioned on these pages. In the second column list any dangers that you know of for each part of the spectrum.

S2 Use your table to help you to explain how the frequency relates to the potential danger.

P2g Inside atoms

ELC P1B.11, P1B.12, P1B.13, P1B.14, P1B.15, P1B.16, P1B.17 **GCSE** P6.1, P6.2, P6.3, P6.4, P6.5, P6.6

Progression questions

- What are the relative masses and charges of the particles that make up atoms?
- What do the atomic number and mass number of an element tell us about its atoms?
- What are isotopes of an element?

A These bars are made from pure gold. What do all the atoms in the bars have in common?

All matter is made up of **atoms**. Atoms are made up of even smaller particles called **protons**, **neutrons** and **electrons**.

- Protons are in the **nucleus** of atoms. They have a **relative mass** of 1 and a charge of +1 (a positive charge).
- Neutrons are also found in the nucleus of atoms. They have a relative mass of 1 and no charge.
- Electrons are very tiny, negatively charged particles that move around the nucleus. They have a charge of −1 (a negative charge). The mass of an electron is so small that we usually ignore it.

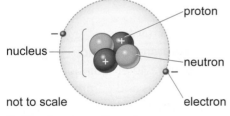

B the structure of an atom

> **1** Where are protons found in an atom?

All the atoms of an element have the same number of protons in their nucleus. The number of protons is called the **atomic number**.

> **2** All the atoms in the gold in photo A have 79 protons in their nuclei. What is the atomic number of gold?

The number of electrons in an atom is the same as the number of protons. The positive charges on the protons cancel out the negative charges on the electrons. This means that an atom has no overall charge. We say it is neutral.

3 All gold atoms have 79 protons in their nuclei. How many electrons are there in a gold atom? Explain your answer.

Most of the mass of an atom is in its nucleus, because this is where the protons and neutrons are. The total number of protons and neutrons in an atom is called the **atomic mass**, or the **mass number**.

4 Which two particles:

    a are found in the nucleus of an atom

    b have a charge

    c have a relative mass of 1?

Isotopes

Atoms of the same element do not always have the same number of neutrons. Atoms of an element with different numbers of neutrons are called **isotopes** of the element.

6 protons + 6 neutrons
mass number = 12

6 protons + 8 neutrons
mass number = 14

C two isotopes of carbon

5 Look at diagram C.

    a What is the atomic number of carbon?

    b The two atoms in diagram C are isotopes of carbon. Explain what this means.

6 An isotope of hydrogen has one proton and two neutrons. What is its:

    a atomic number

    b mass number?

Key points

- Protons have a relative mass of 1 and a charge of +1. They are found in the nuclei of atoms. The number of protons in an atom is its atomic number.
- Neutrons have a relative mass of 1 and no charge. They are found in the nuclei of atoms. Isotopes of an element have different numbers of neutrons.
- Electrons are tiny particles with a charge of −1. They move around the nucleus. An atom has the same number of protons and electrons, so the atom is neutral.

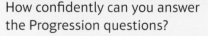

Checkpoint

How confidently can you answer the Progression questions?

Foundation

F1 Draw a diagram of an atom. Label all the parts. Use diagram B to help you.

F2 Give the mass and charge on protons, neutrons and electrons.

Strengthen

S1 Write glossary definitions for these terms: atomic number, electron, isotopes, mass number, neutron, proton.

P2h Radioactive decay

ELC P1B.18, P1B.19, P1B.20 GCSE P6.10, P6.12, P6.13, P6.14, P6.15, P6.18

Progression questions

- What is radioactive decay?
- What happens to an atom when it decays?
- What is background radiation?

A Did you know that most foods are radioactive?

Some isotopes are **unstable**. This means that the nucleus of the atom can easily change. Atoms can change by **radioactive decay**.

We cannot predict when a particular atom will decay. It is a **random** process.

> **1** What is an unstable atom?
>
> **2** Why do we call radioactive decay a random process?

Types of radiation

An unstable nucleus can decay by emitting **alpha particles**, **beta particles** or **gamma rays**. These processes are called alpha, beta and gamma radiation. When a nucleus emits an alpha particle or a beta particle, the atom changes into a different element. When a nucleus emits a gamma ray, the atom stays the same element.

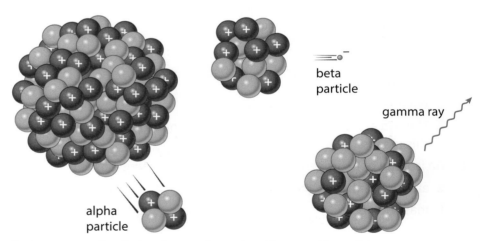

B three types of radiation that can be emitted by unstable nuclei

> **3** Write down two types of radiation that cause an atom to become a different element.

Alpha particles have two protons and two neutrons. This is the same as the nucleus of a helium atom. When an alpha particle leaves a nucleus, the nucleus that is left has a different atomic number and mass number. Therefore, the atom has become a different element.

A beta particle is an electron that comes from the nucleus of an atom. It is formed when a neutron in the nucleus becomes a proton and an electron. The electron leaves the nucleus. The nucleus that is left has a different atomic number, so the atom has become a different element.

Gamma rays are a form of electromagnetic radiation.

Background radiation

We can detect radiation using **photographic film**. This becomes dark when radiation reaches it. We can also detect radiation using a **Geiger–Müller (GM) tube** connected to a counter. The counter clicks each time radiation is detected.

A GM tube detects some radiation all the time. This is called **background radiation**. Most things around us contain small amounts of radioactive substances, including the ground and our food and drink. **Cosmic rays** are a form of radiation that comes from space. Some rocks give out a radioactive gas called **radon**. Radioactive materials are used in hospitals to **diagnose** problems and for some treatments. This also adds to the background radiation.

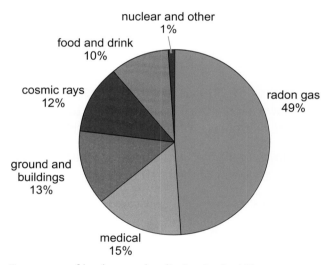

D sources of background radiation in the UK

6 Write down three different sources of background radiation.

Key points

- Unstable atoms emit alpha particles, beta particles or gamma rays.
- Radioactive decay is a random process.
- If a nucleus emits an alpha particle or a beta particle, the atom becomes a different element.
- We can detect radiation using photographic film or a Geiger–Müller tube.
- Background radiation comes from space and from the materials around us.

4 **a** What is an alpha particle made up of?

  b What is a beta particle?

C using a GM tube and counter to measure radiation

5 Name two different ways in which we can detect radiation.

Checkpoint

How confidently can you answer the Progression questions?

Foundation

F1 a Describe three different things that an unstable atom can emit.

  b State which of these makes the remaining atom into a different element.

Strengthen

S1 State three ways in which an unstable atom can decay. In each case, say how this affects the atom that is left.

S2 Describe what background radiation is and how radiation can be detected.

P2i Half-life

ELC P1B.21, P1B.22, P1B.23, P1B.24 **GCSE** P6.23, P6.24, P6.25, P6.27

Progression questions

- How does the activity of a radioactive substance change over time?
- What does the half-life of a radioactive substance tell us?
- How can we use the half-life to work out how much of a substance decays?

A Some radioactive waste is stored underground. How do scientists know how long it will stay radioactive?

When an unstable nucleus undergoes radioactive decay, it changes to become more stable. The **activity** of any radioactive substance is the number of nuclear decays per second. The unit for activity is the **becquerel** (**Bq**). One becquerel is one nuclear decay each second.

> **1** What is the unit for measuring the activity of a radioactive substance?
>
> **2** A substance has an activity of 1000 Bq. How many nuclei are decaying each second?

Every radioactive isotope has a **half-life**. The half-life is the time it takes for the activity of a source to halve. The activity of a source can be plotted on a graph. The shape of the graph is always like graph B, where the line never gets to zero.

> **3** What does the half-life of a radioactive substance tell us?

The half-life is also the time it takes for half the unstable nuclei in a sample to decay. This is shown in diagram C. It does not matter how much of the isotope we have, the half-life is always the same for that particular isotope.

The activity goes down over time. This is because when unstable nuclei in a sample decay, there are fewer of them left to decay.

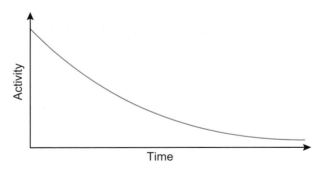

B how the activity of a radioactive source changes with time

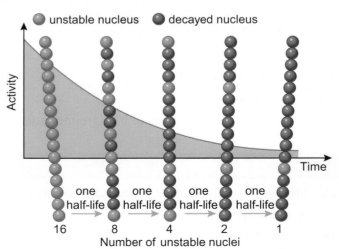

C After every half-life there are only half the number of unstable nuclei left.

Half-life calculations

Graph D shows the activity of two different radioactive substances. You can see that substance A has a shorter half-life than substance B because its activity goes down more quickly.

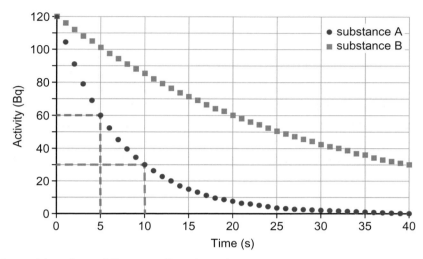

D the activity of two different radioactive substances

Worked example

Look at graph D. What is the half-life of substance A?

At time zero the activity of A is 120 Bq. Half of 120 Bq is 60 Bq.

The activity is 60 Bq at a time of 5 s. This means the half-life of A is 5 s.

You can check this answer by finding out how long it takes for the activity to halve again.

Half of 60 Bq is 30 Bq. The activity of A is 30 Bq at 10 s. It has taken 5 s for the activity to halve again.

4 Look at graph D. Work out the half-life of substance B.

5 At what time will the activity of substance A be 15 Bq?

Key points

- The activity of a source is the number of radioactive decays in 1 s. It is measured in becquerel (Bq).
- The activity of a source goes down over time. The half-life is the time it takes for the activity to halve.
- The half-life is also the time it takes for half of the unstable nuclei in a substance to decay.

Checkpoint

How confidently can you answer the Progression questions?

Foundation

F1 State what these words mean:
   a activity
   b half-life.

Strengthen

S1 Explain what two things the half-life of a radioactive substance tells us.

S2 Look at graph D. At what time will the activity of substance B be 15 Bq?

P2j Dangers of radioactivity

ELC P1B.25, P1B.26, P1B.27 **GCSE** P6.11, P6.29, P6.31, P6.32

Progression questions

- What are the dangers of radiation?
- What precautions should be taken to protect people using radiation?
- What is the difference between irradiation and contamination?

A Why is this person using gloves and tongs to handle a radioactive source?

Radiation from radioactive isotopes can harm our bodies. Radiation can damage cells, such as by causing skin burns. It can also damage the **DNA** inside a cell and cause **mutations**. Mutations in cells can cause cancer. Too much radiation can kill cells.

> **1** State two ways in which radiation can harm cells.

We are exposed to background radiation all the time. However, we are usually only exposed to small amounts so the risk of harm is low. People who work with radioactive materials could be exposed to more radiation. They must take precautions to minimise the risks from radiation.

You are **irradiated** if alpha, beta or gamma radiation from a radioactive source reaches your body from outside. People working with radioactive materials can reduce their risk of irradiation by:

- keeping as far away from radioactive sources as they can, for example by handling sources with tongs
- keeping their exposure time as short as possible
- storing radioactive sources in lead-lined boxes when they are not being used (the lead absorbs the radiation).

> **2** Write down two precautions to reduce the risk of irradiation.

You are **contaminated** with a radioactive source if the radioactive material gets onto your skin or inside your body. This can cause more harm than irradiation because the source is very close to you.

People working with radioactive materials can reduce their risk of contamination by:

- wearing gloves and protective clothing to stop them getting radioactive material on their skin or clothes
- wearing a breathing mask so they do not breathe in any radioactive particles.

> **3** Write down two precautions to reduce the risk of contamination.

B Radioactive sources in schools are stored in lead-lined boxes.

Alpha, beta and gamma radiation are **ionising radiations**. When radiation hits an atom it can make it lose an electron to form an ion. When atoms in our bodies are turned into ions they can react with other atoms and damage cells.

> **4** Why are alpha, beta and gamma radiations called ionising radiations?

Sources of ionising radiation are used in hospitals to find out what is wrong with some patients. They are also used to treat some diseases. Radiation is only used when the benefits are greater than the harm the radiation might cause. The patient is given the smallest possible amount of radiation.

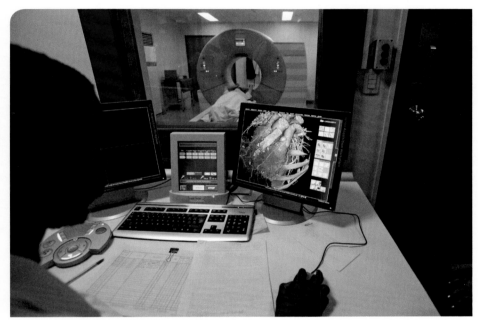

C One way in which doctors can protect themselves is by controlling machines that use radiation from a different room.

> **5** A patient being treated for cancer needs a certain amount of radiation. Explain why the patient is only given this amount and no more.

Key points

- Radiation can damage or kill cells. It can cause DNA in cells to mutate.
- Irradiation is when radiation reaches or passes through the body. Contamination is when a radioactive material gets onto or into the body.
- Precautions to reduce harm include keeping sources as far away as possible, wearing gloves and protective clothing, and keeping the time of exposure to radiation as short as possible.

Checkpoint

How confidently can you answer the Progression questions?

Foundation

F1 Look at photo A. Explain why the person is:

   a wearing gloves

   b using tongs to handle the radioactive source.

Strengthen

S1 What are the hazards posed by radiation?

S2 Describe the difference between irradiation and contamination.

Electromagnetic waves

Infrared and ultraviolet waves have different frequencies. Both types of wave can have harmful effects on humans. Compare and contrast the harmful effects of infrared and ultraviolet waves. **(6 marks)**

Plan your answer

A 'compare and contrast' question means you need to give at least one similarity between the two things being compared, and at least one difference. So a student plan might look like this:

- both damage skin

- IR causes burns

- UV damages eyes as well, and causes skin cancer

....

Student answer

Infrared waves and ultraviolet waves can both damage our skin [A]. Infrared can cause skin burns [B]. Ultraviolet waves can damage our eyes and damage cells in our skin that can lead to skin cancer [C].

[A] This is a similarity between the harm caused by the two types of radiation.

[B] The student has mentioned a harmful effect of infrared.

[C] This mentions the harmful effects of ultraviolet. This is where the answer contrasts the harm caused by the two types of radiation.

....

Verdict

This is a good answer because it mentions the different types of harm that can be caused by each type of wave. It would be a strong answer if it also linked ideas together by pointing out that the higher frequency waves are more harmful.

P3 Electricity and magnets

We rely on electricity for almost everything we do at home and at school. Many electrical devices also use magnets to make them work. Electricity is very useful, but we need to know how to use it safely.

In this unit you will learn how we can measure and control electricity. You will learn how electricity is used in electromagnets, and how it is used safely in our homes.

The learning journey

Previously you will have learnt at KS3:

- how symbols can be used to represent circuits
- about series and parallel circuits
- how to measure current and voltage.

In this unit you will learn:

- how to calculate the charge in a circuit
- about resistance and how the resistance of some components can be changed
- how to calculate the power in an electric circuit
- about magnets and electromagnets
- how electricity gets to our homes and how we use it safely.

P3a Electrical circuits

ELC P2A.1, P2A.2, P2A.3, P2A.4, P2A.5 **GCSE** P10.2, P10.3, P10.4, P10.7, P10.8, P10.9, P10.10

Progression questions

- How do we use diagrams to represent circuits?
- How do we measure current and voltage?
- How do we calculate the amount of charge flowing in a circuit?

A How are the spotlights for this stage controlled?

The **lamps** in photo B are not lit up because the **switch** is open. The open switch makes a gap in the circuit. The lamps will light up when the switch is closed.

> **1** What will happen if the switch in photo B is closed?

B lamps in a series circuit

We can use symbols to draw diagrams of circuits. Diagram C is a diagram for the circuit in photo B.

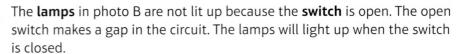

C a series circuit

The circuit in diagram C is a **series circuit**. All the components are in one loop of wire. We say the lamps are **in series** with each other.

> **2** Look at diagram C. Draw the symbols for:
>   **a** a lamp   **b** a battery.

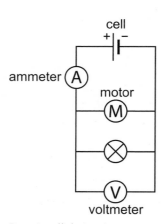

D a parallel circuit

The circuit in diagram D is a **parallel circuit**. There is more than one branch. The lamp and the motor are **in parallel** with each other.

Measuring electricity

The **ammeter** in circuit D measures the **current** in part of the circuit. Ammeters are connected in series. The unit for measuring current is the **amp** (**A**).

The **voltmeter** is measuring the **voltage** across the lamp. The voltage is sometimes called the **potential difference**. Voltmeters are always connected in parallel. The unit for measuring voltage is the **volt** (**V**).

> **3** Name the component used to measure:
>
> **a** current
>
> **b** voltage.
>
> **4** Describe how ammeters and voltmeters should be connected in a circuit.

An electric current is a flow of **charge**. The charge flows around a complete circuit when there is a cell or battery to provide a voltage. The unit for measuring charge is the **coulomb** (**C**). The current is the rate of flow of charge (how much charge flows in a certain time).

We can calculate the amount of charge that flows in a circuit using this equation:

$$\text{charge (C)} = \text{current (A)} \times \text{time (s)}$$

Worked example W1

A current of 5 A flows for 60 s. Calculate the amount of charge that has flowed through the circuit.

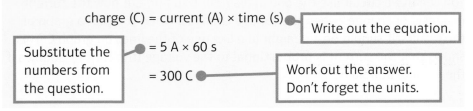

charge (C) = current (A) × time (s) — Write out the equation.

Substitute the numbers from the question. — = 5 A × 60 s

= 300 C — Work out the answer. Don't forget the units.

> **5** A current of 2 A flows for 30 s. Calculate the amount of charge that has flowed through the circuit.

Key points

- A series circuit has one continuous loop. A parallel circuit has two or more branches.
- Ammeters are used to measure current. They are used in series.
- Voltmeters are used to measure voltage. They are used in parallel.
- The charge in a circuit can be calculated using the equation
$$\text{charge (C)} = \text{current (A)} \times \text{time (s)}$$

Checkpoint

How confidently can you answer the Progression questions?

Foundation

F1 Look at circuit E.

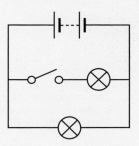

E

a List the components in the circuit.

b State whether this is a series or parallel circuit.

F2 A current of 4 A flows in a circuit for 2 s. Calculate the charge that flows in the circuit.

Strengthen

S1 Draw a diagram of a series circuit that includes a cell, two lamps, an ammeter and a voltmeter.

S2 A current of 0.5 A flows in a circuit for 5 minutes. Calculate the charge that has flowed through the circuit.

P3b Resistance

ELC P2A.6, P2A.7, P2A.8 **GCSE** P10.12, P10.13, P10.14, P10.15, P10.16, P10.18

Progression questions

- What is electrical resistance?
- How does the resistance in a circuit affect the current?
- How can we calculate the voltage needed to cause a certain current?

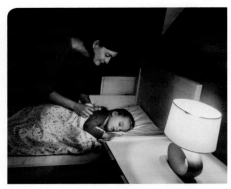

A How can you change the brightness of a light?

The size of the current in a circuit depends on the voltage of the cell or battery. If you use a battery with a higher voltage, the current will be greater and lamps in the circuit will be brighter.

> **1** You change the battery in a circuit to one with a higher voltage. Describe what happens to
>
> **a** the current
>
> **b** the brightness of lamps in the circuit.

The size of the current also depends on the **resistance**. A component with a high resistance makes it harder for the charge to flow, so the current is smaller. The unit for measuring resistance is the **ohm (Ω)**.

A **resistor** is designed to control the size of the current in a circuit. You can change the resistance of a **variable resistor** by moving a slider or turning a knob. The resistance of a **fixed resistor** cannot be changed.

> **2** What is the difference between a variable resistor and a fixed resistor?

Voltage–current graphs

You can use a circuit like the one in diagram B to find out how the current in a resistor changes when the voltage changes. When you plot a graph of the results, it should be a straight line like one of the lines on graph C. This shows that the current is **proportional** to the voltage (the current doubles if the voltage doubles).

The variable resistor is used to change the current in the circuit.

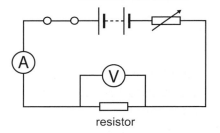

resistor

B This circuit can be used to investigate how the current through a resistor changes when the voltage changes.

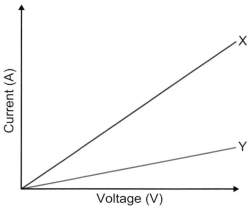

C Voltage–current graphs for fixed resistors are always a straight line through the origin.

> **3** Describe how the current in a fixed resistor changes when the voltage increases.

214

Resistors in series and parallel

If you put two resistors (or other components) in a circuit in series, the total resistance of the circuit increases. If you put them in parallel, the overall resistance of the circuit decreases. This is because there are alternative paths that the current can follow.

> **4** Look at diagrams C and D in topic P3a Electrical circuits. All the lamps are the same as each other. Explain which circuit has the greatest overall resistance.

Calculating the voltage

We can calculate the voltage needed to make a certain current flow using this equation:

$$\text{voltage (V)} = \text{current (A)} \times \text{resistance (}\Omega\text{)}$$

Worked example

The resistance in a circuit is 50 Ω. Calculate the voltage needed to make a 2 A current flow.

voltage (V) = current (A) × resistance (Ω)

    = 2 A × 50 Ω

    = 100 V

> **5** The resistance in a circuit is 8 Ω. Calculate the voltage needed to make a 3 A current flow.

Checkpoint

How confidently can you answer the Progression questions?

Foundation

F1 Describe two different ways of increasing the resistance of a circuit.

F2 The resistance in a circuit is 20 Ω. Calculate the voltage needed to make a 0.5 A current flow.

Strengthen

S1 The resistance in a circuit is 200 Ω. The current is 3 mA (0.003 A). Calculate the voltage being supplied to the circuit.

S2 Look at graph C. Explain how this shows you that X has a lower resistance than Y.

Key points

- Resistance is a way of saying how easy or difficult it is for electricity to flow through a component.
- You can use a variable resistor to change the current in a circuit.
- You can calculate the voltage using this equation:

  voltage = current × resistance

- A graph of voltage against current for a fixed resistor is a straight line through the origin.

P3c More about resistance

ELC P2A.8, P2A.9, P2A.10, P2A.11 **GCSE** P10.18, P10.22, P10.23, P10.26, P10.32

Progression questions

- How do we use electricity at home?
- How does changing the voltage affect the resistance of a filament lamp?
- How does current change with voltage for a diode?

A What is making the grill in this cooker glow red hot?

We use electricity for many different things. Some devices use electricity from the **mains supply**. These include cookers, heaters and washing machines. The electricity is used for heating or to make motors work. All these devices need a lot of energy to work.

Some electrical devices only need a small amount of energy. These can use energy stored in batteries.

1 Name two machines that use electricity from the mains supply.
2 Why do washing machines need electricity from the mains supply?
3 Name two devices that use energy stored in batteries.

All electrical components get hot when electricity flows through them, including wires and resistors. This is useful in electric cookers and heaters. In other devices it is not useful. The thermal energy **dissipated** (spread out in the surroundings) by heating is then wasted energy.

A **filament lamp** is a light bulb with a coil of thin wire inside it. When the wire carries a current it gets very hot and glows. Graph B is a voltage–current graph for a filament lamp.

4 What is a filament lamp?

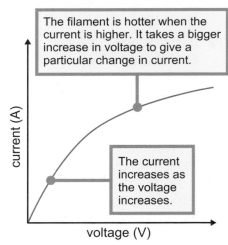

The filament is hotter when the current is higher. It takes a bigger increase in voltage to give a particular change in current.

The current increases as the voltage increases.

current (A)

voltage (V)

B voltage–current graph for a filament lamp

The current in any component increases when you increase the voltage across it. The filament in a lamp gets hotter when the current is greater. This increases its resistance. You can see this on graph B, because the line becomes less steep as the voltage gets higher. This shows that the current is increasing less and less as the voltage increases.

> **5** Describe the shape of the line on graph B.

A **diode** is a component with a resistance that depends on the direction of the current. Graph C shows how the current changes when the voltage changes.

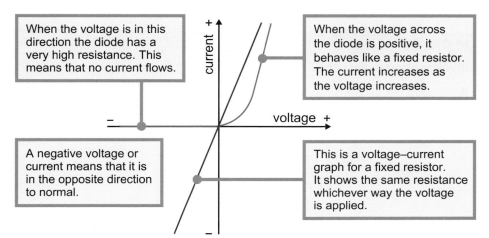

When the voltage is in this direction the diode has a very high resistance. This means that no current flows.

When the voltage across the diode is positive, it behaves like a fixed resistor. The current increases as the voltage increases.

A negative voltage or current means that it is in the opposite direction to normal.

This is a voltage–current graph for a fixed resistor. It shows the same resistance whichever way the voltage is applied.

C voltage–current graph for a diode (red line) and a fixed resistor (blue line)

D diode symbol

> **6** Explain why a diode only lets current flow in one direction.

Key points

- Electrical components get hot when a current flows. Some of the energy is transferred to the surroundings by heating.
- Electrical appliances transfer energy from the mains supply or energy stored in batteries.
- The resistance of a filament lamp increases as the filament gets hotter.
- Diodes only allow current to flow in one direction.

Checkpoint

How confidently can you answer the Progression questions?

Foundation

F1 Look at graph B above, and graph C in the previous topic, P3b Resistance. Describe the shapes of the lines on a voltage–current graph for a filament lamp and a fixed resistor.

F2 Describe how the resistance of a filament lamp changes as the voltage increases.

Strengthen

S1 Look at graphs B and C in this topic. Compare and contrast the graph for a fixed resistor with that of:

    a a filament lamp

    b a diode.

A The filament inside a lamp is a coil of very thin wire. It gives out light when the electricity flowing through it makes the filament so hot that it glows.

The resistance of a component is a way of saying how difficult it is for electricity to flow through it. We cannot measure resistance directly. We must calculate it from measurements of current and voltage. We can use this equation:

$$\text{resistance } (\Omega) = \frac{\text{voltage (V)}}{\text{current (A)}}$$

Circuit B can be used to investigate the resistance of a fixed resistor. The voltage across the resistor can be changed by adding more cells to the battery, or by changing the setting on a power pack.

Method

Investigating resistance

A Set up circuit B. Use a power pack that can provide different voltages (potential differences). Ask your teacher to check your circuit before you switch the power pack on.

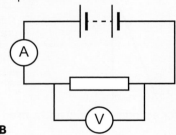

B

B Set the power pack to its lowest voltage setting and switch it on. Write down the readings on the ammeter and voltmeter. Switch the power pack off.

C Repeat step B for five different voltage settings.

D Replace the resistor in the circuit with a filament lamp. Repeat steps B and C.

Resistors in series and parallel circuits

E Set up circuit C. This is a series circuit. Ask your teacher to check your circuit before you switch on.

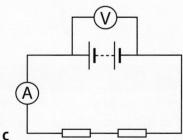

C

F Set the power pack to its lowest voltage setting. Write down the readings on the ammeter and the voltmeter. Switch the power pack off.

Safety ⚠

Bulbs and resistors can get hot.

G Repeat step F for five different voltage settings.

H Now set up circuit D. This is a parallel circuit. Ask your teacher to check your circuit before you switch the power pack on.

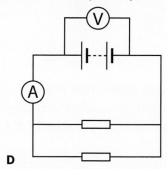

D

I Repeat steps F and G for circuit D.

Exam-style questions

1 What are the units for measuring resistance? *(1 mark)*

2 Table E shows a set of results from the 'Investigating resistance' investigation. Plot a graph to present these results. Show both sets of results on the same axes. Draw a curve of best fit through the points for each component. *(6 marks)*

3 Look at table E. Use the readings at 1 V and at 6 V to calculate the resistance of:

  a the resistor *(3 marks)*

  b the filament lamp. *(2 marks)*

4 Look at your graph from question **2** and your answers to question **3**. Use these to help you to write a conclusion for the results of the investigation for:

  a the resistor *(3 marks)*

  b the filament lamp. *(3 marks)*

5 Describe how you could find out if your conclusion from question **4** applies to all resistors or all filament lamps. *(3 marks)*

6 Table F shows some results from the second investigation, 'Resistors in series and parallel circuits'. Use the voltage and currents in table F to calculate the total resistance in:

  a circuit C *(2 marks)*

  b circuit D. *(1 mark)*

7 Each resistor in circuits C and D has a resistance of 8 Ω. A circuit with just one of these resistors in it would have a resistance of 8 Ω.

8 Use your answers to question **6** to help you describe how the resistance of a circuit changes:

  a when you add a resistor in series *(1 mark)*

  b when you add a resistor in parallel. *(1 mark)*

Voltage (V)	Current (A)	
	Resistor	Filament lamp
0	0	0
1	0.2	0.12
2	0.4	0.23
3	0.6	0.33
4	0.9	0.41
5	1.0	0.47
6	1.2	0.53

E results for questions 2 and 3

Circuit	Voltage (V)	Current (A)
series (C)	4	0.25
parallel (D)	4	1.00

F results for question 6

P3d Electrical power

ELC P2A.12, P2A.13 GCSE P10.27, P10.28, P10.29, P10.30, P10.31

Progression questions

- What affects the power in an electrical circuit?
- How can we calculate power from energy and time?
- How can we calculate power from current and voltage?

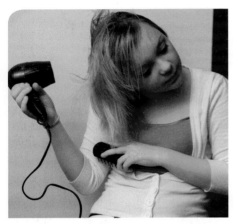

A How can you tell how fast a hairdryer will dry your hair?

B This label from a hairdryer shows that the hairdryer has a power of 1500 W.

All electrical appliances have a label that shows their **power**. Power is the amount of energy transferred by the appliance every second. The unit for power is the **watt** (**W**). One watt is one **joule** (**J**) of energy transferred every second.

> **1 a** State the meaning of power.
>
> **b** What are the units for measuring power?
>
> **2** A hairdryer has a power of 1500 W. How many joules of energy does it transfer each second?

We can calculate the power of an appliance using this equation:

$$\text{power (W)} = \frac{\text{energy transferred (J)}}{\text{time taken (s)}}$$

Worked example W1

A hairdryer transfers 540 000 J of energy in 5 minutes (300 s). Calculate the power of the hairdryer.

$$\text{power (W)} = \frac{\text{energy transferred (J)}}{\text{time taken (s)}}$$
$$= \frac{540\,000\ \text{J}}{300\ \text{s}}$$
$$= 1800\ \text{W}$$

C Blackpool illuminations

> **3** The lights in Blackpool transfer 250 000 kJ of energy every minute. Calculate the power used by the lights.

We can also calculate the power of an electrical appliance from the current and the voltage. The higher the current or voltage, the greater the power. We can use this equation:

power (W) = current (A) × voltage (V)

Worked example W2

An iron uses the mains electricity supply at 230 V. A current of 4.2 A flows while it is being used. Calculate the power of the iron.

power (W) = current (A) × voltage (V)

= 4.2 A × 230 V

= 966 W

4 A microwave oven uses the mains supply at 230 V. The current is 3.5 A. Calculate the power of the oven.

We can combine the two equations to work out the energy transferred by an appliance:

energy transferred (J) = current (A) × voltage (V) × time (s)

Worked example W3

The iron in worked example W2 is switched on for 5 minutes (300 s). Calculate the energy it transfers.

energy transferred (J) = current (A) × voltage (V) × time (s)

= 4.2 A × 230 V × 300 s

= 289 800 J

5 The microwave oven in question **4** is switched on for 2 minutes. Calculate the energy it transfers.

Key points

- Power is the amount of energy transferred each second. It is measured in watts (W): 1 W = 1 J/s
- We can calculate power in two different ways:

$$\text{power (W)} = \frac{\text{energy transferred (J)}}{\text{time taken (s)}}$$

power (W) = current (A) × voltage (V)

- We can calculate the energy transferred by an appliance using this equation:

energy transferred (J) = current (A) × voltage (V) × time (s)

Checkpoint

How confidently can you answer the Progression questions?

Foundation

F1 A motor transfers 500 J of energy in 10 s. Calculate its power.

F2 An oven uses a voltage of 230 V and a current of 9 A. Calculate its power.

Strengthen

S1 A TV transfers 3600 kJ of energy in 5 hours. Calculate the power of the TV.

S2 A torch uses batteries that provide 3 V. The current through the bulb is 15 mA. Calculate the power of the torch.

P3e Magnets and electromagnets

ELC P2A.16, P2A.17, P2A.18, P2A.19, P2A.20 **GCSE** P12.1, P12.2, P12.4, P12.5, P12.7, P12.8

Progression questions

- How do magnets affect each other?
- What is the shape of the magnetic field around a magnet?
- What factors affect the magnetic field around a wire?

A How do these letters stay on the fridge door?

Magnets attract **magnetic materials**. Magnetic materials include the metals iron, cobalt and nickel. Some **alloys** (mixtures of different metals) are also magnetic materials. Steel is an alloy that is a magnetic material.

> **1** Name four magnetic materials.

The magnets in diagram B are bar magnets. The two ends of a bar magnet are called the north pole and the south pole. Magnets can **attract** or **repel** each other, depending on which ends are close to each other.

'Unlike' poles attract each other.

'Like' poles repel each other.

B A north and a south pole attract each other. Two north poles or two south poles repel each other.

> **2** What are the names for the two ends of a bar magnet?
>
> **3** Describe how to arrange two bar magnets so they attract each other.

The space around a magnet where it can attract magnetic materials is called the **magnetic field**. We can use a **plotting compass** to find the shape of the magnetic field around a bar magnet.

- The direction of the field is from the north pole of the magnet to the south pole of the magnet.
- The field is strongest where the lines are closest together.

Magnets are used in electric motors, generators, loudspeakers and other electrical devices. They are also used for simpler things such as door latches and knife holders.

> **4** Give two uses for magnets.

C magnetic field around a bar magnet

Electricity and magnetism

Electricity can produce magnetic fields. Diagram D shows the shape of the electric field around a wire with a current flowing through it.

- The direction of the field changes if the direction of the current changes.
- The field is strongest closer to the wire.
- The strength of the field increases if the current increases.

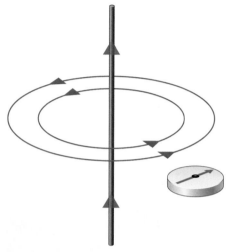

D The plotting compass shows the direction of the magnetic field around a wire carrying a current.

A coil of wire with a current flowing through it is an **electromagnet**. This is also called a **temporary magnet**. Its magnetic field is only there when a current is flowing. Temporary magnets are used in earphones and loudspeakers. Bar magnets are **permanent magnets**, because they are always magnetic.

> **5** Describe the shape of the magnetic field around a wire when a current flows through it.

Key points

- Magnets attract magnetic materials (iron, cobalt, nickel, steel).
- The north pole of a magnet attracts a south pole and repels a north pole.
- The magnetic field of a bar magnet goes from its north pole to its south pole.
- A wire with a current flowing in it has a circular magnetic field around it. The field is stronger if the current is higher. It is also stronger closer to the wire.

Checkpoint

How confidently can you answer the Progression questions?

Foundation

F1 Draw a diagram to show the shape of the magnetic field around:

  a a bar magnet

  b a wire with a current flowing through it.

Strengthen

S1 Describe the factors that affect the strength and direction of the magnetic field around a wire with a current flowing through it.

S2 Describe the difference between a permanent magnet and a temporary magnet.

P3f Electricity in the home

ELC P2A.14, P2A.15, P2A.21, P2A.22, P2A.23, P2A.24, P2A.25, P2A.26, P2A.27
GCSE P10.33, P10.34, P10.35, P10.36, P10.38, P10.39, P13.6

Progression questions

- What is the difference between direct and alternating current?
- What do earth wires and fuses do?
- How does electricity get from power stations to our homes?

A How do we stop fires like this happening?

Electricity from batteries always flows in the same direction. We call this a **direct current** (**d.c.**). Electricity supplied by the mains changes direction many times each second. This is called **alternating current** (**a.c.**). In the UK the mains supply has a voltage of 230 V and a **frequency** of 50 Hz.

> **1** What is the voltage and frequency of the mains supply in the UK?

The mains wiring cables in our homes contain three wires. These are called the **live**, **neutral** and **earth wires**. These must be connected to the correct pins in a plug.

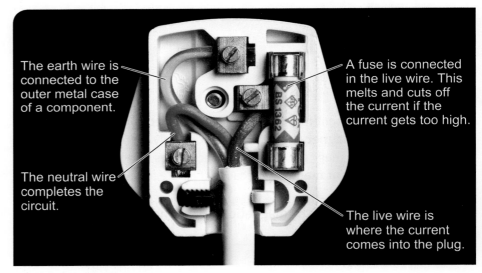

The earth wire is connected to the outer metal case of a component.

A fuse is connected in the live wire. This melts and cuts off the current if the current gets too high.

The neutral wire completes the circuit.

The live wire is where the current comes into the plug.

B the inside of a plug

Electrical wiring has various safety features.

- Switches are always placed in the live wire of a circuit so they can cut off the current.
- The earth wire stops users from getting an electric shock if something goes wrong with the appliance.
- If the current gets too high the **fuse** melts and cuts off the current. This stops the appliance from overheating and possibly causing a fire.
- **Circuit breakers** can be used to cut off the current if it gets too high.

> **2** Name the three wires inside mains wiring cables.
>
> **3** Explain why switches are always put in the live wire.

The national grid

Electricity is sent from power stations to users by a system of wires and cables called the **national grid**. The electricity is transmitted over long distances at very high voltages. This is because it helps to reduce the amount of energy wasted by heating the wires. The voltage of a.c. electricity can be changed using a **transformer**.

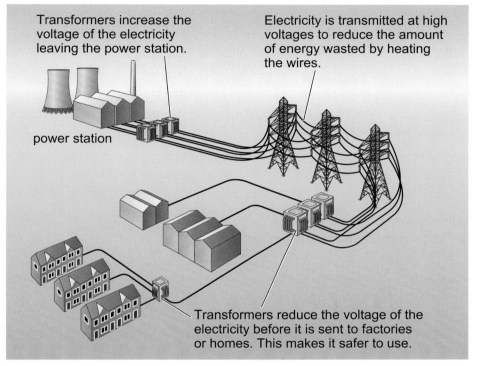

Transformers increase the voltage of the electricity leaving the power station.

Electricity is transmitted at high voltages to reduce the amount of energy wasted by heating the wires.

power station

Transformers reduce the voltage of the electricity before it is sent to factories or homes. This makes it safer to use.

C the national grid

4 What is used to change the voltage of an alternating current?
5 Why is electricity transmitted at very high voltages?

Key points

- Direct current from batteries always flows in one direction. Alternating current from power stations changes direction many times each second.
- The mains supply in the UK has a voltage of 230 V. It has a frequency of 50 Hz.
- Fuses, circuit breakers and earth wires protect people from shocks. They also prevent fires by cutting off the electricity if the current is too high.
- Electricity is sent around the country by the national grid. The national grid uses transformers to change the voltage.

Checkpoint

How confidently can you answer the Progression questions?

Foundation

F1 Describe how these things help us to use electricity safely:

  a earth wires

  b fuses and circuit breakers.

Strengthen

S1 Explain three ways in which plugs and appliances are made safe to use.

S2 Explain how electricity is sent from power stations to our homes.

Electric current

1. Washing machines and other appliances use alternating current (a.c.) from the mains supply. MP3 players and smart phones use direct current (d.c.) from batteries.

   Compare and contrast alternating and direct current. **(2 marks)**

Student answer

Alternating current changes direction all the time, but direct current is always in the same direction [A].

[A] This is correct, and is the difference between alternating and direct current. However, a 'compare and contrast' question needs at least one similarity between the two things being compared, and at least one difference. The student should also have stated that both types of current are a flow of charge.

Verdict

This is a poor answer. The student has correctly mentioned a difference between a.c. and d.c. but has not mentioned a similarity.

Diodes

2. Sketch a graph to show how the current in a diode changes when the voltage across it changes. **(3 marks)**

Student answer

PFYE/P3/SS/FigA –

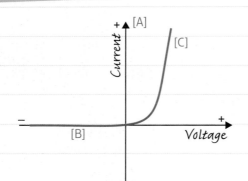

[A] The student has drawn and labelled a suitable set of axes. You do not need numbers on the axes for a sketch graph.

[B] They have correctly shown that there is no current when the voltage is in the negative direction.

[C] They have correctly shown that current increases with voltage when the current is in the positive direction.

Verdict

This is a good answer. The student has sketched a graph of the correct shape.

P4 Energy and particles

When water freezes it turns to ice or snow. What happens to water when it freezes, and why does it eventually melt again?

In this unit you will learn how we measure the energy transferred when forces do work, and how we use the particle model to explain the properties of solids, liquids and gases.

The learning journey

Previously you will have learnt at KS3:

- about the properties of solids, liquids and gases
- how particles are arranged in solids, liquids and gases
- that forces can transfer energy.

In this unit you will learn:

- how to calculate the energy transferred when a force moves through a distance
- how to calculate power
- about the arrangement of particles in solids, liquids and gases
- what happens when a substance changes state
- what causes gas pressure
- what happens when you stretch springs or other materials.

P4a Work and power

ELC P2B.1, P2B.2, P2B.3, P2B.4, P2B.5 **GCSE** P8.4, P8.5, P8.6, P8.7, P8.11, P8.12, P8.13, P8.14

Progression questions

- How can the energy of a system be changed?
- What is work done and how can we measure and calculate it?
- What is power and how can we calculate it?

A The cats are sitting on a warm car bonnet. Why are car bonnets warm after the car has been used?

B The girl is doing work by pulling the wheelbarrow.

Every time energy is transferred, some of it is wasted. This wasted energy usually ends up heating the surroundings. Energy can be transferred in different ways, such as:

- by forces
- by heating
- by electrical equipment.

> **1** State two different ways in which energy can be transferred.
>
> **2** A motor transfers 50 J of energy when it lifts a weight. The weight only stores 48 J of gravitational potential energy. Explain what has happened to the other 2 J of energy.

The girl in photo B is transferring energy by using a force to move the wheelbarrow. The energy transferred by a force is called **work done**. The work done depends on the size of the force and how far it moves. We can calculate work done using this equation:

$$\text{work done (J)} = \text{force (N)} \times \text{distance (m)}$$

Worked example W1

Danny pushes a box 3 m along the floor using a force of 200 N. Calculate the work Danny does.

work done (J) = force (N) × distance (m) — Write out the equation.

= 200 N × 3 m — Substitute numbers from the question.

= 600 J — Work out the answer. Don't forget the units.

> **3** A boy cycles 760 m using a force of 140 N. Calculate the work done.

Power is a way of saying how fast energy is transferred. If you walk up a flight of stairs you transfer a certain amount of energy. If you run up the same stairs you transfer the same amount of energy but your power is greater. This is because you have transferred the energy in a shorter time.

Power is measured in **watts (W)**. One watt is one joule of energy transferred every second. We can calculate the power when a force does work using this equation:

$$\text{power (W)} = \frac{\text{work done (J)}}{\text{time taken (s)}}$$

C This woman is doing work when she runs up the stairs, as she is moving the weight of her body.

Worked example W2

Sarah lifts a box onto a shelf. She does work of 60 J in 3 s. Calculate Sarah's power.

$$\text{power (W)} = \frac{\text{work done (J)}}{\text{time taken (s)}}$$
$$= \frac{60 \text{ J}}{3 \text{ s}}$$
$$= 20 \text{ W}$$

4 Fred does 1500 J of work when he runs up a flight of stairs. He takes 5 s to get up the stairs. Calculate his power.

Key points

- Energy is transferred by heating, by electrical equipment and when forces do work.
- Whenever work is done some energy is wasted. The wasted energy usually makes the surroundings hotter.
- We can calculate work done using this equation:
$$\text{work done (J)} = \text{force (N)} \times \text{distance (m)}$$
- Power is how fast work is done, and is measured in watts (W). We can calculate power using this equation:
$$\text{power (W)} = \frac{\text{work done (J)}}{\text{time taken (s)}}$$

Checkpoint

How confidently can you answer the Progression questions?

Foundation

F1 Fran pulls a wheelbarrow for 10 m, using a force of 40 N.

    a Calculate the work done.

    b It takes Fran 20 s to pull the wheelbarrow. Calculate her power.

Strengthen

S1 A winch takes 2 minutes to pull a log 30 m. The force is 4 kN.

    a Calculate the work done.

    b Calculate the power of the winch.

P4b Particles and density

ELC P2B.7, P2B.8, P2B.9, P2B.10, P2B.11, P2B.12 **GCSE** P14.1, P14.2, P14.4

Progression questions

- How are particles arranged in solids, liquids and gases?
- How do the particle arrangements in solids, liquids and gases explain their properties?
- How can we calculate the density of a substance?

A How and why are the properties of ice and water different?

Ice, water and water vapour are three different **states of matter** (solid, liquid and gas). The three states of matter have different properties because of the way in which **particles** in them are arranged.

> **1** List the three different states of matter.

solid

B particles in a solid

In solids the particles are held closely together in a fixed arrangement. The particles can **vibrate** about fixed positions but they cannot move around. This explains why solids keep their shape and usually cannot be **compressed**.

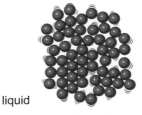

liquid

C particles in a liquid

In liquids the particles are still close together but they are not in a fixed arrangement. The particles can move past each other, through the liquid. This is why liquids flow and take the shape of their container. The particles are still very close together, so liquids usually cannot be compressed.

> **2** In which state of matter are the particles:
>
> **a** close together in fixed positions
>
> **b** far apart and moving around?
>
> **3** Explain why gases are compressible but solids and liquids are not.

gas

D particles in a gas

In a gas, the particles are far apart and moving around **randomly** in all directions. Gases are **compressible** and expand to fill their container.

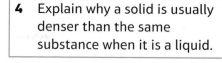

Density

The **density** of a substance is the mass of a certain volume of the substance. A solid is usually denser than the same substance as a liquid, because the particles in solids are closer together. Gases have very low densities because the particles in them are far apart.

4 Explain why a solid is usually denser than the same substance when it is a liquid.

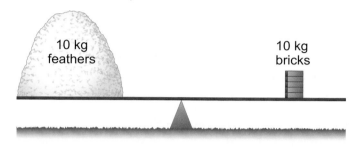

10 kg
feathers

10 kg
bricks

E The feathers have a lower density than the bricks because the same mass occupies a much larger volume.

We can calculate the density of a substance using the equation below. The units for density are usually kg/m³.

$$\text{density (kg/m}^3) = \frac{\text{mass (kg)}}{\text{volume (m}^3)}$$

Worked example

An iron girder has a volume of 0.9 m³. Its mass is 7074 kg. Calculate the density of iron.

$$\text{density (kg/m}^3) = \frac{\text{mass (kg)}}{\text{volume (m}^3)}$$

$$= \frac{7074 \text{ kg}}{0.9 \text{ m}^3}$$

$$= 7860 \text{ kg/m}^3$$

5 A log of wood has a mass of 1250 kg and a volume of 2.5 m³. Calculate its density.

Key points

- The particles in solids are held closely together in fixed arrangements. In liquids they are held close together but can move around. In gases the particles are far apart and moving randomly.

- Density is the mass of a certain volume of a substance.

- A solid is usually more dense than a liquid of the same substance because the particles are packed more closely together.

- We can calculate density using this equation:

$$\text{density (kg/m}^3) = \frac{\text{mass (kg)}}{\text{volume (m}^3)}$$

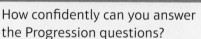

Checkpoint

How confidently can you answer the Progression questions?

Foundation

F1 Describe the arrangement and the movement of particles in:

  a solids

  b liquids

  c gases.

F2 A 500 kg block of aluminium has a volume of 0.185 m³. Calculate its density.

Strengthen

S1 Explain why a substance becomes less dense when it changes from a liquid to a gas.

S2 One litre (0.001 m³) of cooking oil has a mass of 800 g. Calculate its density.

The density of a substance is the mass of a certain volume of the substance. We can find the density of a substance by measuring its mass and volume and then calculating the density.

The units for density are usually kg/m³. However, a metre cubed is a large volume, and when we are finding densities in the school laboratory it is more convenient to measure the mass in grams (g) and the volume in centimetres cubed (cm³). When you calculate the density using these units, the density will be in g/cm³.

$$\text{density (g/cm}^3\text{)} = \frac{\text{mass (g)}}{\text{volume (cm}^3\text{)}}$$

Diagram A shows how to find the volume of an irregular shape.

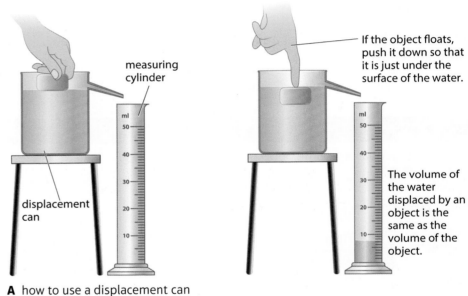

A how to use a displacement can

Method

Solids

A Find the mass of the solid and write it down.

B Stand a displacement can on the bench with its spout over a bowl. Fill the can with water until the water just starts to come out of the spout. Mop up any spilt water immediately.

C Hold a measuring cylinder under the spout and carefully drop your object into the can. If your object floats, carefully push it down until all of it is under the water. Your finger should not be in the water.

D Stand the measuring cylinder on the bench and read the volume of water you have collected. This is the same as the volume of your object. Write it down.

Liquids

E Put an empty beaker on a balance, and set the balance to zero.

F Use a measuring cylinder to measure 50 cm³ of a liquid and then pour the liquid into the beaker. Write down the reading on the balance. This is the mass of 50 cm³ of the liquid.

B a balance set to zero

Exam-style questions

1 Solids and liquids are both made up of tiny particles. Compare solids and liquids in terms of:

  a how the particles move *(2 marks)*

  b the spacing between the particles. *(1 mark)*

2 **a** Write down the formula for calculating the density of a substance. *(1 mark)*

  b Suggest suitable units for each of the quantities in the formula. *(1 mark)*

3 You need to find the differences in density between different concentrations of salty water.

  a List the apparatus you would need to carry out this investigation. *(3 marks)*

  b Write a method for your investigation. *(3 marks)*

  c Explain how you would make sure your investigation was a fair test. *(1 mark)*

4 A student found that the mass of 50 cm³ of cooking oil was 46 g. Calculate the density of the cooking oil. Give your answer in g/cm³. *(2 marks)*

5 A student found that the volume of a stone was 6 cm³. Its mass was 17 g. Calculate its density. *(2 marks)*

P4c Energy and changes of state

ELC P2B.13, P2B.14, P2B.15, P2B.16, P2B.17, P2B.18 **GCSE** P14.5, P14.6, P14.7, P14.12, P14.13

Progression questions

- What are changes of state and how do we make them happen?
- What happens when we heat a substance?
- What causes gas pressure?

A How much energy does it take to melt the butter?

When you heat a substance its temperature rises. If you give the same amount of energy to different substances, some will get hotter than others. This is because different substances have different **specific heat capacities**. The specific heat capacity is the amount of energy it takes to raise the temperature of 1 kg of the substance by 1 °C.

> **1** What happens to a substance when you heat it?

Substances can **change state** when they are heated or cooled.

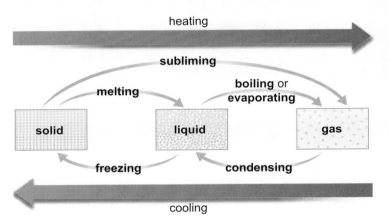

B changes of state

> **2** Look at diagram B. What is the name for the change of state:
> **a** from a gas to a liquid
> **b** from a liquid to a solid?

When a substance changes state the particles end up in a different arrangement. There are the same number of particles in the substance in each state so the mass stays the same. This is a **physical change**, because no new substances are formed and the substance recovers its original properties if the change is reversed. In **chemical changes** the change in the substances often cannot be reversed.

> **3** Explain why melting butter is a physical change.

When you **melt** a solid, energy is needed to overcome the forces between the particles and turn it into a liquid. The amount of energy it takes to make 1 kg of a substance change state is called the **specific latent heat**.

Graph C shows how the temperature of a substance changes as it is heated and absorbs energy.

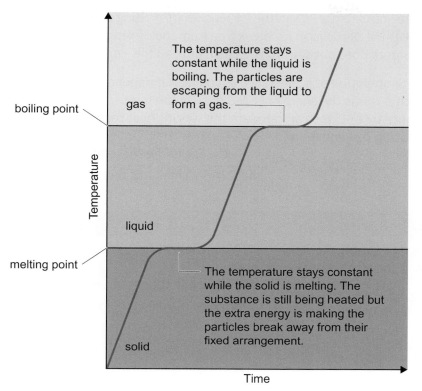

The temperature stays constant while the liquid is boiling. The particles are escaping from the liquid to form a gas.

The temperature stays constant while the solid is melting. The substance is still being heated but the extra energy is making the particles break away from their fixed arrangement.

Time

C how the temperature of a substance changes as it absorbs energy

Gas pressure

Particles in a gas are moving around fast. They exert a force when they hit the sides of their container, and this gives **gas pressure**. If the gas is heated, the particles move around even faster, so they hit the walls of the container more often. They also hit the walls harder. This increases the pressure of the gas.

> **4** What causes pressure in a gas?
>
> **5** Explain why gas pressure increases if you heat the gas.

Key points

- Substances can change state when they are heated or cooled.
- The temperature rise when you heat a substance depends on its specific heat capacity.
- The energy needed to make 1 kg of a substance change state is called the specific latent heat.
- Gases cause pressure because their particles move around and hit the walls of the container. The pressure increases when the temperature increases.

D Gas pressure keeps the balloon inflated.

Checkpoint

How confidently can you answer the Progression questions?

Foundation

F1 Describe four different changes of state.

F2 A container full of gas is heated.

    a Describe what happens to gas particles when the gas is heated.

    b Explain how this affects the pressure of the gas.

Strengthen

S1 Explain what happens to the temperature of 1 kg of a solid substance as it is heated until it becomes a liquid. Use the terms specific latent heat and specific heat capacity in your answer.

S2 Explain what will happen to the pressure of gas in a container if you cool it down.

Ice melts when you heat it. When you first transfer energy to ice its temperature starts to rise. When the ice reaches its melting point, the energy makes the particles in ice break free from their fixed arrangement. The temperature does not start to rise again until all the ice has melted.

The rise in temperature of a substance as you heat it depends on its **specific heat capacity**. This is the energy needed to raise the temperature of 1 kg of a substance by 1 °C. You can calculate the specific heat capacity of a substance using this equation:

$$\text{specific heat capacity (J/kg °C)} = \frac{\text{change in thermal energy (J)}}{\text{mass (kg)} \times \text{change in temperature (°C)}}$$

Worked example

Jamal heats a copper block using 3850 J of energy. The mass of the block is 1 kg and the temperature increases by 10 °C.

$$\text{specific heat capacity (J/kg °C)} = \frac{\text{change in thermal energy (J)}}{\text{mass (kg)} \times \text{change in temperature (°C)}}$$

$$= \frac{3850 \text{ J}}{1 \text{ kg} \times 10 \text{ °C}}$$

$$= 385 \text{ J/kg °C}$$

Method

Melting ice

A Place a thermometer carefully into a boiling tube. Fill the boiling tube with crushed ice, and place the tube in a beaker.

B Adjust the position of the thermometer so that its bulb is in the middle of the ice. Write down the temperature shown by the thermometer.

C Put the beaker onto a tripod and gauze. Pour hot water from a kettle into the beaker, and keep it warm using a Bunsen burner.

D Measure the temperature of the ice every minute and record your results in a table. Stop taking readings 3 minutes after all the ice has melted.

E Note the times at which the ice starts to melt and when it appears to be completely molten.

Specific heat capacity

F Put a polystyrene cup inside a beaker onto a balance and zero the balance. Then fill the cup almost to the top with water and write down the mass of the water.

G Put a thermometer in the water and support it as shown in photo A.

A measuring the specific heat capacity of water

H Put an electric immersion heater into the water, making sure the heating element is completely below the water level. Connect the immersion heater to a joulemeter.

I Record the temperature of the water.

J Switch the immersion heater on. Stir the water in the cup gently using the thermometer.

K After 5 minutes record the temperature of the water again, and write down the reading on the joulemeter.

Exam-style questions

1 Describe how the particles are arranged and held together in:

  a ice   *(2 marks)*

  b liquid water.   *(3 marks)*

2 Table B shows a set of results from the melting ice investigation.

  a Plot a graph to present the results. Draw a smooth line through the points.   *(5 marks)*

  b Explain the shape of the graph using ideas about particles.   *(4 marks)*

3 What does the specific heat capacity of a substance tell us about the substance?   *(1 mark)*

4 Look at photo A.

  a Describe the purpose of the glass beaker and the tripod.   *(1 mark)*

  b Suggest why the water to be heated was put into a polystyrene cup instead of being put directly into the beaker.   *(3 marks)*

5 Sam heated 0.25 kg of water in a polystyrene cup. The joulemeter reading was 11 kJ (11 000 J), and the temperature change was 10 °C.

  a Calculate the specific heat capacity of water (the change in thermal energy is given by the joulemeter reading).   *(2 marks)*

  b A data book gives the specific heat capacity of water as 4181 J/kg °C. Explain why you would expect Sam's result to be higher than this.   *(3 marks)*

  c How could the method described above be improved to reduce these errors?   *(1 mark)*

Time (min)	Temperature (°C)
0	−12
1	−8
2	−4
3	0
4	0
5	0
6	2
7	4
8	6

B results for question 2

P4d Stretching

ELC P2B.19, P2B.20, P2B.21, P2B.22 **GCSE** P15.1, P15.2, P15.3, P15.5

Progression questions

- How do forces cause objects to change shape?
- What is the difference between elastic and inelastic distortion?
- How do we calculate the force needed to stretch a spring by a certain amount?

A How is the person changing the shape of the plastic bottle?

Forces can change the shape of an object by bending, stretching or compressing it. It requires more than one force to distort an object. For example, the person in photo A needs to apply a force with both hands to change the shape of the plastic bottle.

> **1** Describe three ways in which forces can change the shape of an object.

Force meters work because they have a spring inside them. The spring stretches when there are forces on it. The spring in a force meter is **elastic**, because it returns to its original length when the forces are removed. Some materials do not return to their original shapes after they have been distorted. These materials are **inelastic**. For example, if you put too much weight in a plastic shopping bag it will stretch inelastically. The copper pipe in photo A has large forces on it and the bending is inelastic.

> **2** You stretch a rubber band and then let it go again. Explain whether the rubber band was stretched elastically or inelastically.

The **extension** of a spring is the change in length when forces are applied. For small forces, the extension of a spring has a **linear relationship**. A graph of force against extension is a straight line. If you stretch a spring too far the relationship becomes **non-linear** (not a straight line).

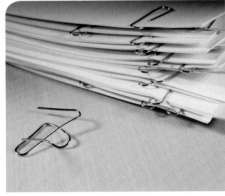

B This paper clip has been inelastically distorted. It will not return to its original shape.

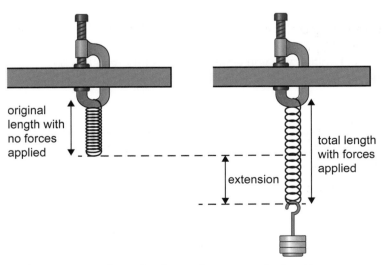

C The extension of a spring is not the same as its length.

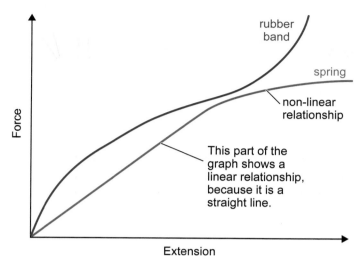

D force/extension graph for a spring and a rubber band

Some springs are much harder to stretch than others. The **spring constant** of a spring is the force needed to produce an extension of 1 m. We can calculate the force needed to stretch a spring by a certain amount using this equation:

force (N) = spring constant (N/m) × extension (m)

Worked example

A spring has a spring constant of 100 N/m. Calculate the force needed to produce an extension of 0.5 m.

force (N) = spring constant (N/m) × extension (m)

= 100 N/m × 0.5 m

= 50 N

4 A spring has a spring constant of 400 N/m. Calculate the force needed to make it extend by 0.8 m.

Key points

- It takes more than one force to change the shape of an object.
- Elastic materials return to their original shape after stretching, inelastic materials do not.
- Extension is the amount a spring has stretched. There is a linear relationship if a graph of force against extension is a straight line.
- We can calculate the force needed to stretch a spring using this equation:
  force (N) = spring constant (N/m) × extension (m)

3 Look at graph D. Explain whether the relationship between force and extension for a rubber band is linear or non-linear.

Checkpoint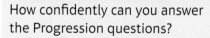

How confidently can you answer the Progression questions?

Foundation

F1 Describe the difference between elastic and inelastic stretching.

F2 What is meant by the extension of a spring?

Strengthen

S1 Describe the difference between a linear and a non-linear relationship between force and extension.

S2 A spring has a spring constant of 500 N/m. Calculate the force needed to make it extend by 20 cm.

You can find the spring constant of a spring by measuring the extension for a particular force. Calculate the spring constant using this version of the formula:

$$\text{spring constant (N/m)} = \frac{\text{force (N)}}{\text{extension (m)}}$$

When you stretch a spring you are doing work, because the force you use moves through a distance. You cannot use the normal equation for calculating work done, because the force you need to pull the spring increases as the spring stretches.

You can use this equation to calculate the work done when you stretch a spring:

$$\text{energy transferred in stretching (J)} = 0.5 \times \text{spring constant (N/m)} \times (\text{extension (m)})^2$$

Worked example

A spring has a spring constant of 200 N/m. A force is used to stretch it until it has an extension of 0.25 m. Calculate the energy transferred to stretch the spring.

$$\text{energy transferred in stretching (J)} = 0.5 \times \text{spring constant (N/m)} \times (\text{extension (m)})^2$$

$$= 0.5 \times 200 \text{ N/m} \times (0.25 \text{ m})^2$$

$$= 6.25 \text{ J}$$

Method

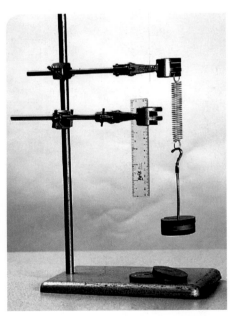

A finding the spring constant of a spring

A Set up the apparatus as shown in photo A. The zero on the ruler should be level with the bottom of the unstretched spring.

B Hang a 1 N weight on the spring. Record the extension of the spring (this is the reading on the ruler next to the bottom of the spring).

C Repeat step B until you have found the extension of the spring with 10 different masses.

D Repeat steps A to C for a different spring.

E Use your results to calculate the spring constant for the spring.

Exam-style questions

1 a State what is meant by the spring constant of a spring. *(1 mark)*

b State the formula you can use to find the spring constant of a spring. *(1 mark)*

c Give the units that should be used in the formula. *(1 mark)*

2 When a force moves an object, the work done in moving the object can be calculated using this formula:

work done = force × distance

Explain why this formula cannot be used to calculate the work done in stretching a spring. *(2 marks)*

3 A spring has an extension of 0.5 m when there is a force of 20 N pulling on it.

a Calculate the spring constant. *(2 marks)*

b Calculate the energy transferred in stretching this spring. *(2 marks)*

4 Write a list of the apparatus you need to carry out an investigation like the one described in the method. *(1 mark)*

5 Table B shows the results of one group's investigation. Plot a graph of force against extension to show their results. *(5 marks)*

6 The readings for springs X and Y were taken by two different students. Use your graph to suggest which student has taken the more accurate readings for the length of the spring. *(1 mark)*

7 a Read a force and extension from your graph for spring X and use these values to find the spring constant. *(3 marks)*

b Explain why you should use values read from the graph to find the spring constant, rather than taking data points from the table. *(2 marks)*

8 Compare the two springs in terms of original length and how easily they stretch. *(2 marks)*

Weight (N)	Extension (m)	
	Spring X	Spring Y
0	0.000	0.040
1	0.034	0.088
2	0.070	0.142
3	0.102	0.192
4	0.131	0.231
5	0.169	0.288
6	0.205	0.343
7	0.235	0.395
8	0.270	0.455
9	0.300	0.488
10	0.335	0.550

Original length of spring X = 0.06 m, spring Y = 0.04 m

B results for questions 5–8

Gas pressure

1 Some air is trapped in a sealed container.

Explain what happens to the pressure of the air if the container is heated. **(4 marks)**

Student answer

The pressure is caused by the force of air particles hitting the wall of the container [A]. When the gas is hotter the pressure increases [B].

[A] This is a good explanation of why gases cause pressure.

[B] The student has stated what happens to the gas pressure when the container is heated. However, the question asks the student to 'explain', so they also need to say that this is because the particles are moving faster and hitting the walls more often.

Verdict

This is a poor answer. When the question says 'explain', you need to say what happens and also *why* it happens. The student has started the explanation in their first sentence, but they have not explained why the pressure is higher when the gas is hotter.

Stretching

2 Describe the difference between elastic and inelastic distortion. **(2 marks)**

Student answer

Elastic distortion is when something changes shape, but goes back to its original shape when the forces on it are taken away [A]. Inelastic distortion is when the thing does not go back to its original shape when the forces stop [B].

[A] This describes what elastic distortion is.

[B] This describes what inelastic distortion is.

Verdict

This is a good answer. The student has described what both terms mean, which shows the difference between the terms.

Glossary

abiotic factor   A non-living factor that affects living organisms, e.g. temperature or amount of light.

absorb   To soak up or take in – for waves, it refers to the energy carried by the wave being transferred away and the wave disappearing.

accelerate   To change speed. The units for acceleration are metres per second squared (m/s²).

acceleration   A measure of how quickly the speed of something is changing. It is positive if the object is speeding up and negative if it is slowing down. Acceleration is a vector quantity.

acid   A solution with a pH of less than 7. Acids react with bases and alkalis, and turn litmus red.

acid rain   Rainwater that is more acidic than usual. Acid rain is usually caused by air pollution from sulfur dioxide and nitrogen oxides.

acidic   Containing or having the properties of an acid.

acquired characteristic   A characteristic of an organism that can change during its life due to something in the environment.

acrosome   A bag of enzymes in the head of a sperm cell. The enzymes help make a hole in the egg cell membrane.

activation energy   The minimum amount of energy needed to start a reaction.

active site   The space in an enzyme where the substrate fits during an enzyme-controlled reaction.

active transport   The movement of particles across a cell membrane from an area of lower concentration to an area of higher concentration. Active transport requires energy.

activity   The number of atoms decaying each second in a sample of radioactive substance. The unit for activity is the becquerel (Bq).

adapted   If something has special features for a certain function (job), it is said to be adapted to that function.

adult stem cell   A type of stem cell that can produce more of the specialised cells in one sort of tissue for growth and repair.

aerobic respiration   A type of respiration in which oxygen is used to release energy from glucose.

AIDS (acquired immune deficiency syndrome)   A disease in which a person's immune system is damaged by HIV so that the person cannot fight off other infections.

air resistance   A force on objects moving through air, which usually acts to slow them down.

alkali   A solution with a pH of more than 7. Alkalis react with acids and turn litmus blue.

alkali metals   A group of very reactive metals. They are found in group 1 of the periodic table.

alleles (one allele)   Different versions of the same gene.

alloy   A metal with small amounts of one or more other elements added to improve its properties.

alpha particle   A particle made of two protons and two neutrons (the same as the nucleus of a helium atom). Alpha particles are emitted by some radioactive isotopes during radioactive decay.

alternating current (a.c.)   A current whose direction changes many times each second.

alveoli (one alveolus)   Small pockets in the lungs in which gases are exchanged between the air and the blood.

ammeter   A piece of equipment that measures the size of the electric current flowing through it.

amp (A)   The unit for measuring current.

anaerobic respiration   A type of respiration that releases energy from glucose without oxygen.

anion   A negatively charged ion formed by gaining electrons (usually a non-metal ion).

anode   A positive electrode.

antibiotic   A medicine that helps people to recover from a bacterial infection by killing the pathogens (the bacteria).

antibody   A molecule, made by a lymphocyte, that helps to destroy a pathogen.

antigen   A molecule on a pathogen that causes a lymphocyte to recognise and attack the pathogen.

aorta   The artery that carries blood from the heart towards the rest of the body (apart from the lungs).

aqueous solution   A mixture that is formed when a substance is dissolved in water.

artery   A blood vessel that carries blood away from the heart.

asexual reproduction   Producing organisms from one parent only. These new organisms are genetically identical to the parent.

athlete's foot   Another name for tinea.

atmosphere   The layer of gases that surrounds the Earth or other planets.

atom   A small particle of an element. All substances are made from atoms.

atomic energy   Energy that it is stored inside materials. Another name for nuclear energy.

atomic mass   The mass of an atom. It is found by counting up the numbers of protons and neutrons in the nucleus.

atomic number   The number of protons in the nucleus of an atom.

attract   Two things pulling towards each other are said to attract.

average speed   The total distance something travels divided by the total time taken for the journey.

axon   The long extension of a neurone that carries the impulse away from the dendron or dendrites to other neurones.

axon terminal   The small 'button' at the tip of a branch at the end of an axon.

background radiation   Radiation that is around us all the time from many sources. Some background radiation occurs naturally but some comes from human activities.

base   Any substance that neutralises an acid to form a salt and water only. May be soluble or insoluble.

base pair   Two parts of a DNA molecule that fit together and hold the two strands of the molecule together.

becquerel (Bq)   The unit for measuring the activity of a radioactive substance. 1 becquerel is one radioactive decay per second.

belt transect   A line along which quadrat samples are taken to investigate the distribution of organisms in an area.

beta particle   An electron emitted from the nucleus of an atom. Beta particles are emitted by some radioactive isotopes during radioactive decay.

biodiversity   The number of different species in an area.

biofuel   A fuel made from plants or animal wastes.

biomass   The mass of living organisms.

biotic factor   A factor caused by organisms that affects other organisms, e.g. competition, predation.

bleach   A substance that is used to remove the colour from materials.

BMI (body mass index)   An estimate of how healthy a person's mass is for their height. $BMI = \dfrac{mass \ (kg)}{(height \ (m))^2}$

boil   (Of a liquid) Turn into a gas in all parts of the liquid, creating bubbles of gas in the liquid.

boiling point   The temperature at which a substance boils (all changes from a liquid to a gas).

breed   A group of organisms of the same species with characteristics that make them different from others of that species.

by-product   An unwanted substance produced in a chemical reaction.

cancer   A disease caused by uncontrolled division of cells in part of the body.

capillary   A tiny blood vessel. Capillaries have thin walls that allow the rapid exchange of substances between blood and the tissues.

carbon monoxide   A poisonous gas produced when carbon burns without enough oxygen.

cardiovascular disease   A disease in which the heart or circulatory system does not function properly. Examples include heart attack or stroke.

catalyst   A substance that speeds up a chemical reaction without being permanently changed itself.

cathode   A negative electrode.

cation   A positively charged ion formed when an atom loses electrons (usually a metal ion or a hydrogen ion).

cell cycle   The sequence of growth and division that happens in cells. Division is by mitosis.

cell division   When one cell divides to make new cells.

chalara dieback   A disease of ash trees, caused by a fungus.

change of state   When a substance changes from one state of matter (solid, liquid or gas) into another.

charge   An electrical property of some particles (e.g. electron, proton) that causes them to exert forces on each other. An electric charge can be positive or negative.

chemical change   A change that forms one or more new substances.

chemical defence   The use of substances made in the body to defend it, such as hydrochloric acid in the stomach.

chemical energy — A name used to describe energy when it is stored in chemicals. Food, fuel and batteries all store chemical energy.

chemical properties — The ways in which a substance reacts with other substances.

Chlamydia — A bacterium that causes an infection, spread mainly through sexual activity.

chlorination — The addition of chlorine to a substance, often to water.

chlorophyll — The green substance found in chloroplasts that traps energy transferred by light.

cholera — A bacterial infection that causes diarrhoea.

chromatogram — The piece of paper showing the results of chromatography.

chromosome — A thread-like structure containing many genes, found in the nuclei of cells. Each chromosome contains one enormously long DNA molecule packed with proteins.

cilia — Small hair-like structures on the surface of some cells that move things across the cell surface.

circuit breaker — A safety device that switches off the electricity supply if the current is too big.

circulatory system — The system that moves blood around the body. The circulatory system consists of the heart and blood vessels.

climate — The long-term weather pattern in an area.

climate change — Changes to weather patterns due to global warming, caused by the addition of carbon dioxide to the air from human activity.

clinical testing — The testing of a new medicine on people.

closed system — An environment that substances cannot enter or leave, such as a stoppered test tube.

combustion — A chemical reaction in which a compound reacts fast with oxygen.

communicable disease — Any disease that can be spread from one person to another. These diseases are caused by pathogens.

community — All the different organisms living and affecting each other in an area.

competition — The struggle between organisms for the same resource.

complete combustion — Combustion of hydrocarbons with enough oxygen to convert all the fuel into carbon dioxide and water.

compound — A substance that contains the atoms of two or more elements joined together by chemical bonds.

compress — To squeeze into a smaller volume.

concentrated — Containing a large amount of solute dissolved in a small volume of solvent.

concentration — The amount of solute dissolved in a stated volume of solvent.

condense — (Of a gas) Turn into a liquid.

conductor of electricity — A substance that allows electricity to pass through it.

conductor of heat — A substance that allows heat to pass through it.

conservation — The protection of an area or species to prevent damage.

contamination — An unwanted addition that makes something impure or damaged, for example a radioactive substance on the skin or in the body.

contraception — The prevention of pregnancy.

contraceptive pill — A pill containing hormones that affect the menstrual cycle and prevent pregnancy.

contract — To shorten.

correlation — A relationship between two variables. If one variable changes so does the other.

corrosion — The gradual deterioration of a substance when it reacts with substances in the environment, for example when a metal oxidises in air.

corrosive — Substances that attack metals, stonework and skin are said to be corrosive.

cosmic ray — Radiation that reaches the Earth from space.

coulomb (C) — The unit for measuring charge.

covalent bond — The bond formed when a pair of electrons is shared between two atoms.

cracking — A chemical reaction in which larger hydrocarbon molecules are broken down into smaller, more useful hydrocarbon molecules.

crude oil — A mixture of hydrocarbons formed from dead microscopic organisms by heat and pressure over millions of years.

crystallisation — Separating the solute (solid) from a solution by evaporating the solvent (liquid).

current — The flow of electricity around a circuit.

daughter cell — A new cell produced from the division of a parent cell.

decelerate — To change speed by slowing down.

decompose — In a chemical reaction, a substance decomposes when it breaks down to form simpler substances.

decomposer — An organism that feeds on dead material or animal waste, causing decay.

delocalised electron — An electron that is free to move and can carry an electrical current.

demand — How much of something can be sold.

denature — To change the shape of an enzyme's active site so much that the substrate can no longer fit into it. This means the reaction can no longer happen.

dendrite — A fine extension from a neurone that carries impulses towards the cell body.

dendron — A long extension of a sensory neurone that carries an impulse from dendrites to the axon.

density — The mass of a substance per unit volume. Units are kg/m^3 or g/cm^3.

deoxygenated — Containing little oxygen, as in blood entering the heart from the body.

desalination — Separating dissolved salts from salty water to produce fresh drinking (potable) water.

diabetes — A disease in which the body cannot control blood glucose concentration properly.

diagnose — To find out what is wrong with someone who is ill.

diarrhoea — Loose or watery faeces.

differentiation — The process by which an unspecialised cell becomes more specialised for a particular function. The cell normally changes shape to do this.

diffusion — The random movement and spreading of particles from an area of their higher concentration to an area of their lower concentration.

digest — To break up complex substances into simpler substances.

digestion — The process that breaks complex substances into simpler, more soluble substances.

diode — A component that lets electric current flow through it in one direction only.

direct current (d.c.) — A current that always flows in the same direction. Cells and batteries provide direct currents.

displacement reaction — A reaction in which a more reactive element displaces a less reactive element from one of its compounds.

dissipate — To spread out and become less concentrated.

distance/time graph — A graph that shows the distance travelled at different times during a journey. Horizontal lines on the graph show the object is not moving. Steeper lines show faster speeds.

distillation — The process of separating a liquid from a mixture by evaporating the liquid and then condensing it (so that it can be collected).

DNA — A very long molecule made of two strands joined together by base pairs. Contains many genes that carry the instructions for running and repairing our bodies.

domesticated animal — An animal kept for use by people, e.g. cows, horses, chickens, dogs.

dominant — Describes an allele that always affects the phenotype when present.

dot and cross diagram — A model of what happens when a bond is formed. It uses dots and crosses to represent the electrons of different atoms.

double helix — The shape of DNA molecules (like a twisted staircase).

drought — A lack of water.

dynamic equilibrium — The situation in which the forwards and backwards reactions in a reversible chemical reaction occur at the same rate (so the proportions of reactants and products remain the same).

earth wire — The green and yellow wire in a cable or plug. It is there for safety.

ecosystem — All the organisms and the non-living factors that affect them in an area.

effector — A muscle or gland that carries out an action when it receives an impulse from the nervous system.

efficiency — A way of saying how much energy something wastes. A more efficient machine wastes less energy.

elastic — An elastic material changes shape when there is a force on it but returns to its original shape when the force is removed.

elastic potential energy — A name used to describe energy when it is stored in stretched or squashed things that can change back to their original shapes. Another name for strain energy.

electrical conductor — A substance that allows electricity to pass through it.

electrode — A rod made of a metal or graphite that carries current into or out of an electrolyte.

electrolysis — The process in which energy transferred by a direct electrical current decomposes electrolytes.

electrolyte	An ionic compound that is molten or dissolved in water.
electromagnet	A coil of wire with electricity flowing in it. An electromagnet has a magnetic field like a bar magnet.
electron	A tiny particle inside an atom. It has a −1 (negative) charge and hardly any mass. Electrons move around the nuclei of atoms.
electron microscope	A large piece of laboratory equipment for magnifying specimens up to 10 million times.
electron shell	An area around a nucleus that can be occupied by electrons.
electronic configuration	The arrangement of electrons in the shells around the nucleus of an atom.
electrostatic force	The force of attraction between oppositely charged particles or objects, and the force of repulsion between those with the same charge.
element	A simple substance made up of only one type of atom.
elongation	When something gets longer, as plant cells do after cell division.
embryo	The ball of cells produced by cell division of a fertilised egg cell. A very early stage in the development of an individual.
embryonic stem cell	A cell from an early embryo. It can produce almost any kind of specialised cell.
empirical formula	A formula showing the simplest whole number ratio of the atoms of each element in a compound.
endocrine gland	An organ that makes a hormone and releases it into the blood.
endothermic	Describes a type of reaction in which energy from the surroundings is transferred to the products, e.g. photosynthesis.
energy	Something that is needed to make things happen or change.
environmental variation	Differences between organisms caused by environmental factors such as the amount of heat or light.
enzyme	A substance produced by living organisms that speeds up the rate of a reaction. For example, enzymes in yeast speed up the fermentation of glucose to make alcohol.
equilibrium	A stable state of rest or balance, where opposite forces or actions are equal and cancel each other out.
erythrocyte	Another term for a red blood cell.
evaporate	(Of a liquid) To turn into a gas (e.g. when liquid water turns into water vapour). Evaporation can happen at any temperature.
evolution	A change in the characteristics of a population over time.
exothermic	Describes a type of reaction in which heat energy is given out to the surroundings, for example combustion.
extension	The amount by which a spring or other stretchy material has stretched. The stretched length minus the original length.
extinct	Describes a species all when its organisms have died out.
family pedigree	A chart showing the phenotypes and sexes of generations of the same family. The pedigree shows how characteristics have been inherited in the family.
feedstock	A raw material; a substance used to make other substances.
fertilisation	The joining of a male gamete (in humans, a sperm cell) with a female gamete (in humans, an egg cell).
fever	A human body temperature of over 38 °C.
filament lamp	A lamp that contains a coil of thin wire. The wire heats up enough to glow when electricity passes through it.
filtrate	A solution that has passed through a filter. Filtration removes any insoluble solid.
finite resource	Something useful that is no longer made (or is made more slowly than it is used up).
fish farming	Growing fish in pens or ponds to supply humans with food.
fixed resistor	A resistor whose resistance cannot be changed.
force	A push, pull or twist.
fossil	Evidence preserved in rock of a species that lived a very long time ago, such as bone turned to rock.
fossil fuel	A fuel formed from dead organisms over thousands or millions of years, such as peat, coal, oil or natural gas.
fraction (crude oil)	A component of a mixture that has been separated by fractional distillation.
fractional distillation	A method of separating a mixture of liquids with different boiling points into individual components (fractions).
fractionating column	A long column used for fractional distillation. It is warmer at the bottom than at the top.
free fall	A fall slowed only by air resistance.

freeze	To turn from a liquid into a solid.
frequency	The number of vibrations (or waves) per second. The unit for measuring frequency is the hertz (Hz).
friction	A force between two objects that are touching. It usually acts to slow things down or prevent movement. It can also cause things to get hotter.
fullerene	A molecule made of carbon atoms each covalently bonded to three other carbon atoms, in a sphere or tube shape.
function	A job; what something does.
fungi	A group of organisms that includes mushrooms and single-celled yeast.
fuse	A piece of wire that melts if too much electricity flows through it. Fuses are used inside plugs for safety.
gamete	A sex cell (e.g. sperm or egg) that takes part in sexual reproduction.
gamma ray	A high-frequency electromagnetic wave emitted by radioactive isotopes during radioactive decay. Gamma rays have the highest frequencies in the electromagnetic spectrum.
gas pressure	The force on a surface caused by gas particles hitting the surface.
Geiger–Müller (GM) tube	A device that can detect radiation. It is used to measure the activity of radioactive sources.
gene	A section of DNA that contains the instructions for making a specific protein.
genetic code	The order of bases on a DNA molecule.
genetic engineering	Alteration of the genome of a species, usually by adding a gene from another species. Also called genetic modification.
genetic variation	The differences between organisms caused by differences in the alleles they inherit from their parents. Most genetic variation is originally caused by mutations.
genome	All of the DNA in an organism. Each body cell contains a copy of the whole genome.
genotype	The alleles of a particular gene in an organism.
giant covalent	Describes a substance in which very many atoms are joined together by covalent bonds.
global warming	The increase in the mean worldwide temperature.
glucose	A sugar produced by plants in photosynthesis, and in animals by the digestion of larger carbohydrate molecules. Glucose is broken down in respiration to release energy for other cell processes.
gradient	The steepness of a line on a graph, described in numbers.
graphene	A form of carbon consisting of a sheet one atom thick, with atoms arranged in hexagons.
gravitational potential energy	A name used to describe energy stored in objects in high places.
gravity	The force of attraction between any two objects. The Earth is very big and so has strong gravity that pulls everything down towards it.
greenhouse effect	The effect of gases in the atmosphere that absorb energy transferred by infrared waves from the Earth, which causes the atmosphere to be warmer than it otherwise would be.
greenhouse gas	A gas that helps to trap 'heat' in the atmosphere. Carbon dioxide, methane and water vapour are greenhouse gases.
group	A vertical column of elements in the periodic table. Elements in the same group generally have similar properties.
growth	A permanent increase in the number and/or size of cells in an organism.
guard cell	A pair of cells that open and close plant stomata.
habitat	The place where an organism lives, e.g. on a particular species of tree, at the bottom of a pond.
haemoglobin	The red, iron-containing pigment in red blood cells that carries oxygen.
half-life	The time it takes for the activity of a radioactive substance to drop to half its value, or for half of the unstable atoms in a sample to decay.
halide	A compound formed between a halogen and a metal or hydrogen. For example, sodium chloride is a metal halide.
halogen	An element in group 7 of the periodic table.
health	A state of being without diseases, being physically fit, and feeling good about yourself and the way you live.
heart	The muscular organ that pumps blood around the circulatory system.
heterozygous	With two different alleles for a gene.

HIV (human immunodeficiency virus) A virus that attacks the white blood cells of the immune system. It often leads to AIDS.

homozygous With both alleles for a gene the same.

hormone A chemical messenger made in an endocrine gland and carried around the body in the blood. Hormones cause changes in target organs.

host An individual that is harmed by a parasite.

hydrocarbon A compound containing only hydrogen and carbon atoms.

hydroelectricity Electricity generated by moving water (usually falling from a reservoir) turning turbines and generators.

hygiene Keeping things clean to prevent the spread of disease.

ignite To start burning.

immune Able to resist infection. A person immune to a disease does not fall ill after infection because their immune system destroys the pathogen quickly.

immune system The body system that protects and defends the body against disease.

impulse An electrical signal that is transmitted along a neurone.

impurity An unwanted substance found mixed into a useful substance.

in parallel The type of connection in which electrical components are connected in separate branches in a circuit. Only part of the current goes through each component in parallel.

in series The type of connection in which electrical components are connected in the same loop of wire. All the current goes through one component and then the other.

incomplete combustion The burning of fuel in a limited supply of oxygen or air. Incomplete combustion of hydrocarbons produces carbon monoxide, soot (unburnt carbon) and water.

indicator A substance that changes colour depending on the pH of a solution.

inelastic An inelastic material changes shape when there is a force on it but does not return to its original shape when the force is removed.

inert That does not react.

infection Another name for a communicable disease.

influenza A disease caused by a virus that produces a high temperature (fever) and cold-like 'flu' symptoms.

infrared Radiation that we can feel as heat.

ingest To take in, as white blood cells take in bacteria to destroy them. Or to eat, as we ingest food.

insecticide A substance that kills insects.

insoluble Describes a substance that cannot be dissolved in a certain liquid (e.g. sand is insoluble in water).

insulate To protect against energy transfer (e.g. myelin prevents the transfer of an electrical impulse in the axon and dendron of a neurone to surrounding cells).

insulin A hormone that causes a reduction in blood glucose concentration.

interdependent Needing each other for resources such as food or shelter (of organisms together in an area).

intermolecular force A weak force of attraction between molecules.

ion An atom or group of atoms with an electrical charge due to the gain or loss of electrons.

ionic bond A strong electrostatic force of attraction between oppositely charged ions.

ionic compound A substance made up of ions of different elements.

ionising radiation Radiation that can make atoms turn into ions. Ionising radiations include alpha particles, beta particles and gamma rays.

irradiation The absorption by a body of radiation from a radioactive substance that is not on or in the body.

isotopes Atoms of an element with the same number of protons (same atomic number) but different numbers of neutrons (different mass numbers).

joule (J) The unit for measuring energy.

kinetic energy A name used to describe energy when it is stored in moving things.

lactic acid The product of anaerobic respiration in animal cells.

lamp Another word for light bulb.

lattice structure An arrangement of many particles that are bonded together in a fixed, regular, grid-like pattern.

law of conservation of energy The idea that energy can never be created or destroyed, only transferred from one store to another.

law of conservation of mass The idea that mass is never lost or gained during a chemical reaction or physical change.

lesion A split in something, such as the bark lesions caused by chalara dieback disease in ash trees.

life cycle assessment An analysis of the effect of a manufactured product on the environment over the whole of its lifetime.

lifestyle The way we live, including what we eat, whether we smoke and how much exercise we do. This can affect our bodies.

light intensity The brightness of light. Light of low intensity is said to be dim.

light microscope A microscope that uses light to view the specimen. Can magnify by up to ×1500.

lignin A substance in the walls of xylem vessels that makes them strong.

limiting factor A factor in short supply that limits the rate of a process.

linear relationship A relationship between variables that produces a straight line when plotted on a scatter graph. The line does not have to go through the (0,0) point.

live wire The brown wire in a cable or plug. The live wire is where the current comes into the plug.

lubricant A substance (e.g. oil) placed between moving surfaces to reduce friction between them.

lubrication The use of a substance between moving surfaces to reduce friction between them.

lungs Organs where gases are exchanged between the air and the body in many animals.

lymphocyte A type of white blood cell that attacks pathogens by producing antibodies.

lysozyme A substance found in tears that protects the eye against infection.

magnet A piece of iron (or other magnetic material) that can attract magnetic materials and attract or repel other magnets.

magnetic field The space around a magnet where it can affect magnetic materials or other magnets.

magnetic material A material that is attracted to a magnet. Iron is a magnetic material.

magnification The number of times larger an image is than the initial object that produced it.

mains supply The electricity that comes to our homes and school from power stations.

malaria A disease caused by a protist that damages the liver and red blood cells.

male condom A barrier method of contraception that stops sperm reaching the egg, and also reduces the spread of sexually transmitted infections.

malleable Describes a substance that can be hammered or rolled into shape without shattering.

mass The amount of matter that something contains. Mass is measured in grams (g) and kilograms (kg). It does not have a direction, so it is a scalar quantity. Your mass does not change if you go into space or to another planet.

mass number The total number of protons and neutrons in the nucleus of an atom.

melt Turn (a solid) into a liquid.

melting point The temperature at which a substance changes from the solid state to the liquid stated when heated, or from the liquid state to the solid state when cooled.

memory lymphocyte (memory cell) A lymphocyte that remains in the blood for a long time after infection. Memory lymphocytes trigger a secondary response if a pathogen infects the body again.

menopause The time when the menstrual cycle stops completely.

menstrual cycle A monthly cycle of changes in a woman's reproductive system.

menstruation The loss of the thickened uterus lining and unfertilised egg at the start of the menstrual cycle.

meristem A small area of stem cells in a plant.

metabolic process A process that happens in the body and that keeps cells alive, such as respiration, diffusion, synthesis.

metal An element that is shiny when polished, conducts heat and electricity well, is malleable and flexible and often has a high melting point.

metallic bonding	The type of bonding found in metals. The force of attraction between the 'sea' of delocalised electrons and positive metal atoms.
metres per second (m/s)	A unit for speed when distance is measured in metres and time is measured in seconds.
mitochondria (one mitochondrion)	Cell structures found in most plant and animal cells. Mitochondria are where respiration happens, to release energy from food molecules.
mitosis	The process of cells dividing to produce two daughter cells that are genetically identical to the parent cell.
mixture	A substance containing two or more different substances that are not chemically joined together.
mobile phase	In paper chromatography, the solvent that moves along the paper carrying the dissolved samples with it.
molecule	A particle consisting of two or more atoms joined together by covalent bonding.
monohybrid inheritance	The passing of alleles for just one gene from parents to offspring.
motor neurone	A type of neurone that carries impulses to effectors.
mucus	A sticky substance produced by the cells that line many openings to the body.
multicellular	Many-celled.
muscle cell	A type of specialised cell that is adapted to contract.
mutation	A change to the DNA in a cell. Some mutations can cause the cell to die or to work incorrectly.
mutualism	A partnership when two species live in a close relationship in which both benefit.
myelin sheath	The fatty covering that insulates the axons of many neurones.
national grid	A system of wires and transformers that distributes electricity around the country.
natural selection	The changes in a population that arise when some individuals have variations in a characteristic that are better adapted to the environment than others. The better variations help individuals to survive and produce more offspring. They pass on the variations in their genes. More individuals in the next generation have these variations.
nerve cell	A type of specialised cell adapted to carry electrical impulses around the body in the nervous system.
nervous system	An organ system that contains the brain, spinal cord and nerves. It carries electrical impulses around the body. This system helps you to sense and respond quickly to changes inside and outside the body.
neurone	A nerve cell.
neurotransmitter	A substance that diffuses across the gap between one neurone and the next when an impulse arrives at a synapse. It triggers an impulse in the next neurone.
neutral	A substance that is neither an acid nor an alkali. Neutral solutions have a pH of 7.
neutral wire	The blue wire in a cable or plug. The neutral wire completes the circuit to allow current to pass through the appliance.
neutralisation	A reaction in which an acid reacts with a base to produce a salt and water only. (Also used to describe the reaction between an acid and a metal carbonate to produce a salt, water and carbon dioxide, and between an acid and a metal to form a salt and hydrogen.)
neutron	A particle found inside the nucleus of an atom. It has no charge and a relative mass of 1.
noble gas	An unreactive gas in group 0 of the periodic table.
non-communicable disease	A disease that cannot be spread from person to person. Examples include diseases caused by genes or lifestyle factors such as diet and smoking.
non-indigenous species	Organisms that have been introduced to an area where they have not been before.
non-linear relationship	A relationship between variables that does not produce a straight line when plotted on a scatter graph.
non-metal	An element that is not shiny and does not conduct heat or electricity well.
non-renewable	Something that is being used faster than it is being formed.
non-renewable energy resource	An energy resource that will run out because we cannot renew our supplies of it (e.g. oil).
nuclear energy	A name used to describe energy when it is stored inside materials. Another name for atomic energy.
nuclear fuel	A substance that stores nuclear energy in a way that can be used in power stations to generate electricity.

nucleus (in cell)	The largest structure in a cell. The nucleus contains the DNA that controls what happens in the cell.
nucleus (in atom)	The central part of an atom, made of protons and neutrons.
obesity	A condition in which someone is overweight for their height, with a BMI of over 30.
objective	The lens in a light microscope that is closest to the specimen.
oestrogen	A hormone produced in the ovaries. Oestrogen helps control the menstrual cycle by triggering ovulation.
ohm (Ω)	The unit for measuring electrical resistance.
open system	An environment that substances can enter or leave, such as a reaction inside an open test tube.
optimum temperature	The temperature at which the rate of a reaction is fastest.
ore	A rock that contains enough of a metal to make extracting the metal profitable.
osmosis	The movement of water molecules through a membrane. Water moves into a cell when the cell is placed in a dilute solution, and out of the cell when it is in a concentrated solution.
ovulation	The release of an egg from an ovary.
oxide of nitrogen	Any one of a variety of gaseous compounds made up of only nitrogen and oxygen atoms.
oxygenated	Containing lots of oxygen, such as blood that has just left the lungs.
pancreas	An organ that contains the cells that produce the hormone insulin.
paper chromatography	A separation technique carried out by spotting drops of samples onto paper and then allowing a solvent to move up the paper. Different components in the samples travel up the paper in the solvent at different rates.
parallel circuit	A circuit with two or more branches that split apart and join up again.
parasite	An organism that lives on or in a host organism and takes food from the host while it is alive.
parasitism	A feeding relationship in which the parasite benefits but its host is harmed.
parent cell	A cell that divides to produce daughter cells.
particles	The tiny pieces of matter that everything is made out of.
pathogen	A disease-causing organism.
period	A horizontal row in the periodic table.
periodic table	The chart in which the elements are arranged in order of increasing atomic number and placed into groups according to their properties.
permanent magnet	A magnet that is always magnetic, such as a bar magnet.
pH scale	A numerical scale from 0 to 14 that measures how acidic or alkaline a solution is.
phagocyte	A white blood cell that is capable of engulfing microorganisms such as bacteria.
phenotype	The effect of alleles on what an organism looks like or how its body works (e.g. coat colour in rabbits).
phloem	Living tissue in plant veins that transports sucrose around a plant.
photographic film	Thin sheet of plastic covered in a chemical that changes when light shines on it.
photosynthesis	The process used by plants to make their food. Carbon dioxide and water react to form glucose and oxygen, using energy from light.
physical barrier	A structure that stops something entering. For example, the skin stops pathogens getting into the body.
physical change	A change in which no new substances are formed (e.g. changes of state).
physical property	A description of how a material behaves and responds to forces and energy. For example, hardness is a physical property.
pitfall trap	A trap used for sampling organisms. The trap is set into the ground so that small animals fall into it as they run around.
plasma (in blood)	The liquid part of blood, which carries dissolved substances.
platelet	A fragment of blood cell that causes blood to clot when a blood vessel is damaged.
plotting compass	A small compass that can be used to find the shape of a magnetic field.
pollutant	A substance that harms living organisms when released into the environment.
pollution	Harm caused to the environment, such as by the release of poisonous substances.

polymer A very long molecule made up of a chain of atoms covalently bonded together in a repeating pattern.

population All the organisms of one species living in an area.

potable Safe to drink.

power The amount of energy (in joules, J) transferred every second. It is measured in watts (W).

precipitate An insoluble substance that is formed when two soluble substances react together in solution.

precipitation reaction A reaction in which an insoluble product is formed from two soluble reactants.

preclinical testing The stages of testing of a possible new medicine before it is tested on people. Preclinical testing includes tests on cell or tissue cultures, and on animals.

predation The killing and eating of one animal species by another animal species.

predator An animal that kills and eats other animals.

prefix Something added to the beginning of a word to change its meaning. In 'kilometre', 'kilo' is the prefix.

pregnancy The time during which a fertilised egg cell develops in the mother's uterus, until the birth of the baby.

prey Animals that are killed and eaten by predators.

primitive Describes early or simple types of something.

progesterone A hormone produced in the ovaries. Progesterone helps control the menstrual cycle by causing thickening of the uterus lining.

proportional Describes the relationship in which one variable or factor doubles when another one doubles. A graph showing a proportional relationship is a straight line through the origin.

protein A type of molecule in organisms that is coded for by a gene.

protist A member of a group of mainly single-celled organisms (e.g. the malaria pathogen).

proton A particle found inside the nucleus of an atom. It has a +1 (positive) charge and a relative mass of 1.

puberty The stage in life when the body develops in ways that allow reproduction (e.g. production of sperm cells in testes, release of eggs from ovaries).

pulmonary artery The artery that carries deoxygenated blood from the heart to the lungs.

pulmonary vein The vein that carries oxygenated blood from the lungs to the heart.

Punnett square A diagram used to predict the characteristics of offspring from two parents with known combinations of alleles.

pure Describes a substance containing only one element or compound that does not have anything else mixed with it.

quadrat A square frame of known size, e.g. 1 m by 1 m, that is placed on the ground to sample organisms living in an area.

R_f value The distance travelled by a dye on a chromatogram divided by the distance travelled by the solvent.

radioactive decay The emission of radiation such as alpha particles, beta particles or gamma rays by an unstable atom.

radon A radioactive gas given off by some types of rock.

random When there is no pattern in an arrangement or in things happening, so that they cannot be predicted.

rate How quickly something happens.

reactivity series A list of metal elements in order of reactivity, with the most reactive at the top.

receptor cell A cell that responds to a stimulus by producing an electrical impulse in a sensory neurone.

recessive Describes an allele that only affects the phenotype when a dominant allele isn't present (i.e. the other allele for the gene is also recessive).

red blood cell A blood cell that contains red haemoglobin, which transports oxygen around the body. Also called an erythrocyte.

reflex A response to a stimulus that does not require processing by the brain. The response is automatic and fast.

reflex arc A neurone pathway in which a sensory neurone passes impulses to a motor neurone, often via a relay neurone. This allows reflexes.

reforestation The planting of new forests where forests used to grow but have been cut down.

relative atomic mass The mean mass of the atoms of an element, compared with 1/12th the mass of a carbon-12 atom.

relative formula mass The sum of the relative atomic masses of all the atoms in a formula.

relative mass The mass of something compared with the mass of a proton.

relay neurone A short type of neurone found in the spinal cord and brain. Relay neurones link with sensory, motor and other relay neurones.

renewable energy resource An energy resource that will never run out (e.g. solar power).

repel To push away.

reservoir A lake formed to store water, usually by building a dam across a river.

residue Solid material remaining in the filter after a mixture has passed through it.

resistance A measure of how difficult it is for electricity to flow through something.

resistance force A force such as friction, air resistance or water resistance that acts to slow down a moving object.

resistant Unaffected or less affected by something.

resistor An electrical component that makes it difficult for electricity to flow. Resistors are used to reduce the size of the current in a circuit.

resource (biology) Something that an organism needs to stay alive, e.g. food, shelter.

respiration A process that occurs in all living cells. Glucose is broken down to water and carbon dioxide. The process releases energy that can be used for other processes.

respirometer An apparatus that measures the rate of respiration.

reversible reaction A chemical reaction that works in both directions.

risk The chance of a hazard causing harm.

salt An ionic compound formed when an acid neutralises a base or reacts with a metal.

sample To take a small portion of something larger.

Sankey diagram A diagram showing energy transfers. The widths of the arrows show the amounts of energy. Wider arrows mean more energy.

scalar quantity A quantity that has a size but not a direction. Examples include mass, distance and energy.

screening Testing to check whether people have a disease, e.g. an STI.

secondary response The immune system response the second time that a particular pathogen enters the body.

sedimentation The process in which rock grains and insoluble substances sink to the bottom of a liquid.

selective breeding When humans choose to breed organisms with certain characteristics. In each generation that characteristic tends to get more obvious.

sense organ An organ that contains receptor cells.

sensory neurone A neurone that carries electrical impulses from receptor cells towards a relay neurone in the spinal cord or brain.

series circuit A circuit in which there is only one possible route for the current.

sex chromosome A chromosome that determines the sex of an organism. In humans, females have XX sex chromosomes and males have XY.

sexual fluids Fluids produced in the reproductive system (semen in men, vaginal fluid in women).

sexually transmitted infection (STI) An infection spread mainly by sexual activity.

solar power The use of energy from the Sun to heat water or to generate electricity.

soluble Describes a substance that dissolves in a certain liquid, e.g. water.

solute A substance dissolved in a liquid to make a solution.

solution A mixture formed when a substance has dissolved in a liquid.

solvent The liquid in which a substance dissolves to make a solution.

specialised cell A cell that is adapted for a particular function (job).

specific Particular. For example, an enzyme is specific to its substrate and will not work with other substrates.

specific heat capacity The energy needed to raise the temperature of 1 kg of a substance by 1 °C.

specific latent heat The energy taken in or released when 1 kg of a substance changes state.

speed	How fast something is moving. The standard scientific units are metres per second (m/s), but speed can also be measured in miles per hour (mph) or kilometres per hour (km/h).
speed/time graph	A graph that shows the speed at different times during a journey. Horizontal lines show constant speeds. Sloping lines show accelerations.
spinal cord	The large bundle of nerves protected by the bony spine, leading from the brain down the back.
spring constant	A measure of how stiff a spring is. The spring constant is the force needed to stretch the spring by 1 m.
state of matter	One of three different forms that a substance can have: solid, liquid or gas.
stationary phase	The surface through which the solvent and dissolved substances move in chromatography.
stem cell	An unspecialised cell that produces more stem cells and cells that differentiate into specialised cells.
sterile (organism)	Unable to reproduce.
stimulus (plural stimuli)	A change inside or outside the body that is detected by receptors. Examples include sight, sound, touch, temperature.
stomata (one stoma)	Tiny pores found mostly on the lower surface of leaves. Stomata can open and close. When stomata are open, gases can diffuse into and out of the leaf.
strain energy	A name used to describe energy when it is stored in stretched or squashed things that can change back to their original shapes. Another name for elastic potential energy.
stroke	A cardiovascular disease in which a blood clot blocks a blood vessel in the brain.
sublime	To change from a solid to a gas without becoming a liquid.
substrate	A substance that is changed during a reaction.
sucrose	The type of sugar transported around plants in phloem.
supply	The amount of something produced.
surgical procedure	A medical procedure in which a doctor cuts into a person's body. This might be to remove diseased tissue or to repair damaged tissue.
switch	An electrical component that turns a circuit on or off by closing or opening a gap in the circuit.
symptom	An effect of a disease.
synapse	The point at which two neurones meet. There is a tiny gap between the neurones at a synapse.
synthesis	Building a larger molecule from smaller ones.
target organ	An organ that is affected by a hormone.
temporary magnet	A magnet that is not always magnetic (e.g. an electromagnet is only magnetic while a current is flowing through it).
testosterone	A hormone produced by the testes.
thermal energy	A name used to describe energy when it is stored in hot objects. The hotter something is, the more thermal energy it has.
tidal power	Using the flow of water in the tides to generate electricity.
tides	The daily rising and falling of the sea level.
tinea	A disease caused by a fungus that digests skin cells, particularly between the toes. Also known as athlete's foot.
titration	Method used to mix acids and alkalis in the correct amounts to give a solution of only salt and water. It can be used to find the concentration of an acid or an alkali.
toxic	Poisonous.
transformer	A device that can change the voltage of an alternating current electricity supply.
translocation	The transport of sugars (mainly sucrose) in the phloem tissue of a plant.
transpiration	The flow of water through a plant – into the root, up the stem and out of the leaves.
tuberculosis	A bacterial disease that damages the lungs.

tumour	A lump formed of cancer cells.
type 1 diabetes	Diabetes caused by pancreas cells producing no insulin.
type 2 diabetes	Diabetes caused by pancreas cells producing too little insulin or by target cells not responding to insulin.
unbalanced forces	Two or more forces on an object that do not cancel each other out, so that there is an overall resultant force on the object.
unit	A standard used to measure things. For example, a unit for length is the metre.
universal indicator	An indicator containing a mixture of different pH indicators. It produces a range of different colours depending on the pH.
unreactive	Tending not to take part in chemical reactions.
unspecialised	Having no special features.
unstable	Tending to change. An unstable nucleus is one that will decay by giving out radiation.
vapour	Gas formed below the boiling point of a liquid.
variable resistor	A resistor whose resistance can be changed.
variation	Differences in the characteristics of organisms.
vector (animal)	An animal that carries a pathogen from an infected organism to others.
vector quantity	A quantity that has both size and direction. Forces are vector quantities.
vein (animal)	A blood vessel that carries blood towards the heart.
vein (plant)	A structure in a plant that contains xylem tissue and phloem tissue.
vena cava	The vein that joins the heart, carrying blood from the body.
vibrate	To move backwards and forwards.
virus	A non-living particle that can only reproduce inside a living cell.
viscosity	A measure of how thick or runny a liquid is. Low viscosity is very runny; high viscosity is thick.
volcanic activity	The release of gases and/or molten rock by volcanoes.
volt (V)	The unit for voltage.
voltage	A way of saying how much energy is transferred by electricity. It is also called potential difference.
voltmeter	A piece of equipment that measures how much energy is being transferred by a current (the voltage, or potential difference).
volume	The amount of space something takes up. Measured in cubic metres (m^3) or cubic centimetres (cm^3).
waist : hip ratio	A measure of the amount of fat in the body. It is calculated by dividing the waist measurement by the hip measurement.
water resistance	A force on objects moving through water, which acts to slow them down.
watt (W)	A unit for measuring power. 1 watt (W) is 1 joule (J) per second.
weathering	The breakdown of rocks by physical, chemical or biological processes.
weight	The amount of force with which gravity pulls things. It is measured in newtons (N). Your weight would change if you went into space or to another planet.
white blood cell	A type of blood cell that defends the body against disease.
wildlife tourism	Travel to an area to see wildlife.
wind turbine	A kind of windmill that generates electricity using energy transferred by the wind.
work done	The energy transferred when a force moves an object. The unit for work is the joule (J).
xylem	Dead tissue in plants formed from long xylem vessels. Xylem transports water and mineral ions around the plant.
zygote	A fertilised egg cell.

The Periodic Table of the Elements

Key

| relative atomic mass |
| **atomic symbol** |
| name |
| atomic (proton) number |

| 1 |
| **H** |
| hydrogen |
| 1 |

Group	1	2		3	4	5	6	7	0
									4 **He** helium 2
	7 **Li** lithium 3	9 **Be** beryllium 4		11 **B** boron 5	12 **C** carbon 6	14 **N** nitrogen 7	16 **O** oxygen 8	19 **F** fluorine 9	20 **Ne** neon 10
	23 **Na** sodium 11	24 **Mg** magnesium 12		27 **Al** aluminium 13	28 **Si** silicon 14	31 **P** phosphorus 15	32 **S** sulfur 16	35.5 **Cl** chlorine 17	40 **Ar** argon 18

39 **K** potassium 19	40 **Ca** calcium 20	45 **Sc** scandium 21	48 **Ti** titanium 22	51 **V** vanadium 23	52 **Cr** chromium 24	55 **Mn** manganese 25	56 **Fe** iron 26	59 **Co** cobalt 27	59 **Ni** nickel 28	63.5 **Cu** copper 29	65 **Zn** zinc 30	70 **Ga** gallium 31	73 **Ge** germanium 32	75 **As** arsenic 33	79 **Se** selenium 34	80 **Br** bromine 35	84 **Kr** krypton 36
85 **Rb** rubidium 37	88 **Sr** strontium 38	89 **Y** yttrium 39	91 **Zr** zirconium 40	93 **Nb** niobium 41	96 **Mo** molybdenum 42	[98] **Tc** technetium 43	101 **Ru** ruthenium 44	103 **Rh** rhodium 45	106 **Pd** palladium 46	108 **Ag** silver 47	112 **Cd** cadmium 48	115 **In** indium 49	119 **Sn** tin 50	122 **Sb** antimony 51	128 **Te** tellurium 52	127 **I** iodine 53	131 **Xe** xenon 54
133 **Cs** caesium 55	137 **Ba** barium 56	139 **La*** lanthanum 57	178 **Hf** hafnium 72	181 **Ta** tantalum 73	184 **W** tungsten 74	186 **Re** rhenium 75	190 **Os** osmium 76	192 **Ir** iridium 77	195 **Pt** platinum 78	197 **Au** gold 79	201 **Hg** mercury 80	204 **Tl** thallium 81	207 **Pb** lead 82	209 **Bi** bismuth 83	[209] **Po** polonium 84	[210] **At** astatine 85	[222] **Rn** radon 86
[223] **Fr** francium 87	[226] **Ra** radium 88	[227] **Ac*** actinium 89	[261] **Rf** rutherfordium 104	[262] **Db** dubnium 105	[266] **Sg** seaborgium 106	[264] **Bh** bohrium 107	[277] **Hs** hassium 108	[268] **Mt** meitnerium 109	[271] **Ds** darmstadtium 110	[272] **Rg** roentgenium 111							

Elements with atomic numbers 112-116 have been reported but not fully authenticated

*The lanthanoids (atomic numbers 58–71) and the actinoids (atomic numbers 90–103) have been omitted.

The relative atomic masses of copper and chlorine have not been rounded to the nearest whole number.